NOT ALL THE FLOWERS TURN INTO PUMPKINS

Julie Trinham

First published in Australia in 2015 by Julie Trinham.

Revised edition 2017

All rights reserved. No part of this publication may be reproduced or transmitted in any form or by any means without the written permission of the publisher.

ISBN 978-0-9943815-0-7

Cover photo by Julie Trinham

To the memory of Aubrey and Lillie

"When we have passed a certain age, the soul of the child that we were and the souls of the dead from whom we sprang come and shower upon us their riches and their spells, asking to be allowed to contribute to the new emotions that we feel and in which, erasing their former image we recast them in an original creation."

Marcel Proust

The names of most of the characters in this story have been changed.

Paris 2013

"You should be a racing car driver" I say rather nervously as I grip the seat and we weave in and out of the traffic at breathtaking speed. "Maybe Grand Prix?" I add, under my breath.

He responds with only an upward turn of his mouth, visible to me from my anxious position in the back seat. He glances in the rear vision mirror as we come to a stop amongst the lanes of impatient drivers heading to work and toots the horn repeatedly, muttering foreign curses aggressively.

After all, it is 8 am Friday morning on the outskirts of Paris and we are in one hell of a hurry, but it's not as if I'm in the last stages of labour or anything. I regret my comment about him being a racing driver which he seems to have taken as encouragement and he swings the wheel and we continue now along the footpath for some distance, until he sees a space between the cars that he can push the nose of the van back into. "Whew!"

He'd called out "Taxi" to me as I'd waded through the exhausted passengers at the Arrivals area of Charles de Gaulle airport and I had followed him like a dog following the offer of a bone. It was only as I climbed in and slammed the door of the van that I realized there was no sign of "Taxi" anywhere on the vehicle, nor was there any ID that I could see. I thought he had said "*Ca va?*" as I got in to the van and I answered "*Ca va bien.*"

He snaps at me "I said *where to?*" I dislike him immediately and he isn't French. He's lost me. I wonder would he really be taking a 68 year-old woman to a white slave-trader. I had been such a willing victim. Maybe I would be robbed and murdered and left in one of the forests. I am indeed wearing two thousand euros under my clothing but he would have to murder me to get any of my clothes off.

I take a deep breath now as we approach St Denis, the entry to Paris through the tradesmen's entrance I always feel, much the same as most airport surrounds, but in this case the burial site of the kings of France for centuries. My throat is dry and stings from the carbon monoxide in the van. I could die in this van, either by asphyxiation or a collision. After a failed attempt to wind the window up I feel a little desperate.

"*Ouvre le window! – s'il vous plait! – monsieur!*"

He snaps out of his "Fangio" role for a moment and looks back at me "You want the window open?"

"Please!"

Without altering speed he twists his arm around and opens the back window. A breeze rushes in with more fumes from the traffic and the roar of cars.

"*Merci*" I cough.

The shops here this season appear to have lots of bold leggings and rather way-out dresses and tops in bright colours, going by the stores I just manage to glance at as we flash by. I'm keen to see what they're wearing in Paris in 2013.

"Here's your hotel" he says as he drops me out on the opposite side of Rue des Ecoles in the Latin Quarter forty-five minutes later, luggage out of the back and now resting in the gutter. I have already given him one hundred euros (he charges me ninety-six and I tell him to keep the change) and he makes no move to get me to the hotel door as I am accustomed to drivers doing. He hands me his card. *As though* I would use him again.

I wend my way across the road through streaming traffic and land at the door of my Hotel in Rue des Ecoles. I notice everyone is in winter clothes. It's only the first two weeks into autumn. The temperature is fairly mild but it's grey and there is a steady misty rain.

It's just gone 9 am and my room "won't be ready until 1.30."

I walk around in the rain for a few minutes and decide to take refuge in the café on the corner and lose myself in a *café crème*. The waitress is very pleasant and friendly and could be the twin sister of the girl who runs the Folkart store in Warrandyte where I used to live, on the rural edge of Melbourne.

I sit and sip my coffee and watch the crowd for a while.

So many English tourists come in and out. They make no attempt at ordering in French and their accented voices are loud. They glance at me for a sign that I might possibly be English. I look away. Let them wonder.

At *Le Fruitier* between the café and my hotel, I browse over what I intend to have as "dinner." I have planned to eat out once a day, most probably lunch and just eat fruit for my evening meal. The grocer looks at the $20 note peeping out of my wallet, the last bit of Australian cash on me. He asks "How many euros for that?" And is quite excited to learn that I only got about fourteen euros for "that."

"Oh, that is very good for France. Very good."

"Yes, but not for me. I think I lose a lot of money this time," (according to the calculations of my right-sided brain.)

I wander around til about 10 am, a little weary after my long journey and all the anxiety beforehand. My car had broken down twice on the Maroondah Highway (that links Melbourne with the mountains) the day before I left. This was the first reliable car I had owned and it had not let me down in ten years. It stalled in the middle lane at traffic lights at peak hour, going uphill, with a huge truck close to my bumper (with the added complication of having two dogs in the car and no leads with me, meaning geographical paralysis for the three of us). It took me ten minutes to persuade the car to cough into action and then it stalled again ten minutes later. I limped home with the RACV man following me and of course it behaved all the way from then on. "I don't like your chances" he had said when I told him, "No, I can't bring the car in for an overhaul as I am going overseas tomorrow morning."

I arrived home despairing about how I would get the cat to the cattery in the morning at 8 am and the dogs to Caroline's (my daughter) without breaking down along the way and eventually missing my plane. Caroline was driving me to the airport but now would I ever make this a reality? However, the neighbours heard me slam the car door and they came to my aid and at 8 am next morning I left for my Paris holiday with little dignity, after struggling to lift the 37.7 kilo Coco into the head height storage spot at the back of their four wheel drive, beside little Lillie and the seething cat in his cage.

"I hope they won't be sick" Max had said, hopefully glancing in the rear vision mirror.

"They're never sick in the car" I reassured him, only to find that the speed he took the corners around the curvy country roads, and the rocking-boat motion of the inner-spring cot-mattress that was to be their bed for the next three weeks, had a negative effect on little Lillie, and I travelled with my arm twisted around quietly arm-wrestling with her gagging response.

"She's alright isn't she?"

"Yes fine." We went over a big bump and Lillie rode it like a surfer but up came breakfast! And so I continued on the first leg of my journey to Paris with my usual innate aplomb.

Now I am at my hotel in the Latin Quarter. I don't feel like walking any further in the drizzling rain and am pleased to be told "Your room is ready Madame."

The girl on the desk is very French, very helpful and speaks perfect English. She gives me the prefix for Australian phone numbers. Of course, I don't have a computer or a phone with me. It's all too hard.

Up to my room. Tiny after the hotel in Rue de Renne that I stayed at last year. Bonnie, from Tennessee, one of the fifteen artists I painted with then, had stayed here and recommended it, but she did say, in her delightful southern accent, that *the rooms were awful small."*

I have a shower and feel better. Feet and legs are a bit swollen although I wore pressure stockings on the flight and my eyes are very sore from the journey. In total, I have been travelling thirty hours from the Yarra Ranges north east of Melbourne to Paris and feel like it! I put on my geometric patterned leggings and black floppy top with my mushroom coloured corduroy jacket and high heels. I manage to get on to Caroline without any problems and the dogs are happy.

It feels like evening coming on. I return to the same café "Royal Jussieu." I choose an *omelette au fromage* with salad and a baguette, which I eat very carefully in small torn off pieces followed by a sip of red wine and water (sign of old age when you're frightened of getting stuck into a baguette in Paris and breaking teeth—which I did in the Loire Valley last year. I often think wistfully of that half-molar resting in the rose-garden at the Chateau, part of my remains already residing in France.)

Three middle-aged French men come in and sit at the table next to mine. I am in a tiny corner looking out at busy intersecting streets (Rue du Cardinal Lemoine and Rue des Ecoles). Musee de Cluny is just down to the left but I am too tired and foot-sore to renew its acquaintance just yet.

I keep feeling it is evening. My body and brain are convinced it's evening. The three men chat on in beautiful French.

Lunch costs me 9 euros for the omelette and 4.30 for the wine. Cheap, very good meal and I'll be making a habit of this. Along with a tip and the fruit I buy for later, which costs me five euros, my meals for the day should amount to twenty euros. See, people wonder how I can afford to come to Paris. I stay an hour and head back to the hotel a few doors away, stopping to pick up a bottle of mineral water on the way.

Prepare to catch up on sleep (*dormer*). Turn TV on very quietly for company and take something to help me sleep.

I wake to the sound of tapping. I call out a croaky "Yes?" but with no answer I fall back into a heap of slumber once more. But the tapping continues, waking me again. It's pitch dark. One of the dogs must need a pee. I call out "Lillie, hang on. I'll let you out." I get up and stumble to an unfamiliar door – "Oh – that's right I'm in Paris!" My dogs are thousands of miles away. Someone is obviously hammering in the room above me it seems. I return to sleep once more, dreaming of my eldest daughter Rachel who lives in Perth.

Wake and look at my watch. It's 6 o'clock and as breakfast is 7 am to 9.30, I'd better get up. Begin to undress. Realize it is 6 *pm* – still the same day! It's night-time still – not 6 *am*! Back to bed. TV news is still on and although it's all in French, it's company, as I hate silence.

Dinner time. It really is dinner time. I eat my pear (pronounced *poir* by fruitier) and over-ripe *banan*. This is how I'll eat in future in Paris.

Very overcast and mild outside. Temperature predicted on TV is mid to high teens for next couple of days. Will continue to rest and watch TV and recover tonight and go seeking the magic Musee de Cluny in the morning which will be Saturday (I think.)

Last July Bonnie and I always met at the Musee de Cluny before joining the others. Sometimes at home in bed, fighting insomnia and longing for Paris, I close my eyes tightly and see Cluny's crumbling ancient Roman brick walls and the view down Boulevard St Michel, as if it were a perfectly clear film running in my mind, the postcard stands, the wet streets and the short walk up from there to Luxembourg Gardens. And the little park just around the corner from it, where on my last day in Paris last year I sat beside an old Parisian woman who watched the sparrows with me and reminisced about the Paris of years ago, in a mixture of French and English, while feeding herself pieces of the plastic bag that she clutched, and tore at and munched away on, in moments of silence. I wondered if that could be me someday – senile and rather outrageous. Maybe it wouldn't be so bad if it was in Paris.

I need to buy an umbrella, maybe somewhere in Boulevard St. Michel. Boy am I tired and sore!

Morning. I wake early and fall asleep again til 4.40 am. Have been dreaming about Rachel again. Rachel seems to be on my mind. I did telephone her the night before I left to wish her a safe and happy trip. She was about to head off to Japan with her daughter Rosy. I told her to give my regards to her old friends and neighbours that I'd been with nearly a decade ago when I spent six weeks with her in Japan.

Warrandyte Victoria 2003

The phone rang with its usual shrill demands and I tore up the steep hill of neglected bushland, where I'd been following the antics of a little echidna as he burrowed through what had once been Nick's attempt at a row of cucumbers. The only sign of Nick's weekend visits to me now were the cigarette butts he'd flicked into the barren earth, angry that there would be no cucumbers to pickle for his Ukrainian palate.

I tripped over the cat as he raced me to the phone.

"Mum – guess what!

...so it all depends on you Mum – what am I going to tell them? I can't say I can go til I get your answer – and I'm *counting* on you."

Rachel was my eldest daughter. She had been accepted into an English teaching program in Japan for twelve months. She'd been hoping for this for a long time.

"Please say you'll do it! We leave Perth in August. My dream has come true. Aren't you excited for me?"

It seemed that Paul, her journalist husband would only be able to stay in Japan for ten months because of his work commitments in Perth and she needed someone there for the children for after school.

I edged on to a corner of the chair. The cat rose, climbed on to my knee, his rear end turned towards my face and waved the snowy plume of a tail across my eyes. I felt I knew what was coming next from Rachel as she continued. "I need you to come to Japan and replace Paul for "after-school hours" for six…maybe eight weeks." There was a pause while this sank in.

"Six to eight weeks!"

"…Otherwise I won't be able to go and I *have* to do it. This is what I've studied for and my degree won't be worth anything if I don't have the experience of living in Japan. I'll never be fluent and my degree will be wasted."

So it seemed that it all depended on me. I extracted a clinging cat-hair from my mouth and thought. I'd probably have to leave work at the hospital – they would never let me go for two months. How could they? But then I hadn't been exactly thrilled about my job lately, well never really. Maybe if the hospital suspended me it would force me in to finding something different – I wonder, or better still, start painting at home in earnest. How many times had I attempted to do that, only to be forced back to working in an office because I had to eat sometimes, and who else was going to pay the bills anyway. It wasn't as if I was risking a career I was passionate about.

Aubrey Beardsley's claws dug through my jeans into my thighs. "Ouch!" Who was to say she would last the full year in Japan anyway. She might not even need me yet.

"Well, can you or can't you?" she went on in an agonized voice.

"Oh Rachel I'd love to but….." My mind was ticking over. I pushed the cat off my knee. I wasn't due for holidays yet and I had a year or so to wait for my long-service leave. Maybe I could put off telling them until the last minute…because they might replace me permanently if I gave them too much notice and then I'd be without income entirely when I returned. They might accept a *few* weeks' notice if I was honest with them – possibly, but I'd probably kiss my long-service goodbye.

"Gosh, I thought you'd be over the moon. Not many mothers get the chance for a holiday in Japan with *free* accommodation. Do you know what it would cost you to stay in a hotel in Tokyo?"

No, it had never entered my mind actually. Had I ever remotely considered going to Tokyo for a holiday? No. I had wanted to go back to Paris. "Just give me time to think Rachel. This is all very sudden."

"Maybe I should have asked Paul's mother. I know *she'd* want to go…but I'm *giving you* the opportunity… and you don't sound excited for me …*at all*."

June 2004

I was sitting on the plane waiting for take-off, reading Rachel's recent letter and chuckling over the school report on Maddie-Rose. (This hyphenated title of hers was a combination of two great-grandmothers. I called her Rosy.) It read:

"Maddie Rose is a very funny daughter. It is possible to become the life of the kindergarten and play happily every day. She holds out to the school lunch of the kindergarten and is challenging. ("This," Rachel wrote alongside it, "means that she only eats plain rice and won't touch anything else.")

Calls own house on the cellular phone at once when a big injury is done or becomes unwell. Tells it is Maddie Rose and come please if it is possible to do so. I want to see the appearance, though thinks the kindergarten also for the thing to injure because a lot of children play to exist as we are careful enough too.

Please inform with the telephone in the morning when missing.

Please hear from the charge when there is a thing about which worries something.

Please write the name in all the properties. Let's write without forgetting even in shoes. The hat is not needed on the day of rain.

Asks the rabbit hutch if receiving rain. Please take the raincoat home.
Does Maddie-Rose say that is happy the kindergarten? Maddie-Rose holds us out so that the kindergarten may become happy.

And not speaking a word of Japanese myself, I thought the teacher's attempt at English was not that bad.

I tucked the letter back into my hand-luggage and gazed out at the tarmac. The day was sunny and blue although it was mid-June, a typically fine Melbourne winter's day. I felt light-hearted and a bit irresponsible being swept away on someone else's mission.

I would never have chosen Japan to visit in a million years. I'd rather be going back to that little hotel ten minutes away from the Eiffel Tower with just a leisurely stroll to Rodin's Museum, The Kiss and The Thinker. I loved his work, but the choice had been taken out of my hands. It did feel rather excessive, to be paying for a ticket to go somewhere I didn't especially want to go to. But it might be quite an adventure being in such a foreign country with my grandchildren and my firstborn, whom I honestly felt a little in awe of these days. I had not seen my daughter for a whole year and it had been far too long.

I sat looking at my nails, clasping and unclasping my hands, unable to quiet the little flock of butterflies that rose and fell softly with the uncertainty of it all, making their presence felt within my breast.

A straggling line of passengers filed in, flashing me looks as they glanced at the seat numbers. I always became conscious at this point when travelling, of the intimacy between total strangers flung together in aeroplane seats, which seemed to be getting smaller every time I flew, and the encroachment into personal space that happened. So now I watched a little apprehensively as the passengers bumped along down the aisle, glancing curiously at each face, they too wondering who they were going to share the cramped space with for many hours, in this case, nine or ten, much easier than the long trip to Europe I had to admit.

A middle-aged man whom I assumed to be Japanese, his arms full of jacket, newspaper and brief case, took the seat next to me. He spent some time struggling to cram this bundle into the overhead storage before he glanced at me rather questioningly, ran his hand through his mop of rather shaggy grey hair and then nodded seriously and settled in to his seat. I squeezed back into mine, while his elbows overlapped into my space and there was the click of his seat-belt.

I had only recently seen the movie "Lost in Translation." I'd borrowed the copy from Caroline to get me in the mood for Japan and my sense of curiosity had been whetted. This and the desire to see Rachel and the kids urged me ahead with the idea and I was at last quite excited about going. Well I couldn't very well get out of it and that was that. I was already on my way and playing truant from work! I *was* going to enjoy this experience.

My neighbour and I sat together, ignoring each other in silence as the plane roared down the runway and soared into the Melbourne sky. It still lifted my heart with the thrill of power as always, even after many flights, carrying me away in its overpowering surge with the strength that reminded me of an army of Hell's Angels riding sedately through town on a Sunday morning and then charging off on to the highway with a menacing roar.

There was a hum of voices and the un-clicking of seat-belts as everyone burrowed into their seats and shuffled through newspapers and climbed up and down re-arranging their overhead luggage. I gazed back at the disappearing green fields of the wintry Victorian countryside and a few of my butterflies flitted lightly again somewhere near my heart.

I had the window-seat and halfway to Sydney breakfast arrived. This consisted of a banana, a packet of Dick Smith cereal, orange juice and coffee and a tiny croissant. I only ate the croissant and drank the bitter coffee and put the cereal and juice in my bag for the kids later on.

I glanced at my fellow traveller and noticed he had only eaten his banana and nothing else. I hesitated a moment and then I touched him lightly on the arm, and smiling at him, pointed at the banana on my tray, thinking he might like another one. I hoped I hadn't crossed some invisible cultural boundary though, with a weird message he might take the wrong way and be horrified at, which only occurred to me once I had made this suggestion, because he turned in his seat to face me, laughed and shook his head. Then he went about tearing open the cereal, still shaking his head amusedly and I shrank a little and decided to withdraw any further effort at becoming familiar, or attempting foreign diplomacy and I gazed out the window once more.

It wasn't long before I felt a light touch on my shoulder with my neighbour gesturing, eyebrows raised with a questioning look as to whether the milk went on the cereal or not. I think he suspected he may have offended me earlier and wished to re-open the line of communication between us. I nodded with a hesitant "Yes." I'd seen the woman across the aisle open her carton a moment before and spray her husband in the face with the milk, so I indicated that great care was needed and illustrated with my hands the possibility of a small explosion. He laughed loudly again at this and I offered him my already open carton which he took, nodding thanks.

From then on I tried to appear occupied, re-arranging my hand luggage, deciding to curb any further friendly but impulsive behaviour on my part which could be taken as rather undiplomatic - or worse. After all, this was my "confident" time of day.

I was used to waking at 4 am and agonizing over my past decisions, relationships and regrets. Rivulets of anxiety and depression had trickled through the family here and there and sometimes I found they lapped around my ankles with a threatening surge, when a high tide of loneliness or self-deprecation rose. I would retreat to my studio with Aubrey Beardsley (the snowy white cat with china-blue eyes and an anxious disposition worse than mine.) Losing myself in creation with oil paints and canvas was the best drug to take my mind on a holiday, thus extinguishing my crushing moods which left me and flew off to sit in the trees with the ravens, well out of sight. It worked for me anyway and I would recommend it.

Now I buried my head in one of the Japanese books my bank teller had lent me. She had spent two years in Japan recently and had given me a ready-reckoner for converting Japanese money into Australian dollars, together with an introductory book on the Japanese culture and a Japanese/English dictionary with lots of handy phrases which I was bound to make a lot of use of. This was the first time I had had a chance to look at any of them.

We arrived at Sydney airport. My neighbour gathered his things together, reaching up to the overhead area and at this point I managed to duck past him to join the others leaving the plane.

As I lined up in the queue once more, boarding for Japan, I was closely followed by a skinny young man who didn't look even vaguely official. He was bent double over my bag as I hurried along, probing the outside of my bag as we went. "What are you doing?" I spun around and snapped at him.

His answer sounded like "Just looking for trace of *expletives*."

"Looking for what?!"

I suddenly had memories of a reckless answering back to someone in uniform and being fined on the spot, not to mention being threatened with a full search of my car and my person, so I left it at that.

At that other time, I had been in a great hurry to drive my 90 year-old father back to his nursing home after spending the day trying to entertain him at home.

Dad had been doing charades of "about to throw up" (brought about by my *women's driving skills* I think), and when the officer announced through my window that I was twenty kilometers over the speed limit, I responded with a very unwise response which was something like *"Why aren't you chasing real criminals on drugs?"* After all, it was my negative time of day and I was feeling extremely anxious, but I didn't think he'd take that into consideration and this unwise comment was met in my face with a growl like meat coming through a mincer and ended up being quite costly, having to re-register my *"un-roadworthy"* car as well as a hefty speeding fine.

Innocent of any criminal intent, an hour later found me back in my seat on the plane and quite pleasantly surprised to see my travelling companion sitting in the same seat as before. I sighed with relief. Now I wouldn't have the concern of wondering who would be sleeping on my shoulder for eight hours and who I'd have to climb over to get to the toilet. Almost old friends now, we both smiled in recognition at our familiar faces as I squeezed past his knees and settled down and buckled up my belt.
I flicked through the pages of Japanese culture with a sigh, wondering how much control the Geisha women had over their lives. Not much I believed. Soon my concentration was disturbed as I could hear the breath of my neighbour looking over my shoulder and leaning a little my way. I continued to read, trying not to be aware of him, but not taking in the words that I was now staring at blankly. With a sudden bound, he jumped from his seat and retrieved a lap-top from the overhead

storage. He set it up and once settled became very engrossed in the screen. I began reading again, feeling that this restless Japanese businessman had decided to get on with his work and ignore me after all.

After a short time there was a slight tap on my shoulder and I looked up from my book. He was jabbing his finger at the screen, smiling broadly at me in anticipation. I squinted at the screen. "First time Tokyo?" it read. I was rather astonished, but our eyes met and after a moment's hesitation I nodded yes. He pointed back to the screen and began typing in Japanese characters as I watched, amazed. He was concentrating and I think, pondering on whether or not it would be correct for him to continue with this pursuit. Then with a click the characters were suddenly translated in to English. I had no awareness, let alone understanding of the extent and absolute magic available with today's technology.

"What is the sight-seeing that you would like to make well known?" popped up on the screen which had been translated for my benefit.

"What is the sight-seeing that you would like to make well known?" I echoed to myself. How quaint. I chuckled and took the offer of the keyboard as he turned the lap-top my way. I bit my lip. What could I say? "I do not know yet" I typed on the uncomfortably small keyboard and I looked at his face thoughtfully.

"You go Tokyo – how many days?"

"Yes, Tokyo, but then to see daughter in rural town – forty-two days – six weeks."

"What do you hope to see?"

I had no idea actually. I didn't know what I wanted to see. I wanted to see my daughter and the children. I'd read about the gardens in Kyoto and apart from that I'd never had much interest in, or knowledge of Japan.

"I would like to see gardens at Kyoto. Where is Kyoto from Tokyo?"

"Daughter has car?"

"No – daughter no car."

"And daughter with you forty-two days - how many children?"

"I have two daughters. This one teaching English."

I didn't quite grasp where his question was heading. Surely he wasn't about to offer me a driving tour. He continued on before I had a chance to say that Rachel had two kids.

"Ah, me two daughters also. Where is the daughter not in Japan?"

"She lives near me in Melbourne."

"What does the daughter beneath you do?"

"She is a psychologist."

"Are all the family members wise of mind?"

I smiled to myself and typed "The daughters are wise of mind. The mother is mad." He roared laughing and I wondered what "mad" had translated to in Japanese.

"Are you Melbourne breeding?"

"Yes" I smiled, amused.

"Ah, you look French."

I was pleased with this idea, although I knew it to be quite untrue but smiled appreciatively.

"Where were you born?" I typed in, enjoying this very entertaining and novel game.

"Nagoya" which provoked a lesson in the correct pronunciation of Nagoya as he retrieved his passport from his bag and pointed to the word. I glanced at his date of birth.

"You are ten months younger than I" I laughed as I typed and watched his astonished face.

"No…not correct!" He shook his head and laughed. I felt that I was being very responsible. I had put an end to any possible suspicion entering my mind that I was flirting with this handsome stranger. He would think me very old now.

There were several dead-end questions from each of us which were just lost in translation, but we laughed a lot and blamed the "software" for our very bewildered and puzzled stares at each other and back at the screen.

We exhausted our conversation on this pursuit and cut the communication line for a couple of hours. I put my head phones on and listened to some music, watched a bit of the movie which was quite violent and didn't interest me and then I dozed off.

I was aware of him putting the lap-top back in to the overhead storage. I hoped I hadn't been talking in my sleep, snoring or worse still – dribbling. I wondered why I had felt the need to tell him my age. No other woman would volunteer that information to a man as readily as I had done.

The movie ended and suddenly he was up at the luggage rack, getting the lap-top out once more, much to the annoyance of the grumpy steward who stood waiting for him to be seated again so he could pass. The stewards looked more like marshals – burly and grumpy, stomping up and down the aisle seemingly preoccupied. I think they were guards. Nine-eleven was still very fresh in everyone's memories. He pointed to the screen again.

"Is Tokyo your first?"

I hesitated, then replied "No – last year Paris for three weeks on my own – and ten years ago…

"Alone in Paris?" His mouth fell open. "No. Woman like you should be in Paris – with man." He shook his head disapprovingly and continued typing.

"I am returning from business trip to Russia, Australia and U.S." appeared on the screen.

"What did you like best in your travels?'

"Australia – Melbourne. What work you do?"

"I work at a hospital. I write letters for doctors,"

"Oh. You doctor?"

"No. Actually what I am doing here now" I said as I slowly tapped on the key-board, "reminds me of my job. Writing letters for doctors who sometimes have English as a second language." I don't think he understood this. And how much had been lost in translation at the hospital I now wondered, as I watched the Japanese characters pop up on the screen. I continued on "It's not what I love doing, but I do like to eat sometimes. My passion is painting."

He stared at the screen and I realized that the meaning in the translation of this rather laborious message was probably lost to him.

My passion had been Aboriginal rights and I had been boring everyone to death for years with it. It had been triggered by a night-school course on Australian History as part of my overdue Year 12 studies at age 35. We had concentrated on the European Occupation. I was hotly indignant with my new-found knowledge of the absence of empathy and respect for the first Australians, and I had become enlightened and would have happily shared my acreage with Aborigines if I had had any acreage at the time.

When we moved to Perth in '86 I'd gone on protest marches and travelled to the other side of the city for my weekly lesson in the Wangkatha language. On one occasion, when the teacher had forgotten about me and gone to Bingo, her twenty year-old son who was home, suggested he take the lesson. I naïvely agreed and we sat on the front verandah of their house on a hot Perth night, while he went over a lot of strange sentences in Wangkatha for the next hour, getting me to repeat them, with him laughing and rolling on the ground. I handed him the thirty dollars for the hour of suspect nonsense and drove home to the other side of the city feeling somewhat violated.

My tolerance and naïve desire to please has proved my undoing in many instances in my life but I went on marching and painting and talking to bemused Aborigines in Wangki language on the Perth train as I travelled to and from my work. They didn't understand the language (nor did the conductor who would come to my aid because he thought I was being threatened) because no-one in Perth apart from the teacher seemed to speak it. Noonga is the language they spoke there if at all, but I couldn't find anyone that gave lessons in it. I wasn't ready to go and live in remote towns like Hall's Creek or Kalgoorlie where Wangki was spoken. I felt isolated enough in Perth as it was but I felt I was meant to be on a philanthropic mission.

So my passion had been Aboriginal rights and I began to express my feelings in my paintings. When I left Perth behind and returned to Melbourne I did eighteen large oil paintings in my own naïve style over the next couple of years which I believed to portray my understanding of some of their injustices, recreating the passion of Nicky Winmar's symbolic protest with "*The Gladiator,*" Kathy Freeman winning her Olympic gold medal, and a dusky maiden standing in a water-hole with a stray empty beer-can floating among water-lilies, symbolic of the white-man's polluting ways, and many other emotions that had poured from my heart. These formed an exhibition for Reconciliation Week which I felt was equal to a long dialogue of debate and I had nothing more to say on the issues other than what my canvases said. My failure to make a speech disappointed some but I was not a speaker.

The comment by the local newspaper's art writer was "exhilarating with empathy and understanding" He also commented on "the varying of method and quality." Nevertheless he understood my message, which is what I was after, rather than impressive brush-strokes, as did several others who bought several of my paintings.

A comment from an Eastern European friend of a friend after her viewing of my paintings was "You know, I never liked *so and so* at all, but looking at your paintings, I feel I understand her now." I felt more chuffed at this than I would have been with another sale. That was all in 2003 following my first 'alone in Paris escapade.'

I looked back at the computer screen at my friend's new comment. "I have been studying watercolors for nine years but I don't get far."

"Maybe you should try oils. It's not as disciplined" (mine weren't anyway.) I had not yet felt a desire to paint in watercolors. I liked the sculptural texture of oils.

I looked out at the silver wing of the plane and wondered what would happen to my dogs and Aubrey Beardsley, if it suddenly fell off. I should have left a list of instructions for Caroline to go by if something like that happened. I wondered who she would give that cat to with his anti-social behaviour. I thought I would like the Bee Gees "Staying Alive" played at my funeral – as the coffin is carried out. That particular track was getting worn out as I played it regularly in the mornings if sunrise hadn't cured my negativity and the feelings of fear that I often woke with. (The mental image of Barry Gibb strutting down the street in his skin-tight jeans would buck anyone up.) My dancing caused the cat to become airborne and the dogs to sit watching with faces full of a somewhat curious but patient sympathy but my mood would lighten. But I think now I would prefer an art show with champagne and nibbles instead of a funeral. In fact, I think I'd prefer to just disappear with no send-off or "send-up" at all.

My eyes welled up in church if I sang certain hymns like "Amazing Grace" which I had for my mother's funeral. In fact my voice would stall with emotion and I couldn't sing for the tears. And the other hymn she loved that went "Though storms may rage about me…" Poor Mum. I understood now. My eyes welled up thinking of her.

Caroline was not really agreeable at all for the Bee Gees "Staying Alive" "It would be such poor taste Mum to be played at your funeral. What are you talking about death for anyway?" I think she had me on the edge of "manic depressive" sometimes and although she adamantly denied it, asked me why I always wanted a label because I would say to her quite often "I think I might have such and such a disorder. I've been typing a letter at work on a psych patient and I have some of their symptoms I think."

"Really Mum, have you thought about getting a little bit of counselling."

"No."

The afternoon wore on. My arm was being nudged gently but persistently and I was separated from my wandering thoughts in to the past with the lap-top screen saying "You draw me now please," and with that my neighbour brought out a wobbly propelling pencil and lined paper folded in half which belonged with his work notes. He placed this on the book I was nursing.

"Please!"

"No, no, no. I cannot now." I shook my head.

"Yes *please*." He rolled his eyes at me, insistent. I tilted his head to profile, took a deep breath and began. I suppose it took fifteen minutes quick sketching. His face was very nice actually. I liked it and a profile was the easiest way of execution.

"You have good face." I spoke this without the aid of the computer and he nodded, smiling and chuckling as if he understood. He had heavy lids and a sensual mouth. He would have been very handsome when he was younger. He was nice looking now – full-stop. Steel-grey hair and lots of it and a lovely smile that lit up his face with soft brown eyes. What a shame. I felt like we should be travelling together. We were, but soon it would come to an end. I rather wished we were going to Paris together, continuing this comfortable relationship we had begun. We'd be perfect companions. We seemed so relaxed together – as though we'd been friends for years. Soul mates, I thought, wandering around hand in hand under the Eiffel Tower or sitting chatting over coffee with the computer on the table between us as our interpreter. I was really enjoying the company of a total and complete stranger.

What *was* I thinking? I looked up from my sketch, momentarily meeting his smiling eyes. He had a wife for sure - forget it. I was indulging in romantic fantasy - as usual.

He looked at the pencil sketch, a delighted look of recognition and pleasure on his face.

"Ah - portrait - portrait - please sign."

I laughed and signed it with a great flourish. "You have good face."

He carefully put his "portrait" away in his briefcase, retrieving it several times during the remainder of our journey for more admiring looks, smiling each time and shaking his head.

"Please, your name," and he presented me with a small notebook. I wrote it in full and he spent the next few minutes working on the correct pronunciation.

We then turned to the phrase book I had with me and read some sentences to each other, with me chuckling delightedly as I found appropriate things to say to him in Japanese. We both laughed together as I stumbled over the Japanese sentence for "I want red wine. Can you send the head waiter over?" He roared.

We were having such fun and I noticed curious, rather suspicious glances from the steward or guard or whatever he was as he passed by us each time. I had been feeling that it must be about drinks time and felt in a celebratory mood, but he told me via the phrase book that he didn't drink wine - "Not at all. No alcohol!"

He shook his head seriously and wagged his finger to emphasize this, so I was surprised to see him take a bottle of white wine from the trolley minutes later. I looked curiously at the wine.

He indicated with a gesture of fingers "Just a tiny bit." He grimaced at the first sip and we continued to read nonsense to each other from the phrase book quite uninhibitedly. He looked at me and shook his head with a very dreamy expression and said "Happy, happy."

I read out to him in Japanese "Thank you for the evening. I have enjoyed myself."

"I am very, very happy" he murmured huskily

"So am I" I smiled, then laughing, adding from the book the Japanese phrase "May I take you home?" He rocked back and forth laughing, patting my arm and leaning closer to my side of the seat.

Dinner arrived. Curried fish and pumpkin – *kabochya*. We went through the Japanese and English for everything on our plates. I noticed, feeling a little concerned, that he was downing the white wine with great gusto. I said, shaking my head, "Bad wine. Too much not good. You say you not drink wine." He was getting very flushed in the face. I hoped there wasn't a medical reason that had kept him from drinking alcohol up until then. He might collapse or die and it would be my fault. I had led him astray, off the wagon maybe. I went to top up my glass but nothing came out of the bottle. "All gone?!"

He burst into guffaws of laughter pointing at the cap screwed on the bottle and wagged a finger at me again "tut-tutting" me in Japanese. I'd only had half a glass of red and he thought I was drunk already. Maybe I was. Then I noticed he'd finished his bottle entirely. His face was a strange colour. He seemed to be having a very hot flush. He stroked my hair and breathed huskily "Juree - you beautifor, beautifor."

I pointed to the empty bottle. "It's the wine."

He shook his head and said "No. You beautifor. I happy, much much happy."

I was *much much happy* too and, maybe he was not married. Maybe at worst he was separated, or better still widowed. I didn't want to never see him again.

"Phone number....address *prease* Juree."

The steward walked by giving me a "*What are you two up to …you're not going to disappear into the washroom together are you?*" look. And I returned his stare with one that hopefully meant "Don't worry we're not completely out of control. I'm behaving." My gaze followed him down the aisle to make sure he had read my thoughts.

The plane began to descend. I began to write my address in the little black book he had produced, but then I stopped…I flicked through my Japanese phrase book. I asked carefully in clumsy Japanese "Who is – meeting you – at airport?" Then, pausing for a moment and waiting for the inevitable... looking at the soft brown eyes I asked softly, casually …"Your wife?"

But there was no hesitation with his answer - "Yes – wife!" he grinned broadly.

The pen screeched to a halt. The plane was coming down to earth slowly. So was I. I had had him widowed for ten years and free and charming and my soul mate – I knew it!

Fog and mist and suddenly the coast of Japan. A golf course. I believe it costs a fortune to play golf in Japan. So much green! "I'm in Japan!"

He shook his head somewhat sadly as we gathered up our things.

"Good luck Juree" he offered and I can't remember now whether we shook hands or if he gave me a brush of a kiss on the cheek.

"No, no address, no. Goodbye." I joined the growing queue of passengers impatient to get off the plane. I felt irritated, or disappointed or angry, I don't know which. Maybe all three, and we went our separate ways.

I saw him again at the Customs counter and he stood staring at me. His face wasn't red any more but the smile had been replaced with a concerned expression. He was probably questioning the accuracy of his computer and wondering what incorrect translation it had been guilty of.

The plane arrived at Narita airport thirty minutes early and I went straight through Customs without a hitch. I couldn't believe it. The Customs man looked at my Disembarkation form. I had written my "regular work" as "Medical Transcriptionist," so whether or not they thought I was a brain surgeon – I don't know.

"Here on *horror day*?"

"Yes" I said. "My daughter teaches English here."

"Oh well you have nothing to *decrare* then," as though he didn't believe for a minute that anyone with a daughter teaching English and with me straight out of an operating theatre could be guilty of carrying drugs, weapons or exotic birds.

Rachel had warned me that I'd probably take two and a half hours to get through. That's how long she took to get through Customs, and *she* was the English teacher. But, straight through like a shot. It must have been the "medical background."

And there was Rachel looking wearier than I'd ever seen her, waving and smiling amongst the crowd of Japanese faces. The humidity hit me.

We hugged. "You're early Mum. How was your flight?"

"I got through Customs in a flash. And the flight – the flight was just wonderful. I sat next to this Japanese man…," I began and laughing, struggled out of my jacket, feeling the humidity consume me. I was dying to tell her about my first experience with a Japanese person. I needed to make light of it, to convince myself that I wasn't experiencing a feeling of disappointment or maybe regret, at not having given him my address or maybe guilt right on my arrival in Japan for my innocent flirtation that I knew my daughter would not approve of.

Rachel hurried me along after she had asked a passerby in Japanese for directions. She seemed fluent in Japanese. I was impressed. "We have to hurry Mum. The train to Tokyo leaves in three minutes. It's so good you're early."

"Don't make me run Rachel or I'll wet myself." We ran anyway.

"There are toilets on the train."

It was Saturday night. The train was quiet. "Do you need the toilet now?"

"No. I'll sit tight. I'll go later." I attempted to chat about my travelling companion. She wasn't interested. She wanted me to look at dozens of photos of Japan: Rosy at kindergarten, and cherry blossoms in spring.

I stopped pursuing my line of conversation and my voice trailed off ...."Rachel, I'm going to be here for six weeks..." After all, looking around me, I felt like I'd just arrived on another planet and the sudden change in circumstances and surroundings and the instant severing of a friendship, left me feeling a bit like an abandoned puppy.

"Don't show me photos of everything *now* Rachel. I want to see it all for myself as a surprise."

"We won't be going here so look at these" she said showing me photos of a beautiful hotel they had stayed at in the mountains in autumn. In the photos the children looked as though they had grown a lot. Paul her husband had become far too thin. He was only fifteen years younger than me. I forgot I was getting old fast and he was really not that far behind me.

I was keen to see the approaching lights of Tokyo but Rachel wanted me to look at more photos. All I wanted to do was relax and absorb my daughter and maybe watch the lights of Japan at night served up to me behind her as an exciting backdrop. I'd missed her so much. I just wanted to sit and look at her. After all it had been over a year.

We arrived at the station in Tokyo. There were toilets on the station.

Well, this was different. A hole in the ground and stinking. I stood astride it and splashed the cuffs of my linen slacks. There was a first time for everything wasn't there. How did this thing flush? I pulled a couple of levers and nothing happened. I opened the door and peeped out. There was a long line of about twenty Japanese women peering at me anxiously and impatiently, shifting uncomfortably from one foot to the other.

Rachel rang her Japanese neighbours on her mobile. They were going to meet us at the station. We changed trains. The next one was packed. All the women had reddish-brown hair. Rachel said they all dyed their hair "Western Brown." That was the look. I was in fashion then for the moment.

She conversed with two giggling teenage girls who sat across the aisle from us. They reassured her that we were on the right train. She looked so tired. She told me the trip would take an hour.

Not many people had computers there according to Rachel. They all had facilities on their mobile phones instead.

"Why didn't you give that Japanese man your address Mum?"

"Because he was a *married* man."

"They're all like that here Mum."

"Well I'm not interested in a *married* man."

"*Really*." followed by a short silence which was broken by Rachel. "Do you know they can get used high-school girls' undies from vending machines here?!"

I blinked at her. "What? Who?"

We were going to a suburb or a town that was pronounced like "Cookie." The train lurched occasionally. The floor slid back and forth.

"That's what an earthquake is like" she explained, quietly replacing the photos into her bag. "If there's an earthquake while I'm at work, just stand in the front doorway. That's the strongest structure in the building. We have earthquakes all the time here and the kids do earthquake drill every day at school but they get under the desks. The first one we had was when I was at work. Paul was alone upstairs using the computer and the whole place started shaking and he came rushing down the stairs screaming "Earthquake earthquake!" (I could just imagine the six foot five inches of him leaping around like a grasshopper.) "He jumped literally right out of his sneakers which went flying in two directions and he ran out into the street yelling. Our neighbour Megumi had seen him fly past and said that that was the most dangerous thing he could have done because of falling roofs and glass...just stand in the front doorway until it's over. That's the strongest structure to shelter under."

Rachel as a little girl was always hoping for a volcano in the suburbs. She wanted excitement and drama. She didn't want *me* to provide the drama though. But an earthquake every day - she was in the right place. That was probably the real reason she was drawn to Japan.

"Alright Rachel. I'll remember."

We got to Kuki. There was something familiar. Did it remind me of somewhere in Paris? Two old men sat by a food vendor. The air was hot and heavy. A black, very overweight poodle sat puffing and panting on a bench beside the men. A busker strummed his guitar and wailed away in Japanese. There was a buzz of traffic. I left my luggage to pat the dog. The smell of sweat on the man holding him made me reel backwards. I decided not to force my way through the rancid air surrounding him and stood awkwardly looking at them both. Rachel moved in and chatted to the men, going up close, squatting down to pat the panting poodle, seemingly unaffected by the smell. The man commented on her Japanese. They were impressed. I was impressed.

"I'm not really fluent at all – maybe another year and I'd be right" she assured me.

The neighbours arrived. My grandchildren arrived with them. Suddenly it was hugs and "Nanny" and squeezing of hands and pressing of cheeks to breasts. Everyone was bowing and smiling.

2013 – Good Morning Paris!

The TV is still going but now with a French comedy. I'm still weary. At least time is back to normal again now for me and I'm not feeling totally upside down.

Showered and dressed, having kept my precious money pouch that I wear on a long cord around my neck at arm's length the entire time, I apply moisturizer and a little foundation. My lines don't show up quite so much in this mirror as they do at home. I'd always hated having a "wide face" as I describe it. It was a fat face actually and as I grow older, despite the desire to somehow acquire the looks of a retired ballet dancer, at sixty-eight and a half I have the figure of Mick Jagger and as for the wide face, most of it is determined to end up underneath my chin, not arranged as I had planned at all. Life was cruel. My youngest grandson age five loved to arm-wrestle me. He thought it appropriate because I was built like one of the kids and he always won—not because it was right to let him win but because the arthritis in my hands and wrists screamed for mercy. Life was indeed cruel.

I sigh and put the eyebrow pencil between my teeth to pull the metal cap off which I have done a hundred times at home – too mean to buy new pencil and it is actually only an inch long. One's eyebrows and body hair in general seem to diminish with age I have found. Caroline gave me this eyebrow pencil years ago, a remnant from her make-up course before she changed to Psychology – maybe I hang on to it for sentimental reasons – and – CRUNCH! – What the...NO!!

I gasp at my reflection in the mirror over the bathroom basin. I have broken a piece right off my front tooth! A quarter of my tooth is gone. NO!!!!! Not my first day in Paris!

Perhaps I'm dreaming – I hope so – and I will wake up in a moment and it will still be last night!

I can't believe it! Why me?! What have I done? – Recently! I shriek looking skyward.

Well, I'll be the non-smiling Australian trying to look French for the next three weeks. I'll just have to look haughty and not open my mouth. That will look French maybe. No, I will look just like my passport photo! And how am I going to eat? *Mon Dieu!* Why does it happen in France?! Well, I'm just going to have to grit my teeth (gently) and bear it.

First breakfast. Cracked cup – another one on the tray. (I didn't crack it! Is there a message here?)

Bonnie did say "It's a Spartan breakfast, cup of tea, baguette and croissant," not like last year's smorgasbord in Rue de Renne. Of course, I could not consider the baguette. The whole tooth may explode. So breakfast is finished in record time.

"Room number Madame?"

I concentrate and then "....*quarante cinq.*"

She gives me a "Well done" smile. I try not to smile back at her.

On the way to the lift I pass Americans at the desk complaining about their small room and another woman from the U.S. is begging for "a room to spend just the day in" as her mother-in-law has just died. I've got much worse news to deal with closer to home. My tongue goes to my tooth's jagged surface.

It's still semi-dark outside. Wearing new navy clingy dress, black leggings, shoes from Cambodia (like tapshoes Caroline commented) and navy, grey and white animal print scarf as the temperature is predicted to be 50°F today – moderate/cool.

By the way, note to myself – remind me not to come via Hong Kong again. They sprayed pesticide heavily half an hour before landing and I'm still coughing.

2004 – Meeting With Japan.

I don't know how Rachel would have survived without her Japanese neighbours. They were always in and out of the apartment chattering and giving concerned advice and when Maddie-Rose was sick earlier on, they had helped nurse her back to health. She had been so very fortunate to have been placed next to such a helpful and friendly family.

They drove us back to the apartment in their van, the car full of smoke from Megumi's husband Yuuta who puffed away chain-smoking, and blowing clouds of it around us while the kids laughed and chatted loudly in Japanese, not seeming to mind the choking air. The screen at the front of the dashboard showed on a map where we were. (I had thought thirty years ago that this would be a wonderful invention and why hadn't somebody thought of it and now here I was, seeing my idea in action in Japan.) Then it was transformed to a computer game that the boys' eyes became glued to. The same thing was happening in the car travelling beside us. Everyone had a movie going on or a computer game on the dashboard while they drove.

The apartment was in a block of units. Sandy from North Carolina, who was there, also in the same language program as Rachel, called out "Hi" from the upstairs apartment as we bundled in.

"Such a tiny area to be in for twelve months." I gasped as I walked in, dropping my luggage. No wonder "tall Paul" was glad to get out. He would have taken up most of the space. I scanned the "Paris B&B"-sized bathroom where, when you showered, the entire space was sprayed. There was a separate toilet with a hand-basin on the top of the cistern, so that when you flushed, water also came through a tap on the top of the cistern and into the basin where you washed your hands and the water then filled the cistern again. An invention I hadn't seen in Australia or anywhere else for that matter.

A kitchen/family room was at one end with a low table and low seats. The table had a heating coil attached to it underneath, radiating downwards for chilly legs in winter. That could have disastrous consequences. I couldn't imagine safety standards ever allowing that in Australia.

The "*tatami* room" (or room for sleeping) was covered with straw matting. It was quite empty but at bed-time out came folding rubber mattresses two inches thick. On top of these, futons were laid, which were just soft bedding about the same thickness as the mattresses and then a sheet and a very heavy blanket. These were all stored in the bedroom cupboard and each morning they were taken up and put out to air, all their bright colours hanging from balconies and windows, flapping up and down the street in a riotous and blatant flag-waving statement.

"First rule"... and a very rigid one as Anthony informed me. "Shoes off Nanny!"

Shoes were everywhere at the door. This spot was called the "*genkan*." As for walking into the *tatami* room in shoes - instant death I think. I got the message.

"I can feel a tiny piece of gravel on the floor. Did you walk outside in bare feet?"

"Oh, I forgot. I'm just learning. I promise I won't do it again."

The second bedroom was really tiny and was used as a dressing-room and all the family's clothes were kept there. The whole family shared the tatami room. Rachel reassured me that the neighbours *all* shared their tatami room with their children, the teenage boys as well. "How did they ever get to have three children?"

Rosy had been helping to clean the apartment all day. Rachel had picked some pink, blue and mauve hydrangeas. The Japanese loved hydrangeas and they were everywhere just then. Every talk show on TV had a huge arrangement of hydrangeas behind the presenter. There was no garden at the apartment, but a pot of lavender and geraniums at the door which Rachel had placed there.

I could cope with any sleeping arrangements as long as I had my special pillow that supported my arthritic neck, but I couldn't cope with the snoring. That night the two children, base and deeper base made sounds like asthmatic donkeys. After falling asleep with exhaustion listening to Anthony's braying, I was woken by this sound again at 2 am. He settled after about half an hour but then began again at 4 am and the air weighed suffocatingly, like wall to wall damp cat. After all, there were four of us in a tiny enclosed room. I dragged my blanket off to the dressing-room and curled up on the floor which was cold. I then migrated to the living area and the couch.

Rachel was very disappointed with me in the morning. "You *would* get used to it. You're not trying."

"But the windows are kept closed at night and I'll suffocate. Can't we keep them open?"

"The neighbours wouldn't dream of opening their windows at night. We'd be murdered in our beds. Mum, the children have been looking forward to having you sleep beside them *Japanese* style. We wanted you to experience Japanese culture."

"Will they be disappointed if they wake up next to a dead woman – Australian style? I won't last six hours let alone six weeks doing this. I'm sorry but I need oxygen – and I need to experience sleep!"

####

On Sunday we walked to the main area in town which was pretty grim and reminded me of the town in Bali where Caroline and I had joined in a funeral procession going to a cremation that we were invited to as a "special tourist experience."

This town was a little shabby and bleak but there were some streets with some very stylish Japanese houses. Most of them had ornate fences in concrete and wrought iron to match the theme of the house. Each roof had tiles which were like little waves and these trimmed some of the tall concrete fences too. There were bamboo-roofed carports covered in creepers and others were tiled to match the house. The windows were all quite small and clean-cut, the fancy decorative touches being reserved for the doors and surrounds and rooftops. Gardens were compact and ordered, sometimes with just a solitary tree of green pompom foliage in exactly the right spot. There were lots of pink hydrangeas and every tree and hedge was shaped and clipped like a poodle straight from the salon.

The actual town had no shops to browse through or inviting shop windows to entertain one. There was not a sign of fashion, just the barest necessities of life. It was certainly not a touristy town but I found it very interesting to see people living as they did every day with no tourists in sight. I would be seeing the Japanese as they really were, going about their ordinary lives with no artificial touristy facades. That thought really appealed to me.

The streets were quite narrow and those people not driving vans pedaled bicycles. They bowed or nodded as they passed us in the street, even while astride their bikes. If I was going to start riding a bike as Rachel expected me to, I'd have to practise the art of bowing while riding or I'd fall off and break something for sure. It was many years since I had been on a bike.

We arrived at a shrine and walked through a line of lamps that looked like red-lacquered bird-houses. These led through a tall archway. It was silent but for our footsteps scuffing the gravel. This place was a memorial to the soldiers from many wars. The writing on the stone walls was of course all in *Kana* characters so I understood nothing.

Rosy stared up at me as I waved the persistent mosquitoes away from my face. She was looking at the chunky silver head on a leather string that I was wearing around my neck. "Oh Nanny, you're wearing Buddha." came the deep little voice full of awe.

"Are you sure Rosy?" I whispered, fingering it and bending down to let her look more closely.

"Yes. It *is* Buddha" she reassured me. "He's a god you know." We blinked at each other gravely.

It was complicated for Rosy at mealtimes. They had always said grace before meals and in fact Anthony, inclined to be a touch fanatical, went through the process before each course, not just before his meal and got a right ragging at school. This was a Buddhist area and Rosy reminded everyone of his importance in the world and particularly in *her* world. When "Christian" grace was finished and the eating began, a little indignant voice would be heard piping up at the table…*"And what about Buddha?!"*

The children would also mumble something that sounded like "*Eat a ducky mouse*" following grace. I was obviously very ignorant because I thought they were insulting each other, sort of like Bart Simpson's "eat my shorts!" (I still don't know what it means.)

The gardens were lovely and green at the shrine. Autumn would be really beautiful with the red and gold maples and in spring with the cherry blossoms. With summer, it was green and full of azaleas, hydrangeas, and lots of bamboo. (My friend on the plane had said Japan was at its best in March and April.)

There was some form of ritual going on in the temple. There were loud booming sounds like thunder which turned out to be drums and Rachel and Anthony said they were learning to play a smaller version of these and I would be going to watch them perform this on the coming Thursday night which was their "Taiko drum lesson night."

In the centre of the park there were some very unhealthy forlorn looking chickens enclosed in an aviary together with a moulting rooster and a pair of peacocks and we plucked the only shreds of grass that made it out of the gravel path and fed it to them. They watched us until we were out of sight, wanting more. I wondered who cared for them.

It was a rather depressing sight heading back down the road to "home." There were electricity lines and poles everywhere, all at slightly different angles like the skeletons of skinny scarecrows, due I supposed to the many earthquakes. They looked very untidy and the street scene looked like a black and white photo.

When we returned to the apartment Megumi, Rachel's neighbour, joined us. Rachel and she chattered on, laughing and joking. Rachel's voice when speaking Japanese to Megumi was much higher and more lilting than when she spoke English. I tried to contribute to their conversation with mostly sign language and to make conversation, asked with Rachel as interpreter, what the typical Japanese lunch was. Without another word, Megumi scurried off to her apartment chattering in Japanese as she went and returned some minutes later with noodles and fish in soy sauce with green beans in a sesame sauce. She also proudly showed me some pink tomatoes from her parent's *"farm."*

We sat on the floor and ate our lunch with chopsticks. Rachel warned me then, that in future to be careful what I enquired about to Megumi, otherwise she was inclined to take it as a "request" and just go and organize it, and that I had probably made her feel she had to prepare lunch for me. Megumi squatted on her heels, smiling at each of us in turn as if watching a tennis match, quite unaware of what we were saying and amused at the fascinating English conversation going back and forth with her eyes following closely.

This area we were in was zoned "semi-rural" and about an hour's drive from Tokyo. All the houses had their "farms," which were as big as the smallish Melbourne suburban garden, crammed with vegetables, herbs, a fruit tree and some chickens. Rice grew in any spare land along the streets. These streets were just a maze and had no names, so to avoid becoming very lost, one had to become extremely observant and note landmarks such as a red wall, a rock painted bright yellow or a junk shop on a corner nearby, or a one-eyed dog that sat outside a gate regularly. I had no idea how my letters had ever managed to get there.

Megumi returned after lunch. Rachel turned to me translating "Would you like to see outlet? You might like to look at shops" and Megumi nodded at me enthusiastically waiting for my answer.

It took us one and a half hours to travel the 45 km. The streets were narrow, the pace slow. The scenery once out of town really reminded me of Bali, but a very flat Bali and very brilliant green with rice paddies everywhere. It was a generally Asian world with its bamboo and ordered landscape, but the carefully shaped trees in the gardens made it uniquely Japanese and this was one of the most characteristic features of Japan that I remember.

We wandered through stalls containing everything the well-dressed dog should wear, from Hawaiian shirts and sun-frocks to pullovers and all over thirty dollars apiece. Rosy stopped to pat and interview every dog we met. Dogs here were made a real fuss of, and thank goodness they didn't eat them. That was one of the first questions I asked Rachel when she begged me to come to Japan and she was very indignant that I should suggest that the Japanese ate dogs or cats. They don't, but they do dress them up and paint their nails and treat them differently to what we do in the Western world.

We piled back into the car which was filling with smoke from Yuuta's excessive smoking habit, and rather unpleasant on a long journey. He stayed in the car, the ever patient chauffeur and watched movies while we did the shopping.

Shopping was Megumi's only passion or "hobby" according to Rachel.

We went to another centre like Westfield's Shoppingtown. We wandered around a store laden with blue and white china and I bought a *"noren"* which was a two-paneled curtain to hang in the hallway of the home. When I did hang it up when I got back to Melbourne, my handyman commented as he ducked under it and entered, "You didn't really have to put bunting up just for me." Nobody but me appreciated the effect my *noren* had.

Rachel was almost obsessive about blue and white china. "As long as it doesn't have MADE IN CHINA somewhere on it" she'd say, turning over every bowl to check where it had been made. Each time she did this I smiled to myself, thinking of her father, who one morning during a fierce argument with me (he was like a cat in a bathtub before breakfast) finished his porridge and looked like he was about to hurl the bowl at the floor. He hesitated and turned it over to find my name looking at him and said sheepishly "Thought I'd better check first." I was quite touched at his thoughtfulness at not wanting to smash in anger, something I had made with my own two hands, and at that point we met each other's gaze and both burst out laughing.

I loved the blue and white Japanese pottery and would have loved to have taken a collection of it back home. Rachel had a book on Japanese décor. Everything was blue and white and hand-dyed, like rolling seas with billowing curtains at every opportunity, the theme of the sea being predominant in Japan. It gave a wonderful feeling of serenity and order.

I thought how I would like to buy presents for Megumi and her family before I left Japan. I was so grateful for the way they had been there for Rachel, but for now I bought them coffee all round and we headed off home to the apartment.

The computer showed a message had arrived from Angela, a friend I'd worked with for years and who was house-sitting for me and minding the dogs and cat. She'd just broken up with her husband and had jumped at the suggestion of an empty house to stay in for six weeks and she loved dogs. This solved the animal problem for me and I was very grateful and hoped she was managing. They were a bit of a handful if you weren't used to the three of them. Coco, my biggest dog was "waking her up at 4 am and not going back to bed again." She always woke at 4 am, Coco that is. She knew I was always awake before 4 am and worrying. Many years ago Ed used to arrive home at 4 am from gigs. That's probably where my insomnia began.

At midnight I dragged my blanket behind me and headed off to the couch. I *had* tried. The asthmatic donkeys had driven me out again. I wished I had Coco with me. We could talk.

####

Monday was a school day. In Melbourne it was the Queen's Birthday holiday and another day for Angela to learn to cope with the dogs and cat and catch up on some sleep before she returned to work on Tuesday. I couldn't help but be a bit worried about my four-legged babies at home and how they would be thinking I had deserted them.

At 7.30 the children were about to leave. I kissed Rosy and off she toddled. They all walked in a group, picking up more kids along the way to school, a pedestrian bus-load, wandering off like blank-eyed sheep, some with serious faces like Rosy's, some grinning yet anxious, ready to boldly face the firing squad. I decided to wait until everyone had left the house including Rachel, so I would not be in anyone's way and then have my shower in peace. I had to get in to a regular routine so as not to hold anyone up.

I waved goodbye from the dressing-room window like a good grandmother, wearing a thin nightdress over which I modestly wore a short light-weight satin dressing gown. My hair was undone and unruly, but no-one could see me through the curtains as I called out my goodbyes and waved amusedly to the line of children.

A long gleaming black car suddenly pulled up. I heard Rachel outside in the street in front of the window say in a surprised voice while climbing on to her bike.

"Goodness, it's the Headmaster. This is odd. Maybe he's come to meet my mother."

I shrank. The car door opened and out jumped an athletically built man. He stood at attention beside it, slim and handsome in a dark suit, immaculate, bowing deeply in my direction. Well, I was in my nightclothes and had been caught. I could not go out to meet Gregory Peck's double wearing my dressing-gown and looking totally unkempt, so I stood there, believing myself to be shielded by the curtain only a couple of metres away from him.

"Mum, bow to him!"

"Oh Rachel *please*." I whispered aloud, trying to dissolve in to the background. "He doesn't know I'm here."

He and I stood, with me wrapping my arms about my torso in a protective and defensive stance at the window, both of us dipping and bowing silently back and forth for what seemed like an agonizing age. With a final deep bow to me he returned to his car. With a few words to Rachel he bowed once more, clicked his heels and saluted. The car sped off and I watched him, still bowing back and forth over the steering wheel whilst looking back in my direction.

"How embarrassing" I groaned red-faced to Rachel who was still adjusting her feet on to the pedals. "Still, he couldn't see me through the curtain, thank goodness."

"He said he was checking on the children's pick-up program. Still, he's never done that before – and yes, we could both see you perfectly well through that curtain. He's never come to the house to check on the children before. That was most unusual. I think he must have wanted to pay my mother a visit to check on *her*."

I groaned in despair and off she went, calling out as she disappeared in to the distance "And don't go wandering around on your own. You'll get lost!"

I felt mortified. Trust my luck. I so wanted Rachel to be proud of me. Hopefully I would catch up with him at school the next day. It was Open-Day and Rachel said I had to go in her place. Maybe I could make amends and let him see I was civilized after all – well sort of.

I got stuck into cleaning the flat. I hadn't realized that I was *"not pulling my weight."* I was not really here for a holiday but to be Rachel's right-hand man, which I proved not to be very good at over the ensuing weeks and my duties involved more than just keeping an eagle eye on the children.

I could not read any of the bottles under the sink as all the labels were in *Kana* and this meant I had to inhale everything to identify it before I dared use it. I couldn't find a vacuum cleaner or even a broom and went over every inch of the floors with a tiny hand broom and shovel that belonged amongst Maddie-Rose's toys. I folded the mats in the tatami room. The futons were heavy and I strained my wrists lifting them. I put a couple of loads of washing on and remembered this time to slip in to the rubber thongs at the back door before I walked on the gravel. The clothes line consisted of a small portable frame hanging from the porch. I hid my articles of underclothing behind the children's clothes. I already felt exposed and vulnerable. I was still in shock following the incident with the Headmaster.

I was wanting to start a diary and I didn't have anything to write in. I thought I'd go for a wander later and see how far I could go, before I got lost, and buy something – anything, to write in.

The day began heating up. I strained my ears at the sound of Japanese pop music in the distance, getting louder and louder and noticed a van slowly cruising by. Rachel said they were mad on loud-speakers for advertising and announcing if anyone was lost or if there was a public warning of some kind and they drove around giving descriptions and instructions.

Rachel kept referring to the *"Yakuba"* being in control of the community and that at 5 pm every day they played music and all the children had to run home. I didn't believe it. That sounded like the Hamlin story to me. That and schoolgirls' used knickers – really?!

I had bought some nail-polish at the outlet place on Saturday. I had a split thumb-nail that had remained split ever since a brush-tailed possum bit me while I was feeding it bread one night some years ago. A continually splitting nail resulted and the nail-polish seemed to strengthen it and hide it.

    I put on a black singlet top, beige cargo pants and a floppy cream hat as it was hot out there and headed off down the street bowing to an old woman who passed. She looked at me grimly and bowed. I stopped and looked at a garden with rows of onions, tomatoes, pumpkin (*kapochya* or was it *obacha*), beans and strange herbs as well as wind-flowers, holly-hocks and aster daisies and watched a woman tending them. She looked weary and bedraggled and leant on a rake glaring at the crows. The place was alive with crows and there were crow-calls day and night. I was awakened by them each morning. That was the first sound I heard cutting through the drone coming from the *tatami* room. I would never have associated that with Japan in a million years. Crows reminded me of parched Australian paddocks in summer and Graham Kennedy, (the most famous variety show host in Australia who in the moderate old days of Australian TV tried to get away with the expletive "faaaaaaaark" as "just a crow-call" but resulted in him being banned from live television from then on.)

    I decided to turn left. No street names to note. I carefully observed things.

I arrived at a junk shop and turned right in to more of a main street. It was full of big blocks of apartments.

Everyone's futon was out airing. Damn, I forgot to put our futons out. I walked to another corner and there was the main road. There was a collection of vending machines in a line. My eyes glanced at each one quickly and there was nothing remotely like "used undies" displayed anywhere that I could see. That was probably a fantasy of my son-in-law.

I waited to go across the street on the painted white lines. I knew what reputation Asians had as drivers in Australia. I didn't trust them here either. Rachel had said "They don't usually stop for pedestrians" which I thought was a rather untoward state of affairs, so I waited until there was not a sign of a car in either direction and then crossed.

I found a pharmacy. I needed some cold cream. I ventured in feeling very brave on my own. The attendant was a middle-aged, very charming lady. (Funny that I didn't feel middle-aged. What was middle-aged *plus* supposed to feel like anyway?) She watched patiently while I performed my face-cleansing charade and then guided me to some tiny jars of expensive looking stuff and I asked her if she had any "Baby-oil." She burst out laughing at the macabre suggestion from the middle-aged-plus foreigner and I said "I come back later," and we both bowed and I scooted out.

Down the street through the leaning electric light poles I saw the entrance to the shrine. Well done! Imagine what Rachel would say when I told her that I went down to the shrine and had a look around today. Who said I shouldn't go off anywhere as I'd get lost straight away?

I smiled at a couple of people as I would normally do at home in Australia, a man and a couple of women. They ignored me. Then I remembered Rachel saying that you *never* did that in Japan. I had given the wrong message. I wasn't to invade their privacy. I should have just bowed. If you were going to acknowledge their existence on the planet you bowed. If you smiled you got a blank alien and indignant expression for almost committing indecent exposure. It would be hard to get out of that habit when I got home, I mean bowing. I always smiled at complete strangers when I walked the dogs and rarely did they look straight through me. The French were reputed to be the same but I couldn't help myself there either. I couldn't play the haughty role without fair reason.

Gosh, I offered my man on the plane a banana as my first greeting! What message was *that*? I blushed.

I walked through the paths at the shrine and sniffed at the odd white azaleas still in bloom. They smelled of nothing. I walked through an opening in the trees and could see a man tending plants in a hot-house. There was rice growing there and a very murky looking stream running by, with the train line a stone's throw away. I came back through a curtain of bamboo into the green of the gardens again. There were little shrines everywhere amongst the trees. The paths that led to them were mossy and crumbling with age. I pictured how it would be in autumn and spring or even in winter, when it would be covered in a blanket of snow.

There were loud reverberating sounds of *taiko* drums coming from the direction of the main shrine again.

The rooster in his enclosure worried me. I stepped back when he came close to the wire. He looked as though he would have drifts of mites around him for a two-meter radius. The peacock stood surveying me, its tail trembling with a whirring sound. I pulled up some grass and stuck it through the wire and wandered off, worried because there was no sign of food in their cage. I wondered if they were ever properly fed. There was an almost empty filthy water dish there too.

I stopped at a shop that smelled of fish. There were plastic bags of shrunken looking fruit and other things I could not recognize. Everything was presented in cardboard or polystyrene boxes and a family of watermelons huddled together on a bench, the only things familiar to me. There was someone out the back in the semi-dark gloom preparing something. I thought maybe I'd rather not like to know what they were preparing.

I found a shop that sold pens and papers and school books. A nice middle-aged woman again. She was very polite. (There were a lot of us middle-aged plus women in the world.) I got my exercise-book to write in and it was midday, a good time to head home for lunch before the heat really set in.

The phone rang as I opened the door. Rachel had a flustered tone in her voice. "I've tried you several times. I was starting to get really concerned. I was wondering what on earth you had found to occupy yourself with."

"Oh, I did some washing - walked up to the shrine had a look around" said as casually as possible.

"Walked up to the shrine?"

"Yes and I found a place that sold exercise books so I'm just starting on my diary" I added.

There was a bit of a silence. "Oh, well that's good then. I'll see you about 4.30. I've got to go. There's a child waiting to see me."

I had been managing up until then, remembering my experiences to date, from when I flew out of Melbourne beside my Japanese man until Rachel's phone call just then, and had been scribbling them down in an urgent almost illegible scrawl all over Anthony's ragged papers he'd finished with before I forgot the exact details. (At least my short-term memory was still intact.)

Je t'aime Paris – 2013

9 am. Head out towards Musee de Cluny. Stop to ask directions along the way from a shopkeeper in white apron setting up shop. I thought I'd be able to see Cluny from outside my hotel. "Straight down the street near the Sorbonne" I think he says to me in smiling French. Cluny will be my icon like the Eiffel Tower was last time to keep me from getting lost.

Arrive at the little park opposite the *Musee* – the one I spent lots of time in last year, writing in my diary about the sparrows luxuriating in their dust-baths. Now to be in there once more warms my heart but I am freezing cold and breathing in the misty rain of Paris. I find myself humming Frank Sinatra's "I love Paris." My, what you might call 'corny' theme is interrupted by a family of rather swarthy people near me who begin screaming at each other in wild abuse. The people outside Cluny waiting for admission look in my direction, alarmed, and I make my way out of what was once my little place of solace and reflection last year, still overgrown with grasses and wildflowers and take refuge in the doorway of the corner bookshop. One of the male members of the angry group begins physically assaulting the screaming woman. Children and babies howl. Where's a gendarme when you need one?

I pass the *Musee,* half expecting a smiling Bonnie from last July to arrive on the scene. I wonder if I should go back to the hotel and get my jacket. It's freezing. I wouldn't dare face the crowd in the park again so I continue on, stopping to pet a little black fluffy dog an Asian woman is leading. She smiles and says *"Salut."*

Stroll to Boulevard St Michel, my favourite street. Look at lots of very chic shop windows. An outfit with a bulky chestnut coloured jumper, belted with wide band and worn with scarf over shirt and brown winter slacks, ankle boots and socks bulked up above them and I am drawn closer to take a photo. I must try for that look next autumn.

(TRYING TO FORGET THAT I HAVE A BROKEN FRONT TOOTH!!)

Stop at postcard stall that sells umbrellas and buy a black one for eight euros, my first Paris souvenir which I shall treasure.

Have to check Luxembourg Gardens. The planting around the lake in the Gardens is now in the softest dusty pinks, greys, greens and white – beautiful. Last year it was yellow, violet, blue and white. Take photos around the Gardens. The clock in the Palace is striking

10 o'clock like a cue in an opera production, and I take it as a summons directed at me and I make my way to "Le Rostand."

Here I feel glowingly warm again. Spent much of my time in this café last year drinking *café crèmes*. Can't believe it - here I am! – back in my favourite Paris haunts.

Get a couple of "looks" from women. Do they think my dress is too short for my age? I am wearing black leggings. Maybe they noticed the tooth.

I order my *café crème* and now sit, sipping very hot coffee (with a little silver jug of hot creamy milk) and listen to pouring rain and watch the traffic and the people. This is where I belong. I don't ever want to leave this moment.

Get out my pen and notebook and jot my feelings down - an editor's nightmare, full of exclamation marks and words in capitals to express my every moment in Paris in briefest diarized form.

A family of several adults and a couple of children in next cubicle are having breakfast. One of the women is adjusting a bright blue tie on her husband who just can't get the knot in the right position. At last, satisfied with the effect, she sits down again beside him. Only then does he notice me through the glass panel and flushes with embarrassment, so I give him the thumbs up and a wink and they all laugh.

10.10. A big bus with "Vega tour" on the side goes past. I wonder if that's for vegetarian tours.

10.45. Walk on back down Boulevard St Michel and enter several shops just for *"regarde."* Visit very cheap shop and browse through lots of curious things including batteries called *"Varta Piles"* - rather odd. I choose big T-shirt top with *"Je t'aime"* and the Eiffel Tower on it – not *too* "touristy," a pen, long olive-coloured cardigan (Made in Morocco) which I have now put on and will wear to lunch. So much is labelled "Made in China", which is disappointing. I return to my hotel.

12.15. Back at "Royal Jussieu" café near my hotel. My pen from the cheap shop works and ah, red wine hits the spot! Sitting in the same tight little corner I'd sat in yesterday (was that yesterday?) Traffic buzzing outside. Rain falling again and I left new umbrella in my hotel room. *Stupide*!! But only short walk through the rain to hotel from here.

Little did I know when last sitting in this spot yesterday that I'd have a broken front tooth! Fancy, first day in Paris and I look like a heroin addict! I could cry. I'm dipping bread in red wine on the quiet. I have to, in order to cope with the crust. Can you imagine if the whole tooth gives way!

"Bette Davis Eyes" is playing in the background. The irony of it. I wonder what her teeth are like.

Outside a young woman walks a West Highland terrier, like "Poppy" the one that I painted for a friend years ago. Man walking with long bread stick under cover of umbrella. Hope it won't get soggy.

I LOVE PARIS!

Waitress clears my dishes speaking to me in French. I say *"Non merci Madame"* to offer of coffee. I must try and stick to my budget of 20 euros a day and I need to buy fruit and mineral water yet.

A woman on bike rides by, with tiny but stalwart terrier sitting in basket staring ahead like a dutiful but drowned rat, seemingly undeterred by the rain. A jogger in a red shirt, a ginger-coloured West Highland terrier on a lead and young man walks rapidly with sticks one uses for cross-country skiing.

I am where Rue des Ecoles meets Rue *Jussieu* and Rue du Cardinal Lemoine and as usual it is *"Jus' me."*

What is it about Paris? It all moves so quickly, with such vibrance. Dogs, people, lime-coloured Renaults and motor bikes. No signs of boredom. Everything buzzing like bees around the hive over every inch of deliciously sweet and tasty Paris.

2 pm. Return to Hotel. Watching TV - *"Tellement Vrais"* ("A Matter of Truth" – I think), interrupted by African maid arriving to service my room and she seems embarrassed to find me here. She smiles shyly as I take the hint and remove myself and stand on the staircase and inspect the huge old tapestry on the wall while she cleans the bathroom and replaces towels and soaps.

*I continue on now in my Japanese diary....
moment to moment!*

    This afternoon I expected Rosy around 2.30 and I kept going out and standing like a lost mother, waiting. By 3.25 I heard noises of other children and I wandered out for the umpteenth time. Along came the little thin waif, long skinny legs in jeans and a big yellow sun hat, looking like a sunflower herself, sniffing at flowers in a neighbour's garden across the road. I clapped my hands feeling too inhibited to call out as I glanced up and down the street and she remained engrossed in nature and ignored me. I clapped my hands again and she looked up and a smile widened her face as she remembered and she ran awkwardly to me, throwing her arms around me. Then, "I'm going to the park", and she dropped her bag inside the door.
    "No not on your own."
    Anthony arrived behind her. "I've got homework."
    "Well we're going to the park until Mum gets home."
    "OK, I'll do my homework there."
    "Guess where I've been today? I went to the shrine," I boast as we walk along.
    "Nanny, how did you know where to go?"

"Well I didn't really intend to go to the shrine, but all of a sudden - there it was!"

"Oh Nanny!"

The park was just around the corner. It consisted of an area of concrete with a strip of grass and bushes around it and some swings, and big enough for a few kids at a time to play ball games. Rosy and I played on the swings for a while and then we tossed a large pink ball back and forth. No-one wanted to talk about their day at school.

Some boys ran up with a baseball and glove and one took the ball from Rosy. In a flash Anthony was nose to nose with him, homework book tossed to the ground, snorting.

"Come on its 4 o'clock. Let's go kids. Mum will be home in a minute."

"Mum, what's that on your nails? You haven't painted them have you? Do you know the Japanese are very suspicious of painted nails? They'll think you're a – you know what! And that top is too bare. That would really be *frowned* upon" she said frowning.

"Well, we don't have any polish remover in the apartment so I'm afraid the Headmaster will be further appalled tomorrow when I front up to the school as "the woman with painted nails," who also stood in the window in her nightie this morning."

"Nanny went to the shrine today" grinned Anthony. "But she didn't mean to go there. She found it by mistake!"

It was 4.45 and the flat was full of kids and Megumi was visiting again. We sat around the table on the floor and drank iced green tea. The children were tumbling around in the *tatami* room and I was aware of music being played on a loud-speaker outside.

"Oh, 5 o'clock" Rachel said, looking at her watch, and with that, there was a stampede to the door like the rats of Hamlin disappearing into the street and it was almost quiet in the flat except for Anthony sniffing loudly.

Megumi's friend Miko who was driving me to school the next day arrived and carried on ridiculously about how young I looked and how Rachel and I could be sisters. Then the conversation turned to whether or not I had yet tried "*Natto.*"

"It's fermented soy beans" said Rachel pulling a face, "and they're *disgusting*."

I didn't understand the cultural significance of *natto* but felt sure I would find out before long.

We contacted Caroline on the Internet after dinner and I tried to explain my experiences so far, beginning with the plane trip and my Japanese man and what a hilarious time I had had. She seemed bewildered and Rachel was getting impatient with me as I could not type properly with the lap top on the very low table. I was sitting on the floor and using only two fingers and my hands were too big at that angle for the keyboard, not to mention my arthritis. "You're hitting the keys too hard.

You'll damage the keys!"

"Oh, for goodness sake Rachel..."

Caroline's reaction to the thought of me riding a bike in future was one of amused disbelief. "Mum, how long has it been since you rode a bike? I hope there'll be photos."

I love Paris in the fall.

4 pm. Need to get out and walk Paris streets. I close the door and realize my key is inside. I go down and apologize to the receptionist who is very obliging and returns with me and another set of keys to my room.

I am wearing high heeled shoes (old ones) as they are more comfortable but they are too sloppy to walk far in and I clip-clop around the block to Rue St Germaine and back to Rue Morge where I stop at a bistro to escape the rain and have a *chocolate chaud*. The boy behind the bar must be new and is not used to inventing anything but alcoholic drinks it seems and calls for assistance.

The rain has been falling horizontally and although it is only light rain and despite my umbrella, it has drenched me. I decide I've had enough of watching the weather, thank the boy behind the bar for his *chocolate chaud* and leave.

"……I love Paris." That song from the fifties is stuck in my mind now and the lyrics flow with the rhythm of my steps. Yes, I love Paris.

I can't believe it's a whole year and more since I was here in the sizzling summer. I wonder who turned up at Claude's July session this year. It was hot last July.

This is the first time I've been to Paris in the autumn.

5 pm. Collect my key from the receptionist and I pour out my sad tooth episode to her.

"Madame, I would not have noticed had you not told me."

How un-French of me to draw attention and then make explanations. Even Johnny Depp is quoted as saying *"Don't complain and don't explain"* and I had intended to keep that bit of Hollywood philosophy in mind in future as a good guide, but of course in this situation he would have just popped into one of the celebrity cosmetic dentists and *voila!* I suppose she thinks I always look like this anyway. She is friendlier and more helpful than the usual French receptionist I have encountered, even since I have shared my humiliation with her.

She asks me about the recent fires near Sydney and I tell her about how close the 2009 ones were to me in Victoria and how I had to leave my property but lucky for me the wind changed – so overall we're confidants.

Poir et banan for dinner again.

Very noisy people have arrived above me, speaking Chinese and I think they're complaining about the size of their room. I have a double bed but I wonder how on earth two people would manage in this little space if it's the same size as mine. Their raised voices continue along with the loud staccato of the rain, smacking like lead from a shot-tower in to the courtyard four floors below.

5.10 am and back to normal hours like home. I wake stiff and sore from this hard mattress and can hardly turn over I'm so stiff. The bed is almost as hard as the floor - and the pillow (bolster) almost the same dimensions as a draught-stopper you'd put at the door.
6.15 am – rise. Today I will have to wear my sneakers. Cannot walk far in anything else. I dress in grey sneakers, grey jeans, black and silver jumper and mushroom cord jacket.
7 am. Girl on desk questions "You say you live in Melbourne but you live in mountains?"
I go on to explain that Melbourne is not really residential like Paris and if one lives with Melbourne as their city, one says they "live in Melbourne" when overseas.
She says "Same in Paris. None of us live right in Paris but it is easier to say – *I live in Paris* – only the rich live in Paris or have investment properties here."
I point to my tooth and say *"Non baguette merci Madame"* and she offers me an apple (which I feel is a strange alternative) to replace it along with my *croissant*

(this time with a little soft cheese.) I cut the apple into manageable slices and nibble at it with some difficulty.

10 am - Just finishing *café crème* in "Le Rostand" having left hotel at 8.30 am and wandered, camera in hand down Rue Des Ecoles taking photos. Drawn again to Musee Cluny and thence to Boulevard St Michel. Take pictures of fashions to show Caroline. Ambling down further than I've been before, past Luxembourg Gardens, I am yelled at by an old angry derelict French woman who shakes her fist at me. Move on to the Gardens and some sunshine.

It's really quite cold in Paris now and to think I left my most comfortable flat black boots at home and put sandals in instead, along with my straw sunhat with the floaty pastel coloured scarf. This now lies on my bed as if it is my latest art-form. I won't be wearing it. Lots of boots and heavy jackets being worn. Thank goodness I've got the cord jacket. I almost didn't bother to bring it. I'll be living in it.

Open Day at school in Japan – 2004

This morning I ironed my long white linen wrap-around skirt on a miniature ironing board that was like a toy. I had bleached the skirt startling white before I left home and here I was ironing it almost on the floor, the skirt sweeping it as I ironed. I put on a mauve and white tie-dyed top, and wondered if I could borrow a bag of Rachel's to squash the soft indoor shoes into that she had leant me. Either that or take a plastic bag to carry those and my diary. You have to take indoor shoes everywhere with you i.e. virginal shoes – scuffs (*srippers*), that have never touched the outside ground *ever*. I had not packed a handbag at all and I found a neutral coloured one of Rachel's in the mess in the dressing-room. I imagined she would prefer me to use that instead of a plastic bag. I didn't want to make another *faux pas*, particularly in front of the Headmaster.

Miko called in with her car at 12.30 to take me to the school. She was going too, to observe her daughter's activities. We drove in silence.

It was Open Day for parents and *kapochyas* (grandmothers or was that the word for pumpkin*)* and I was to go in place of Rachel. I was glad I was equipped with indoor shoes as I was told I would be hopping from indoors to outdoors many times over. Megumi joined us and they took me to Rosy's class and left me outside the door feeling quite strange and very much a foreigner in a strange land.

A sea of curious little Japanese faces greeted me as I entered the classroom and a shy but pleased Rosy smiled at me. I hoped I was dressed to please her and I instinctively hid my nails.

It was their lunch-time and a squad of tiny boys and girls had just finished dishing up the meals, gowned and masked in white as if they had all performed brain surgery in miniature. They were eating what looked like a fricassee of sorts with beans and carrots, bread and butter. Rosy put her hands together beneath her chin and said grace. I wondered if this was to God or to Buddha. I took a photo and felt very proud of her. It would be Buddha of course and it seemed she was the only one who bothered to thank him for the fricassee.

Her classmates all behaved just like kids anywhere. The teacher was a tiny woman with a traditional Japanese basin-style hair-cut that was black - not dyed Western brown. She looked everywhere but at me. Her lunch had arrived too and she ate at her desk at the front of the class, ignoring me as though I were invisible. A slight young woman approached me, reassuring me of my visual being, smiling and questioning in very careful English, "Rachel is your daughter, and you are Rosy's *Obachan*?"

She took me to look at the work on show and pointed to Rosy's. The writing of course was all in Japanese characters and I couldn't imagine what Rosy's writing said, but she carefully and quietly translated it into English for me. Evidently Rosy and her daughter had been at the Buddhist kindergarten together last year. This was equal to our Prep grade. She had been to Australia, "Ayres Rock and Gold Coast for honeymoon" she told me in her musical voice.

Rosy stood up and asked the teacher's permission for another piece of bread and then sat down with her two chopsticks in her right hand, carefully and expertly spreading the butter evenly with them as you would with a knife.

I counted thirty-four kids in the class. There were twelve grades and a total of 408 pupils in the school.

Immediately the children had finished their meal, despite our presence, they collected rags and buckets of water and Maddie-Rose, together with the other little pupils, got down on her knees in the hallway outside the class-room and began scrubbing the floor. I felt quite taken aback and helpless as to the welfare of these tiny children. Their lunches would not have gone down yet. Evidently each child had an allotted area and this was scrubbed each day. While this was going on, the teacher walked around inside the classroom with a toothbrush protruding from her mouth, doing her own bit of cleaning. A recording of the "Blue Danube" played loudly over the loud-speaker and they all scrubbed their own square meter area to waltz-time and I wondered if this was an exercise in reflection and humility, or maybe penance set to the strains of Western classics, but Rachel assured me later "It's an exercise in economy as there are no school cleaners."

Rosy took me upstairs to Anthony's classroom. Along the way teachers and students bowed and I bowed. I checked again with Rosy the pronunciation of *Obachan* and the word for pumpkin (*kapochya*) that had been stuck in my brain from my lesson with my Japanese man on the plane. I realized I had been introducing myself as "Rosy's pumpkin" up to this point. Anthony was delighted to see me and learn the name he would give me in future.

When he contained himself he ordered "Nan you have to be at my 6th hour and Rosy's 5th hour and I am going swimming now and you have to come to that too."

Rachel had to take his temperature every morning before he went swimming and write it on his personal card to give permission. "No-one went swimming if their temperature has not been recorded in the morning."

Rosy had gone back to her class and I stood outside Anthony's room trying to look occupied, staring at the display of *Kanji* characters and looking for Anthony's name amongst it all. Rachel's two neighbours arrived and it was decided we should go and watch Miko's daughter and Anthony in the pool. The three of us together trying to communicate was quite hilarious. Their English was as good as my Japanese. Wide-eyed and gesticulating madly, we all burst out laughing and they indicated "tearing their hair out" and I did the same.

They led me to where I had left my outdoor sandals. We changed shoes and Miko indicated to me to bring my indoor shoes. We crossed the large playground and arrived at the pool where we got back into our indoor shoes and went inside. It was actually an outdoor pool but only indoor shoes were worn there. Would I ever get used to this footwear culture?

A friend of Miko's arrived and they chatted for some time, and then I think the conversation turned to me, because the friend started oohing and aahing that someone so young could be the *"Obachan."* "So young, so *beautifor*." I think because I was fifty-nine they expected the *Obachan* to be wizened up and bent over a stick. I would never have thought in a million years that the Japanese would find me remotely attractive! This came as a surprise. Was it just out of a desire to please me or as a polite opening comment, or what? I eventually decided that compliments were part of the Japanese culture and I don't remember ever commenting on anyone's beauty to their face. I must have actually seemed very lacking, even though the gracious but unwarranted compliments on my beauty kept coming.

"It's only because you have blue eyes Mum. They'd kill to have blue eyes" Rachel reassured me regularly.

I should have come to Japan years ago and not wasted my late fifties catching up with that Ukrainian, after all those years that I'd been romanticizing over him. There were many charming men in Japan that I found attractive.

####

Dad had decided to make a "sea-change" when I was thirteen which actually disrupted and changed everyone's lives but his and we moved away from the leafy Eastern suburb of East Ivanhoe and my little gang of friends, down to the Mornington Peninsula (where he had precious childhood memories of holidays at Seaford, a long steam-train ride and then a coach and horses to their beach-house. That was in 1915.)

So began 1958 and he commuted to Melbourne every day to work, his various clubs and his golf, his life unchanged.

I was thankful to be leaving my old high-school behind, which I hated with a passion, brought about I think because the English teacher was introducing debating to our lessons and I would rather have gone swimming with sharks than stand up and deliver a talk in front of the class.

At the time Elvis' "Teddy Bear" was a hit and the music teacher had made the prediction that this Elvis fellow would not last out the year.

I was bitterly disappointed to find that I hated my new school even more than the one I'd left behind. All I wanted to do was draw and write compositions. Algebra and geometry were languages I was seriously handicapped in and it seemed the curriculum insisted on including public speaking which had me quietly disappearing into the sick-room daily until the threat had passed. School was an agony.

Our new neighbours were from Texas so things were looking up but I was a little disappointed to find that they had not the slightest connection to, or appearance of characters from the Wild West. But I did learn some wild new dance moves and make a couple of life-long friends.

As time went on the Mornington Peninsula began to turn into somewhat of a migrant settlement.

Up until seventeen all I had wanted in life was a horse, and apart from that dream, I was proving to Mum to be a homebody, and at seventeen, destined to become a "horsey old maid." Mum was under the impression that local dances were like church socials and I finally gave in to her unrelenting demands that I "*get out and socialize*" as she did as a girl.

While tripping the light fantastic, a Dutchman called Hank promised to take dancing lessons, so he could "sweep up de floor wid me."

Then I stumbled upon Nick in the barn-dance and experienced "love at first sight." He drove me home with no goodnight kiss to follow and I was certain that he was the man I wanted to marry. I was a child and he was twenty-three, jumped out of planes for sport, was tall, handsome, charming, well-dressed, well-mannered, cigarette in hand and with an air of nonchalance. He was like Dad except for the appealing foreign accent and a wife he said he was divorcing (a fact that I was yet to learn).

"Stop crying! I hate to see a woman cry," and a silent pause that went on for what seemed forever, interrupted only by my tragic blubbering, then Nick added "I've seen too many women crying in refugee camps." I gulped. This was not how the script was to read was it? Seventeen and in love for the very first time! Up until then I'd only been in love with Rowdy Yates and Crash Craddock. This I had thought was the real thing. I'd already announced to Mum that this was the man I wanted to marry.

I remember my brother Bruce opening the fridge and exclaiming "Ugh! What's with the laboratory specimens!?" Mum had prepared food for entertaining my Eastern European boyfriends, assuming that there were no European borders to taste when it came to pickled rollmops.

"Who have we got from the League of Nations tonight?"

"He's a White Russian sky-diver."

"An exotic butterfly! I can't wait to meet him."

But that never came to pass as Dad sent him packing without a word of goodbye to me when Nick explained his marital status and his intended divorce. Occasionally our paths crossed but he avoided me and our relationship had only consisted of an innocent kiss up to that point.

I think it must have been Magda the much-married, warm- hearted but hot-blooded Latvian woman who lived across the road who introduced us to the *"lab specimens."* She was quite practiced at pickling and bottling specimens of many kinds. She confessed to me many years later how one Christmas she had found a beautifully gift-wrapped present evidently meant for another woman going by the attached card, hidden in her husband's shed. Enraged, she unwrapped the expensive bottle of perfume, transferred its contents to one of her own bottles and substituted it with a specimen of her own urine and then painstakingly wrapped it up as beautifully as before.

"Can you imagine!" she shrieked. "Am I not a *terrible* old woman?"

It was a Saturday morning in 1963. The mid-morning sunlight fell upon me as the curtains were wrenched back. This heralded the arrival of a hovering image of Mum at my bedside surrounded by a pink aura. (I had just finished painting my bedroom walls in a rosy hue.) Instead of *"Behold...."* She gasped "Wake up – President Kennedy has been shot – in Dallas – in Texas! This could mean war!"

I blinked at the offending sunlight. President Kennedy, killed? Gosh! For a few moments I heard the childish yet very sultry voice of Marilyn, *"Happy birthday... Mr President..."*

"Do our neighbours know yet? They're from Texas." I curled up once more and wondered if Houston was near Dallas.

Mum panicked too much.

I stood at the front of the crowd of hysterical girls outside the Southern Cross Hotel the following year, clutching a drawing I'd done of John Lennon. Was there something that reminded me of Nick? Maybe his arrogance. Apart from that he was the Beatle whose brain I most fancied. Someone in plain clothes patrolling the crowd stopped and spoke to me, commenting on my sketch. "Give it to me and I'll see if I can take you up to meet them." He returned some minutes later. "Sorry, Security says *No way. It would cause a riot if they let one girl in* – but they'll see he gets your drawing."

"Now, you had your tonsils taken out only a week ago…" (As if I could forget. I think the hospital staff thought I was holding a United Nations meeting at my bedside. Over the tops of the ever mounting flowers carried in, I cringed, hyperventilating as each one arrived and stood glaring at the others.) "…and if you scream you'll haemorrhage to death. You're nineteen, not a fourteen year-old so you won't scream will you… promise me!"

"Oh as if I'd scream!"

I couldn't hear a thing. John, Paul and George could have been singing "Ol' McDonald Had a Farm." My screams were drowned out with the tsunami of female vocal lunacy that swept over my head and caught me up in its wave. I was part of the mass hysteria. Why was I screaming? It would have been awful and very messy – but luckily I didn't haemorrhage.

"Sydney……" Miko's friend's gentle voice broke through my faraway thoughts and she stumbled along in struggling English in an effort to tell me her impressions of her honeymoon to the Gold Coast and Sydney.

"Sydney"….She waved her arms and made circles in the air… *"Buzz.. bzz…"*

"Mosquitoes" I offered.

"No - no" she shook her head.

"Oh…flies?"

"Yes, flies, many *many* flies."

I did the "Australian salute" (to fight off the flies) action. After a while they all laughed politely, but not understanding.

The swimming demonstration was over, with Anthony swimming very well, looking so much the foreigner, big and blue-eyed. We exchanged shoes and went back to the classroom where we changed shoes again. Rosy arrived.

"Nanny I'm going home now."

"No Rosy – you're coming home with me."

"No. The children are lining up. I *have* to go."

"No Rosy I have the key."

"I have my own key Nanny."

"Good grief Maddie-Rose. I am here to look after you now.

You'll go home with me today. This is why I am here. You're not a latch-key kid. You don't have to use your own key." Much scowling from under the huge sun-hat and the heavy back-pack.

"Take your bag off and let me carry it before your back breaks." She ignored me and sat down in the corner of the room taking a selection of books from the shelf all in *Kana*.

Anthony came up proudly with a sheet of paper covered in huge *Kanji* characters in black ink. "This is your present Nan."

"It's beautiful. I'll frame it and put in on the wall at home next to my *noren*."

I think the teacher was pleased with my show of enthusiasm. She introduced herself at last just as I was about to leave and was very formal and there was a lot of bowing to each other. I'd been standing around for an hour and I was tired. Finally, I collected my street shoes and pulled them on after much "Sayonaring."

Someone passed me on the way out and said brightly "*Bon soir*." I completely forgot the appropriate "*Konichiwa*" (good afternoon) and instead said something that was a combination of *obachan* and *kapochya*. I'd never pick up the language in a million years. And I didn't get to see the Headmaster after all that.

On the way home we passed a Japanese woman and child who both looked admiringly and amused at the little Western girl and the mother nudged her daughter. They bent down and "oohed" and "aahed" at Maddie- Rose the cute puppy who was actually scowling fiercely and they laughed together at the little foreigner under the big hat.

Rachel was already home. Rosy wanted to go to the park alone and began arguing again. Anthony was waiting anxiously for a girlfriend to come over for a visit.

"Oh Mum, you used my bag the kids gave me for Mother's Day! It's special, she grumbled, turning it over for inspection of damage. "How could you."

"I'm sorry Rachel. I thought you'd be angry if I turned up at school with my things in a plastic bag. I couldn't fit anything more into my luggage and I didn't really think about a selection of handbags when I was packing." I wasn't yet at the stage in life where a woman can't check the mail-box without a handbag over her arm, like the Queen.

Rachel gazed in to the refrigerator thinking about dinner. "Surely you'll eat vegetables that have been cooked with beef tonight. You wouldn't eat pork last night and I'm not cooking different meals for everyone."

"I'm not eating meat. You know I'm vegetarian. What's the big deal?"

"Nan's a vegetarian Mum. What's that Nanny?"

"I don't eat meat."

"Why?"

"Because I don't like eating animals."

"Well you might *have* to."

"No I won't Rachel and that's that. Just let me have some rice and I'll cut one of those pink tomatoes and mix it in."

"You can't eat that – and don't put the children off meat for goodness sake. They need it. They're growing."

"I need meat as I'm going to be a big man Nan. Did you eat meat when you were a kid Nanny?"

"Yes. I had no choice." I thought how I wasn't allowed to leave the table as a child until my plate was clean. Otherwise I would hear night after night the story of the women standing in cess-pits in Colombo collecting food scraps in their skirts. This was a much used form of persuasion my father used for getting me to clean my plate. He'd been on his way to the Middle East and the War, and those women would be standing in the cesspits forever, because of me.

"When you're grown up you can make your own choices. Meat-eating might have been OK once. It's a cruel industry now. Pigs are more intelligent than dogs and they never see daylight, except when they're on their way to the slaughter-house ....and they can't even turn around in their cages. As though I'd eat *pork!* All I want is a bowl of rice and I'll be happy." I looked up at the three faces staring at me, each one affected differently. There were a few seconds of stunned silence.

"Now you've probably put her off pork for life and it's the only meat she eats."

Anthony's friend arrived. She seemed quite shy but didn't hesitate in running to the TV as soon as she was in the door and plugging her play station in without a greeting or word to anyone, let alone a "Do you mind if I enter and take over the apartment everybody?"

I was amazed at their language achievement as they chattered away, all of them, excitedly, exclaiming, teasing and joking fluently in Japanese. Then off she tore to visit the twins around the corner. Shortly after though, the *Yakuba's* music was heard, broadcast over the rooftops and Rosy came flying back in the door.

"That was quick Rosy."

"I heard the music" she gasped.

One of Megumi's boys arrived, wanting to join in the play station action.

"I thought they had to run home when the *Gestapo* played their music. What are they doing here?"

"They don't *have* to obey it Mum. It's more a reminder that it's 5 pm rather than an *order*."

"I can't keep up."

Megumi arrived with little dishes and packets, "a little bit of this and a little bit of that for *Mummy*." She held up a tiny bowl.

"*Natto*. You must try it" was translated by Rachel. It's revolting stuff – in slime."

"I'll try it Megumi, just a *tiny* bit" I indicated with my fingertips. She stirred it with chopsticks. I blinked at it. It looked like small beans wrapped in mucus.

"Smell it Mum!"

I picked up a piece with chopsticks and closed my eyes so I couldn't see the mucous affect. It tasted OK but when I opened my eyes there were fine strands of the mucus floating around in the air, clinging to my chin and the chopsticks like fine cobwebs. Megumi was desperately making a winding-up motion at me.

"You've got to *wind it up* Mum."

Megumi was delighted that I hadn't been repulsed. I had passed the first part of this cultural test.

"Very good for you. Very good" she assured me. She chopped up some spring onions and added them to the bowl in my hand and stirred in some mustard powder. I stared a little horrified at her busy chopsticks wondering if I would be up all night with my stomach. At least I could say I had tried *Natto*.

Rachel said everyone asks "Have you tried *Natto?*" Sort of like "What football team do you barrack for?" Well, it's no big deal and I would not put it on my shopping list but if it is served up to me again here I could put it in my mouth fairly bravely. Still, it had to go down yet - and stay down. I thought Megumi must have heard Rachel and me arguing over the meat issue earlier and had come to introduce a few local alternatives as a peace offering. She then began to dish up a portion of black slimy seaweed, some tiny onions and a mixture of I-don't-know-what with grated white radishes. We mixed this in with our bowls of Rachel's sticky over-cooked roux she'd made and Megumi sat back on her heels to watch. The small amount of food was very filling and a sort of "good cultural experience" or so I told myself.

We sipped green tea together. I liked that. It was more like water that vegetables had been cooked in rather than the insipid green Chinese tea that I felt tasted like cardboard back home. Rachel added some left-over pork to Rosy's rice.

"No. No pork!" came from an indignant Rosy and she placed her little hands across her plate. Rachel rolled her eyes at me.

Rachel and Anthony began a clapping game that was popular at school. I was really tired after the day's school visit. The clapping brought next door's kids back in together with Megumi. Everyone tumbled around in the limited space we had and it was really rowdy and the clapping games continued, played by the four of them. I wanted bed. I was too tired to join in.

The TV was going full blast and there was a travel show on about Japan. I would rather have watched that and sat back and relaxed but there was nowhere to relax while they were all there. The show was hosted by a handsome Japanese man in a cowboy hat – Country & *Eastern* style. I questioned Megumi through Rachel on the area of Japan being shown to which Megumi looked blankly at me and shrugged. "Megumi is not interested in travel or geography. She's only interested in shopping Mum."

The boys tumbled into the tatami room and sumo wrestling and grunting battles ensued. One of Megumi's boys was built like a sumo wrestler, intended to be one and liked to practise on everyone. I think it is the ambition of every Japanese family to have one boy become a sumo wrestler like the Irish donate a child to the priesthood. Eventually they all filed out and Rachel made up my futon on the living room floor. Anthony flashed me an injured questioning look.

"I can't sleep in your room for your snoring Anthony. I'm sorry."

"I'll try not to *very hard* Nan."

"No, you can't help it. Just let me sleep out here."

Rachel wanted me at school with her the next morning and I had to ride a bike there. I had to be ready to leave at 7.30 am.

Paris Scents – 2013.

I pick up a free English-speaking "Marketplace" magazine/newspaper on my way and am glancing through it. Rent here seems very high but I couldn't live in a Paris apartment with two dogs and a cat anyway. It would be out of the question. I mean, where would Aubrey Beardsley go to the toilet? I couldn't entertain the thought of a litter tray in a tiny apartment - unless I had one with a balcony - but he'd go crazy anyway.

Very interestingly there are many, many ads for English speaking ("French not required") nannies to care for kids in all kinds of situations, live-in and live-out. This might be my way of experiencing French life and learning French in later years if I could arrange a temporary working visa. I might one day look in to this possibility – you never know. Otherwise, it might make more sense to sell my house in the mountains when my pets have all gone and buy a unit or apartment closer to Melbourne and then rent it out and rent an apartment in Paris. I couldn't bear to think of my pets gone. A walking frame on cobblestones would be my means of getting around by the time I was ready - I don't think so. A beautifully carved walking stick would look more "fashionable."

I head off on my well beaten track from last year right down Rue de Vaugirard. That's where my hotel was. Everything was as I left it a year ago and it seems like yesterday that I was hurrying to meet the painting group, paints and brushes in a bag over my shoulder, past those same little antique shops that I always had to stop and look at through the windows, with mediaeval hunting scenes, old lace cloths, china hares and silver knives with carved ivory handles. They always seemed to be closed, but the florist stalls were open and bursting with fragrance and dewy flowers and cafes exuded the wonderful early morning aromas of Paris. Now I hope to buy an already prepared, delicious tuna and mayonnaise roll at one of the shops in Rue du Rennes which I used to frequent.

I walk right to the Hotel from last year, which I won't name and it looks like the same grumpy Frenchman is still at the desk, the one that said when I came back after the week of painting in the beautiful Loire Valley (having made a booking for my return week's stay), "I am sorry but I have no booking for you Madame." "Well then, are you going to put me out in to the street?" I had snapped. I could see he wasn't going to take responsibility for the stuff-up and he blamed instead the incompetence of the African receptionist and suggested I make a formal complaint to management about him. "No I will put you in a room, don't worry." He then sent me to a small room with a stinking sewerage problem. I suffered in silence for the three days that I had left, feeling this could be a kick in the pants for finding them at fault. A shame, because the first room I had there was huge and the breakfasts were out of this world – French music playing and all – perfect.

There are no food vendors open today so I head back the way I came, passing the spot where the beggar with the little puppy used to sit last year. That used to break my heart each time I passed and I would toss some coins their way in the hope that the puppy might share in the takings and not just support the beggar's smoking habit. Once I asked in a voice verging on despair "Do you love him?" He didn't understand me and I longed to snatch the puppy away from him but how could I do anything about it—I couldn't take a puppy home. I wonder where that puppy is now. All the beggars had dogs last year.

I stop to photograph a shop window where an antique doll with red hair and an emerald green crinoline, gazes out at me with a look of disdain and pursed red lips.

"Are you going to photograph the dolly?" A street cleaner in fluorescent green suddenly appears from the back of a truck. He takes a camera out of his overalls pocket. "Thanks for the idea." He adds "I am a photographer too. The light is just right."

He grins and I take a photo of him taking a photo and he laughs a little. (And the light on the dolly turned out to be very bad actually.)

I head for the food vendors in Boulevard St Michel. I choose a *crepe fromage* with champignons and a mineral water. It comes to less than five euros.

Well, here I am, back in my Luxembourg Gardens once more. The Palace clock is chiming 12 again and with it the sun is suddenly quite hot. I've been chilled to the bone all morning. So now I am sitting enjoying the warmth.

Tai Chi is performed by many here in the gardens and one fellow who is definitely an exhibitionist has been "air-boxing" and punching for ages to a disinterested audience and no-one watches except me, from the distance. The joggers are still jogging and one has to get out of their way continually.

1.30. I'm photographing boys fencing with sticks. There are people playing tennis and basketball. I sit and watch the ponies being saddled. One of the ponies whinnies so loudly it makes everyone turn and stare. Then the pony shakes violently from head to tail with a creaking of harness and jingling of the bit and the tiny girl sitting astride him, is being shaken out of her tree, her body shuddering along with the pony. What a scream. Everyone in the vicinity roars laughing. It should have been captured on video - the vibratory reaction of the little girl's chubby cheeks below huge blue eyes and bouncing blonde curls was priceless.

2.20. The streets and cafes are now packed with tourists and an organ grinder continues to play his music outside the gates. The weather suddenly turns cooler which drives the crowds off into the cafes.

3 pm. Back at hotel. Room has not been touched except my wet towels have gone but not replaced and bed is unmade and rubbish is still in bin. (The fourth floor of the hotel is not cleaned until 4 pm I find out later.)

6.35. Just finished dinner at "Royal Jussieu." Handsome young waiter tries to sell me a whole bottle of wine instead of a *verre de vin rouge* and a cheese platter instead of an *omelette fromage*. His art of persuasion has failed and he shows his final disappointment after producing a big blackboard with the array of desserts for the third time to my determined "*Je ne mange pas desserts monsieur.*" He settled for providing me with a cappuccino, even though he suggested "*un café crème?*" I love this café and the situation it is in and I can rely on the food being safe and the staff are very friendly (even though I wonder if the suggestion of a *café crème* after dinner is in a bid to indicate that he sees me as just another vulgar tourist.)

I like to be on the edge of the hive of industry that is going on outside. It re-charges my *Varta piles* for my love affair with Paris, whereas if I am in my hotel room alone for too long I begin to feel a little alienated from the Paris I love.

A testing day for Mummy.

I must have been very tired last night. I woke still wearing my dressing gown. I have been lying on my "bed" waiting for my turn in the bathroom. Anthony has been reading in there as usual. He reads on the toilet for hours – Japanese comics, and no-one can get in there. I slept like a log and my tummy feels happier than it has for a very long time, even after last night's potion of natto mustard and radishes. Maybe I'll change to Japanese food when I get home.

I had woken at the same time that I did in Melbourne. Japan was an hour behind Melbourne, so in Japan it was 6.30 when I hopped up, having waited until I heard Rachel stir.

"Now we're going to have to hurry Mum" said Rachel locking the front door behind us. "It's late."

Megumi came out and I tried to remember "*Ohayou gozaimas.*"

I said "*Ohayou gomazu*" and the two of them burst out laughing. They corrected me good-humouredly and I climbed on to the bike. I felt about as confident as I felt when I last climbed on a horse at Margaret River in

Western Australia after not having ridden for twenty years.

Megumi gave a bit of a grimace and turned and went back inside, closing the door behind her, not wanting to witness an embarrassing incident with *Mummy*.

When did I last ride a bike? It was at King's Park in Perth for about half an hour seventeen years ago and before that - I was sixteen years old, I thought as I took hold of the handle-bars and fumbled with my feet on the pedals. I used to ride my bike everywhere once upon a time as a young teenager.

We set off with me wobbling a bit. I had my camera, my diary and my "inside-shoes" in the attached basket.

People in Japan actually ride bicycles with babies in the basket and no-one has remotely heard of helmets of course, let alone safety seats for babies. The babies just share the tiny space with the cabbages and fish.

"Now hurry Mum! I'm late."

Was that my fault? "Rachel I'm not hurrying."

The further we got away from the apartment the better the surroundings. I decided I would get on the internet to Caroline that night and update her on the improvement in the local landscape. Then I noticed there were suddenly cars on the road.

"What side of the road should we be on?" I called out to Rachel who was a block ahead of me.

Keeping up with Rachel had always been like that. My mind flashed back to the America's Cup in 1987. We were living in Perth then and every time Rachel, Caroline and I went in to Fremantle, she'd take the lead once off the train and stride off like Joan of Arc might have if she'd been thrown off her horse. She was eighteen then and Carrie and I would be running to keep up like bridesmaids. She hadn't changed.

"It doesn't matter which side! She yelled back. "It just depends what side the car is coming on."

"What?" Oh great! I'd never worn a helmet anyway, not even horse-riding. I hopefully would survive the journey.

"Mum you're just going to have to do your best. I can't be late" she called back to me as she turned and sped swiftly through a crossing without me, her long hair blowing in the breeze.

The streets were narrow, rutted and cracked. There was a low wall at the side of the road about a foot high between the traffic and me and if I had thought too much about how narrow it was, I would have fallen off, but I knew I must not hold Rachel up.

With clenched teeth I concentrated on "*Ohayou gozaimas, Ohayou gozaimas*" rehearsing for the day's experience at Rachel's school. We came to an intersection. There was a truck sitting there. Rachel whizzed through and at that point the incompetent timid Mummy dismounted.

"Rachel – I can't – wait!" I pleaded. I ran across wheeling the bike and mounted up again once I felt safe to do so. She didn't wait. She pedaled on.

The houses lining the laneways were very pleasant. The whole area was very attractive and very clean and very "Japanese" and not at all like Bali really.

We entered the High School grounds and I was impressed. One, the fact that I actually had arrived in one piece and two, there were rice fields there and a shrine. We stopped at the shrine and Rachel said "Quick, I'll take your photo!"

I felt I should be finding a statue of Buddha and thanking him profoundly and reverently for getting me there in one piece.

"With the bike please" I puffed. "I'll need proof for your sister."

Several teenagers called out in greeting to Rachel.

"Ohayou gozaimu, ohayou gozaimasu, ohayou gozaimasu" I practised.

We changed our shoes and Rachel led me to the staff room. I felt like I was in a play, a local production about Oriental people. I could have been dreaming. All the teachers turned and stared at the new foreigner. I felt hot and flushed and quite breathless. *Ohayou gozaimasu, ohayou gozaimasu, ohayou gozaimasu.* My thin white cotton trousers felt damp. I thought I would probably have a black bike seat imprinted on my bottom.

Rachel introduced me to a line of happy faced beaming men.

"Ohayou gozaimasu, ohayou gozaimasu, ohayou gozaimaso" I said repeatedly and carefully as I passed each smiling face.

"Hullo" they offered. "Pleased to meet you," with bowing and more bowing.

At Rachel's desk there was a bowl of steaming green tea waiting and a tea lady scurried off and returned bowing, with a bowl of tea for me too. It was very good.

The school nurse came and introduced herself and asked me if I had seen Mt Fuji. She pointed out over the roof-tops.

"It is out there." We stared out at a hazy humid pearly white sky that matched the limb she so gracefully extended towards the distant horizon. "But in summer you cannot see it. You can only see it in winter when the air is clear," she continued in a lilting dreamy tone, her arm dropping languidly.

"Where do you wish to go to in Japan?"

"What is the sight-seeing that you would like to make well known?" and I wondered what he was doing right then. Did he take out that pencil likeness of himself and wonder why I had not been more cooperative?

I answered "Kyoto," and this prompted a discussion between her and Rachel that I could not make head nor tail of. Evidently she had just returned from a school excursion to Kyoto. She was very friendly and pleasant. I liked her. Then she began a scintillating description of the physical attributes of Rachel's husband Paul. Giggling, she summed him up, hiding her face behind her hands – *"Just like - Hugh Grant."*

Hugh Grant – it was the blue eyes. I didn't tell her that I couldn't stand Hugh Grant. I nodded at her with a weak smile.

I remembered the night Paul arrived to take Rachel out on their first date. I had expected a somewhat pimply adolescent high school type of boy that she had met at the gym. I opened the door to this huge, mature-looking man with movie-star looks. He was the image of Hugh Grant!

"You want to see Disneyland?"

"Not *really*, that's US culture. I wish to see *Japanese* culture."

"Come and I'll show you around the school Mum." We walked outside on a walkway and I freaked out when I realized I was in my inside shoes!

"No, the walkway is OK, as long as you walk on the yellow stripes and not on the gravel in between."

"Oh for Pete's sake!"

I took a photo of the school and the garden. Rachel sang out over her shoulder "I'm going to the loo before I go to class. Do you need to go?"

We walked into the staff toilets. "They're holes in the ground again. I'll wait til I get home. I don't really need to go."

"Mum they're OK. Just stand facing the higher bit that's at the back."

"Then I must have done it back to front at the station the other night."

"Well, go now the right way."

"No way. My slacks will end up wet again."

We headed back to the staff-room and a big gravelly-voiced Headmaster called us in to his office which was like a large boardroom, the walls lined with what looked like leather. It was all brown - very male. He invited us to sit. I noted that he was of an older generation to that of the children's Headmaster. He cleared his throat.

"I want to talk to Rachel's mother" Rachel translated with a rather intimidating smile at me.

I hoped I'd done nothing terribly wrong already.

"My Eng*r*ish very bad" he laughed and lounged back in his chair. He fumblingly told me "How good Rachel has been," or I sort of translated what he said as such and my eyes wandered to the wall behind him with large photographs of men I supposed to be previous Headmasters from long ago. I thought how my father and these men would have killed each other if they had had the opportunity sixty years earlier.

I heard Rachel say "The Headmaster's father's cousin lives in a retirement village on the Gold Coast." and I brought my gaze back to the Headmaster and the present time with a jolt. He was beaming at me expectantly and I hoped he wasn't counting on me knowing his father's cousin.

"How do you like Japan?"

"Each day I like Japan more and more ... Ummm, Japan very good" which sounded like I was doing another *natto* tasting.

"What is the sight-seeing that you would like to make well known?" But he phrased it differently.

"I would like to see Kyoto" I replied rather timidly.

Again the possibilities of getting to Kyoto were discussed.

"Not enough time and not enough money" said Rachel turning to me with under her breath, "What is this obsession you have with *Kyoto* Mother?"

Yes, I was beginning to sound like a parrot and a lame one at that. I didn't know what I wanted to see. It was the only place I could think of when asked out of the blue.

Actually, I'd love to take a trip to Nagoya and catch up with that spunk I sat next to on the plane Rachel!

Of course I kept those words within my head, smiling at her all the while I thought them. We both smiled back at the Headmaster together. I cringed because she told him we didn't have enough money to travel as far as Kyoto. Now he would think she came from a family of paupers. Well, and that was close to the truth wasn't it. I wondered how her father the country music singer would be assessed by the Headmaster and how would Ed behave. He was a born mimic and would have been having a field day had he been here.

They threw back and forth the word *"mata,"* which is pronounced like "Mudda" but means "not yet," many times and they both laughed when I asked Rachel what she was saying about me. He told Rachel about other famous gardens closer to us. Good, I thought to myself. I might get to see some Japanese gardens after all.

Then out of the blue he asked "What are your hobbies?"

"Oh - er - painting."

"Ah… painting!" tilting his chair back on two legs, the fingertips of both hands meeting. "What you painting?" in a deeper gruff tone.

"Oh – ah – Portraits – oils."

I wondered if I should have been quite so specific. I painted all sorts of things but my very recent art work commissioned by a certain middle-aged Japanese man came to mind. He might find some paints for me and ask me to paint a portrait of him at recess - I certainly hoped not.

"Ah…Your mother *on her own* living?"

"Yes."

And looking at me with what I felt was undeserved scrutiny …"Don't you get - *lonely?*"

I felt the Headmaster was being a little inappropriate with this question as it came out with such an emphasis on *"lonely?"*

"One could forgive almost anything in one who is a victim of loneliness" my mother used to say. She knew what loneliness was. And yes, of course I was lonely. Maybe loneliness was a genetic condition. Better to be lonely than with the wrong person. Anyway, had I come to meet the Headmaster for a counseling session or what?!

Discreetly hiding my fingernails and with a tone of more self-assurance, and defying the guilty expression I felt sure my face was betraying, I finally answered him "Sometimes – lonely. When painting – not lonely."

"Ah…" He looked unconvinced but continued "and other child?"

Rachel attempted to reassure him that Caroline lived not far away from me.

"Other child *not living with mother*!?" His voice rising an octave.

"No, not living with mother," Rachel told him and turning to me "Japanese mothers *actually live* with their children when they're old."

It was Rachel's last session at that school and she said *"Sayonara"* to him and they exchanged pleasantries and Rachel told him if he came to Australia he would be welcome to come and stay with them. I thought it an unnecessary suggestion for her to make but I said nothing. After much bowing all round and me with my hands hidden behind my back to hide the nail polish we were ushered out.

We went back to the staff room to wait for the English teacher to take us to his class. I was perspiring with the heat, not to mention the anxiety.

The kids had been corresponding on the internet with students at Rachel's old high school in the Yarra Valley. They were working on answering emails in English.

I was introduced to Ryota the English teacher. He bowed and said "I am very *pull*eased to meet you." I was knocking on the doors of my brain, looking for "good morning" but I couldn't find it. I was still recovering from the anxiety of meeting with the Headmaster and I made a strange strangled sound in my throat and bowed.

"You are *welc*ome to come to my class."

Evidently it was Rachel's role to assist him as he was not fluent in English.

Once more the price of travelling around Japan was brought up, this time by Ryota.

"Yes, it is costly and we don't have the time really" volunteered Rachel almost impatiently this time and I could understand that. While she was teaching and with the kids too, it would just be too expensive for us all and I was not really on a *horror-day*.

There was another bowl of green tea waiting at the desk. We drank our tea and followed Ryota to the classroom. A roomful of fifteen year-olds all in navy blue uniforms greeted us. On the way to the room Ryota asked me to repeat my name and then repeated it over and over to himself. *"Juree. Juree, Juree."*

He turned to me, peering over his spectacles. "I think you introduce yourself....OK?" and then made the announcement in English to the class.

"We have special visitor today. Rachel's mother. She is from Australia," (murmur murmur from the class.)

"*Ohayou goz... goz...*"

"*Gozaimasu*" prompted Rachel rolling her eyes impatiently at me, her silliest pupil. This was very difficult for a woman who used to play truant from school to avoid speaking at the front of the class. I had no idea when I said I'd come to Japan to mind the kids that this would include public speaking!

"My name is Julie." Rachel wrote it on the board and with it the Japanese version. "I am Rachel's mother and I live in Victoria, Australia, Warrandyte."

Ryota looked at me with a patient thoughtful face, not unlike the look I get from Coco sometimes, which I read as *"I've already told them that. The mother is certainly not as bright as the daughter.*

There had not been many replies to their emails according to Rachel and she was disappointed. "We'll have to divide the kids up so there's three kids to each email." There was much jeering and laughter as they were placed with other pupils.

Ryoto came and stood beside me. "Juree, please translate." He pointed to the name "Lachlan" on a piece of paper.

"*Ratchey?*" He tried in a questioning tone at me.

The boy from Melbourne had requested they call him *Lachy* for short.

"*Lockey*" I enunciated to him "is how it is pronounced."

"Ah…of course…..Rocky."

"No. Lockey, Lockey."

I looked over the shoulders of a few students after Rachel suggested I "mingle," to help supervise what they were doing. One girl wrote "I do truck and field." I pointed out her mistake feeling rather unqualified to do so.

They seemed very nice polite kids. One Australian boy had asked one of the Japanese boys if he wore a *kimono* every day. Rachel heard this and laughed.

"Hardly. Do you *ever* wear a *kimono*?"

"Yes, many times" he answered rather indignantly. "I wear *kimono* every day for sleeping in summer."

I took a photo of Rachel and the English teacher while they were supervising the students and before she left the lesson she made quite a long goodbye speech in Japanese. There were lots of "*Sayonaras*" from everyone. She would have two different groups that afternoon and it would be the last time she would be with that particular group of fifteen year-olds.

Class over, we headed off on our bikes. Rachel had to get me home and get back for two more lessons. How she ever found her way around on a bike when she first arrived I had no idea. She amazed me. Easy to see she had come from pioneer stock.

The paths were narrow again. This time, there were rice-fields with lots of water to fall into should I wobble off.

Rachel left me at the door of the apartment and pedaled off back to the school once more.

I walked around inside, deep in self-critical thought for fifteen minutes before I realized I was wearing my outdoor thongs! I leapt out of them and placed them outside while looking up and down the street. Was I being watched? I carefully dragged the straw broom across the floor to cover my tracks. I was nervous about the Yakuba (I was informed much later when I'd left Japan that they were just the local council and not a sinister organization of faceless men as I had depicted them) but I certainly didn't want to have Rachel finding another bit of grit on the floor.

####

I was at the park this afternoon, again filling in time until Rachel's return. We were throwing the ball back and forth with Anthony's friends joining in and along came the tiny boy with piranha-like teeth who had sidled up to me in Rosy's classroom, tickling my arm. I had moved away then as Rachel had warned me about a little horror who snuck up and tickled one's arms and then moved to the direction of one's bottom! I ducked out of his way.

"I know all about you. Go away!" I backed away from the small monster and he trundled off.

"Nanny, that boy's mad. He stood up on the window ledge at school and showed everyone his willy" said Rosy stormily.

"And as though anyone would want to see it Rosy!"

"Will you still be alive when I'm grown up Nanny?" she queried as we walked home hand in hand, "and will you come to my wedding?"

"Let me see, when you're twenty I'll be seventy-three. Maybe. And, yes, I'll come to your wedding, hopefully. Just don't ask me to carry you" I added, rubbing my wrists, my arthritis niggling from throwing the ball in the park.

When Rachel arrived home I asked her if we could maybe talk to Carrie on the internet.

We were eating dinner when the youngest boy from next door burst through the door. "Here we go again" said Rachel shaking her head. "As sure as Paul and I were having a "cuddle" the kids from next door would burst in. If we locked the door they'd rattle it like crazy and then when we eventually opened the door, they'd run in and yell *"WHAT DID YOU LOCK THE DOOR FOR?!"*

Anthony asked me what "animal" I was.

"Maybe a rooster, I'm not sure" I replied. "I'm not into Chinese birth-signs. I prefer the zodiac signs and I'm an Aquarian."

"Oh that's all nonsense. Japanese star-signs are quite different - it's all to do with what blood type you are here."

What next!

Rachel retrieved the laptop and I waited for her to offer it to me to contact Carrie but there was no offer. Still I was able to relax for once in my pyjamas on the living-room floor as there were no cheeky boys bouncing around me nor sumo wrestling on top of me.

Rosy decided she had to make a quick visit to the shop for an obvious sugar fix but it was long after 5 pm. She had exhausted herself pleading in the form of a tantrum and a display of cajolery, rage, threats, tears, moaning and wailing. I couldn't stand it any longer and hurled in her direction at the top of my voice - "THAT'S

IT! I'M NOT COMING TO YOUR WEDDING MADDIE-ROSE!"

She threw me a thunderous glance as she tore through the door clutching a fistful of small change, having succeeded in her manipulations. Rachel gave me a long and puzzled stare, one hand on her hip and I heard her sigh as she turned back to the rice cooker.

Rosy came curling around me later like a cat, the remains of the sticky sugar fix still obvious around her mouth, and she gazed up at me with her typical six year-old's toothless smile.

I said very quietly "You made me very sad to see you put on such a tantrum before," which was not my true feeling at all, but it was all I could say without further blowing on the coals of the family dynamics at her earlier take off of Liz Taylor in *"Who's Afraid of Virginia Wolf."*

Rachel had been typing on the computer to Caroline for half an hour, typing at a furiously rapid pace. (Just because I told her I was referred to as *'The Gun'* at work due to my typing speed, was there any need to try and outdo me?)

"Do you want a very quick word then.... Mother?" she called over her shoulder. I pulled the blanket over my head and said casually from my refuge on the floor "Oh - tell her I'll write." My hands were too sore to type anyway and I couldn't get used to that tiny keyboard.

She continued on for a while and then eventually switched the computer off.

"Caroline says that Angela is having problems with her wisdom teeth. I don't know why she doesn't just get the dentist to *yank* them out."

I answered from under the sheet "You don't just *yank* wisdom teeth out. I had to go to hospital to have mine pulled."

"You don't have to go to hospital for wisdom teeth. I had mine pulled out in the dentist's chair in Karratha."

"I'm sorry" I said sitting bolt upright, but I went to hospital – full anaesthetic!" I lay down again.

"Anyway, the dogs are OK, but when Angela got home last night there was vomit and poo in your lounge room."

Well, I thought, at least the dogs are showing signs of missing me. "I don't care" came my muffled reply. Right then I was thousands of feet up in the air, heading towards Paris with my Japanese man. I turned over again and pulled the covers over my head.

Long after the apartment was in darkness and Rosy's snoring had invaded the Kleenex I had wadded in to my left ear, I lay tossing and turning, rehearsing what I would say should he land on my doorstep and how, if he could find my phone number, what a strange phone call it would be with no laptop as interpreter. Sleep overtook me.

2013 – The Painters.

Wake at 6 am. Didn't get to sleep last night until about 10.30 which was surprising as I had walked all day, had wine, two Panadol Osteo for my hand pain and half an anti-anxiety tablet and at 10 pm decided to take another quarter.

Wash hair and style it well, dress in grey jeans and sneakers. I put on about three light-weight black tops as it's still really chilly and muffle myself in a blue/black/grey animal print scarf.

At breakfast a rather attractive middle-aged man sits at next table - vaguely acknowledge each other. A different waitress brings me a baguette with my croissant. She ignores my *"non baguette s'il vous plait Madame."* I have to go and ask the girl on the desk for sugar. The man next to me gets up, leaving his croissant untouched. I am about to grab it discreetly with no one there to witness as I am starving hungry on my one croissant, but the waitress glides past and removes his tray. As she passes me I do the unthinkable – *"Madame – le croissant!"* bursts out of me and I hand her the baguette and snatch the croissant in the swooping action of a sea-gull. When further threat to my teeth occurs and I am in need of some sustenance for today's first meeting with the group, there are no limits to my behaviour.

I can't believe I did that. What an ill-bred peasant I am. She would know that anyway by the condition of my teeth!

10.00 am Arrive at Musee Cluny.

I smile carefully. Claude recognizes me instantly of course, even though I am a blonde this year (something I had not planned on either and the first of my pre-Paris disasters.) He shows great pleasure at my arrival and welcomes me with a kiss to both cheeks. It is wonderful to see him again and of course it has only been fourteen months. He says Ralph didn't turn up this July for the first time in many years and I told him Bonnie had said that the delightful, happy and gay Ralph was going on a trip away with Mat this year. "Interesting" smiles Claude.

There are only five of us in the group this time instead of the fifteen young and vibrant people I was with last year. I remember how I had stood nervously in the grounds of Musee Cluny last July, being the first to arrive and suddenly a beaming handsome American with unruly hair lunged at me, shook hands and said "Hi, you must be a painter too. I'm Steve." What a turn my life was suddenly taking. My mind fast-forwarded through the chapters towards a pre-conceived happy ending. I thought my luck had changed. But by the time the whole colourful crowd got together he was instantly bewitched by an attractive young Italian woman, young enough to be my daughter and another prospective conquest for him.

Bonnie arrived and then Mat and the very animated, fluently French-speaking Ralph and the collection of friendly smiling people from Spain, Portugal, Italy, the U.S. and Canada.

We had a wonderful time in the French sunshine of mid-summer, taking up a couple of tables everywhere we went for lunch, spending two hours all speaking in different languages, trying to order food and wine with frustrated waitresses whose language skills were pushed to the limits and beyond.

During our first introductions amongst each other over wine, the subject of age arose and Steve admitted to us in sad tones that he was forty-seven. Nobody made any comment and then as we were about to leave, standing in line waiting to pay our *additions*, he announced to us all quite surprisingly, "Hey, I have to make an apology to you all. I was really surprised that everyone believed I was forty-seven. I lied to you. I am actually fifty-three." Disappointed that none of us showed any surprise or amazement at his confession he added rather uncomfortably "It's just that according to all the dating sites - nobody wants anyone over forty-seven." I rolled my dinosaur eyes in his direction and glared.

Later that evening a few of us met on Steve's suggestion of cocktails after class. The conversation turned to the latest dating sites which I had had no experience with nor interest in, my only contribution to this discussion being that seeing as the "cut-off age" was forty-seven I'd hate to think what response I'd get— probably Methuselah when I would have been hoping for Johnny Depp. Steve hopped in with "See – Johnny Depp is forty-seven!" Well, evidently Johnny Depp had sadly reached his 'use-by' date and I answered "The liar is probably fifty-three!"

The very bubbly Bonnie from Tennessee spoke fluent French but with such a Southern accent. I picked her accent up almost immediately, which was not what I had expected I'd be doing in Paris. When I opened my diary each night it read in a broad Southern accent.

This year there are two women and one man from the U.S. and one young woman from Spain. They are a friendly, pleasant but sober little group compared to last year. I have prepared myself for the fact that the trip this year will be a completely new and different experience to last July. Am I to expect a perfect continuation from where I'd left off in Paris so grudgingly last year? I had gone home then with the burning desire to somehow move to France permanently. I know everyone's first question to me when I get home this time will be "Was it as good as last year?" and I intend to begin a completely blank page with an open mind.

It has become very cold and I am really not prepared at all for cold weather.

We set off to Square Viviani across the way from Notre Dame where I've painted before but after half an hour it starts to rain.

Can't say I like the water-colour pens that I've brought this year. Last year I painted in Paris in acrylics and then in oils when we went on to the Chateau in the beautiful Loire Valley.

We pack up and head for shelter in the 13th Century St Severin Church. I have come in later than the others and didn't realize we were supposed to be painting in "*one colour only.*" Claude frowns at me in the silent half-light. How can one paint in one colour when one is surrounded by glorious stained glass windows?

We take a break to go for lunch at an East African restaurant. I pay more for lunch than I usually do (25 euros). I had noodles and vegetables – very nice, with lots of ginger and a red wine and a cappuccino.

Finally we leave St Severin at 5 pm and I find my way back to my hotel quite easily with instructions from Claude to ring him at 9 am tomorrow, to find out if it will be the dry venue or the wet weather venue. I think it's been forecast to be wet and cold.

2004 – Miko and Megumi take me shopping.

Megumi and I went to Miko's house first and rang the bell. The small "golden retriever" of unverified parentage was tied to the door handle. He evidently spent his days like that. He looked in great need of a good brushing, and heaven knows what else. His hair was shedding in tufts. He smiled good-naturedly and I stroked his nose. He smelled bad and when I patted him there was a cloud of loose faded hair released. He eyed off my nail polish very suspiciously, sniffing my fingertips one at a time.

"What's his name?"

"Long."

"Long? Hi Long."

Miko's voice came from the interior. "OK, OK" answered Megumi. Miko had her "cute" little Hyundai van that she was leasing today. "Tonight a new car. Every ten years the Japanese car is crushed and you get a new one," so we had worked out through Rachel's translation the other night. My old Ford back in Melbourne would be due for its third crushing then.

In the car Miko was sniffing and I heard the request for "tissue." I thought the Japanese only sniffed and that it was indecent to blow one's nose. She just dabbed at her nose and turned and said "Nose running." Megumi and I produced our phrase books and I looked up hay fever *"kafunsho desu?"* "Ahh..." they both exclaimed in unison, delighted and smiling at my attempt at pronunciation.

We walked into the supermarket armed with our phrase books. It was just another supermarket, except I was the only foreigner and the food was distinctly Japanese with rows of unidentifiable bright pink and red things in the meat department, those little white sperm-shaped fish and eels and more eels. Every form of Japanese food possible. Food as difficult to understand as the writing and the speech and with sushi in every form.

As usual, I was worried I was not going to have enough money with me, and I wished I'd brought more but wasn't this just the same at home? I only wanted to buy a few things and I had nearly 6000 yen with me and 2000 yen of Rachel's which I would give back to her. I looked at my money converter again and again. I had nearly $70 of my own money. But then I had to get a bottle of wine for Friday night as Megumi and Miko had planned a little "get-together." The wine labels were unrecognizable to me but Megumi ran to me grinning broadly with a bottle of red, jabbing a finger at the kangaroo on the label. Hardy's Shiraz. It was only about

$6 but I thought my calculator might be wrong. I'd better go easy with the food I was going to buy.

"Tatami mat…smell!" An order to me as we passed the household items.

"Yes" I sniffed "dry-grass."

We puzzled over the deodorant Rachel had instructed me to get. She'd given me an empty spray can and we tried to match it. I felt so handicapped when looking for anything in the supermarkets. All that *Kana* and *Katakana* writing. As Rachel instructed me "*Katakana* for foreign words, *Hiragana* phonetically, *Kanji* characters and writing in general, *Kana*." It all looked the same to me, like Pittman's shorthand and that was much easier to learn and only took me a year.

"Don't let her talk you into getting an expensive one Mum. This is the only one that works for me here" were my instructions. I was sure I'd get the wrong thing.

"Oh, cold cream. That's what I want… *Softymo Super Cleansing Wash*." As long as it wasn't oven cleaner I guessed it wouldn't hurt. I held it up for their approval and waved my fingers in my face. They both nodded wide-eyed and unsmiling. I looked at their faces. Not a trace of make-up. How would *they* know. I gesticulated "My face fall off – you big trouble." Megumi shrieked seeming to understand.

The food area was certainly interesting. Rachel had been disappointed that they'd be taking me to the supermarket. She wanted to be the one to take me through it and introduce the food to me. I looked at the sushi.

"You try?"

"I try."

I bought a few squishy rolled up items I had no idea what to do with and Megumi gabbled off instructions in Japanese, then "You try!"

"I try" I assured her. I began searching the aisles for soy milk which was all I drank at home. "Soy milk" I pondered wandering along the aisle.

"*Soy* milk" - blank faces. "Soy *beans*, tofu, soy *milk* - soy milk - sorry, sorry - soy *sauce*."

"No. Soy milk."

"Ah…soy sauce."

"No, no, no." "I can't put soy sauce in coffee."

"Ah… sorry, sorry, *coffee!*" We all scampered off to another site. "Powder one?"

"No not coffee. Soy *milk*." I pointed to the cows-milk carton covered in bright green Kanji characters, a small cartoon cow at the bottom.

"Oh *milk*. Sorry. *Soy milk*? Sorry not know *soy* milk" and two blank expressions.

Mildly frustrated but amused I gave up. I was sure that they drank soy milk at home all the time!

With the help of the phrase book I asked "Food for party tomorrow night – Friday night… I buy what food?"

Megumi replied "No no no, sorry. After eat...after eat, dinner gone...party."

Now, they thought I was inviting myself to a meal. I pointed to some potato chips. "This one....with drinks."

"Ah yes." They looked pleased.

I bought some tomatoes and began to add up the cost so far. I looked at my calculator again. We checked our phrase books once more and I pointed to a packet of what looked like pickled mushrooms.

"*Nasu, nasu*?" I looked it up "Eggplant." They pointed to packets of little eggplants. "No, I want other eggplant. BIG one!" I didn't think I'd confuse them further with the suggestion of "aubergines."

"OK" Miko dumped a packet of little eggplants into my arms. "Don't know *BIG* eggplant!"

The apples were huge and the eggplants tiny. It was all back to front but the vegetables were quite cheap compared to home.

"You want *Natto*?" Megumi pointed as discreetly as if she were referring me to the condom shelf.

I said a long "Noooooo." She looked hurt. The converted was back-sliding already. I bought a packet of film, a packet of five. I made a mental calculation again.

We headed for the check-out after we had found the cheese. The Japanese thought cheese disgusting Rachel had told me and there was practically nothing to choose from. I bought something that looked like cheese labeled Camembert, again cheaper than home. I had spent 4,337 yen. Phew – what did that convert to?

There was a very correct way of doing everything in Japan. You got your basket off the trolley. The girl allowed you so many plastic bags. You went to a stainless steel bench and you packed the bags.

Miko started the car. "You" she motioned to me and then to the back seat, "STAY!" My name was not "Long" but I got in and sat alone for another fifteen minutes with the air conditioner and the motor running. They came back with more bags and Megumi handed me a bottle of iced green tea.

"Thank you. Thank you" and then I added "Very bright sun" pointing in its direction.

"Sun, what *sun?*"

I looked it up. "*Taiyo.*"

"Ah...sun."

"Typhoon coming – on TV?"

"Yes" said Megumi. "On TV...typhoon come." And with this they talked covertly together. I wondered what they might be keeping from me.

Having returned from the shopping expedition and alone once more, I felt a bit lost and wished I had some Bee Gees music to listen to and went to the fridge, opened it and stared at the contents and decided to have a swig of green tea. I would have preferred a swig of red wine but there wasn't any.

Earlier that morning I had attempted to send Carrie an email. I was not sure at all how to do it, as really, I was a bit unadventurous when it came to technology, especially Rachel's. But I was not going to "write" as I said I would. I related to Carrie *"Open Day at the school."* I hoped when I sent it off that it was on its way.

I thought I would probably be in trouble for using the computer unsupervised, knowing what a tangle I get myself in with anything to do with technology, but I asked Rachel that morning "When can I send an email to my friends at work? They'll be hanging out for some news."

Rachel had gone to a meeting with the Yakuba. Maybe she should work for them – as an interrogator I pondered, frowning to myself and taking another swig of tea. A year in Japan had equipped my quiet little girl with the mind-set needed for survival amongst Japanese professionals it seemed. The Yakuba employed Rachel in the English language scheme as well as playing music at 5 pm for the *Rats of Hamlin.* She stressed that if *Yakuba* was not pronounced correctly it came out as meaning something akin to the *Mafia,* and why was I not surprised? "One had to be careful" she added "or you will offend."

"What did you have at lunch today Anthony?"
"Squid."

"You always have squid."

"I'll show you how to play Japanese chess Nan."

Megumi had come in for coffee as soon as Rachel returned from her meeting. She brought with her some strange squashy green cakes, rather rubbery to bite into with a sweet filling of red bean. They raved over them. I said one would do me for a meal. They were very filling, coloured with green tea and dusted with icing sugar. They tasted to me like uncooked cake mixture and took a while to slide down and were horribly synthetic-tasting. An hour later I was still swallowing. I wouldn't be able to eat again for twenty-four hours.

"Your mother very slender. Not eat much food" said Megumi eyeing me rather disapprovingly with Rachel translating.

"Why did you spend $50 at Tommy's for goodness sake?" asked Rachel, picking up the receipt from the shopping I'd done. "We didn't need tomatoes, or broccoli or cucumbers."

"I know, I know, I've doubled up. It was my money. I'll just have lots of tomatoes and cucumber with my rice – OK?"

We sat down to seaweed and noodles, rice, tomatoes, broccoli and cucumber and the sushi. "And I'll keep eating the tomatoes broccoli and cucumbers til they're gone!"

I confessed to my attempt at sending the email. "Why did you E-mail Caroline? I thought you were going to email your work-friends?"

"I just thought I'd have a practice on Carrie before trying the girls at work. She probably didn't get it." Why did I have to report on everything I did? I wasn't the pupil. And who was the daughter in this relationship anyway? Thank goodness her term in Japan was coming to an end.

I asked if we could watch the news. "I'd like to see what's going on in the outside world. All we watch is Japanese cartoons *every* night."

We got the latest on the war in Iraq through an interpreter, replays of September 11th and the latest information on how Bin Laden had wanted to crash planes into Japanese sites as well. Bush came on and then the Japanese PM came on the screen. He had rather shaggy hair and a pleasant face but with very puffy eyes. I liked him.

"He wears his hair like that to represent a lion" said Rachel.

"Really! – seriously?"

"He should dye it yellow and grow it longer then" said Rosy morosely in her very deepest bass voice.

The next news story was about a man who was in court on the charge of looking up a high-school girl's skirt with a little mirror in his hand. He was caught at the station. "There Mum, now do you believe it about the vending machines?"

"Oh really Rachel, my mother used to have an old man drop his bowler hat on the floor of the train every morning when she was going to work, so he could bend over and look up her skirt. That was Melbourne in 1927. I don't think men have changed. Anyway, are they going to behead him for that – or *Carry Harry* or whatever they call it?"

I tried the facial cleanser at bed-time. It was a clear gel. When I spread it over my face it went into a lather. "Maybe this is shaving-cream." I moved it towards my eyes and it didn't budge the mascara. The children came and watched and roared with laughter. "Rachel, I'll need to use just a *tiny* bit of your cleanser. This doesn't seem to work on my eyes." I remembered the visits to the dermatologist and the allergist in Perth and the warnings of trying out any new skin preparations on the inside of my elbow for forty-eight hours before attempting to use them. After the patch testing showed my violent reaction to the native plant Grevillea, I was given a warning about similar allergy-producing irritants that were also contained in many cosmetics.

At last I set up my bed on the couch. I was lying staring at the ceiling waiting for the usual deafening "preparations-for-bed" from Anthony to end, with every light left on as he passed through like a whirling dervish, stumbling over my bed as he went. After much repeated yelling and pleading the dazzling lights eventually were turned off and darkness finally reigned. I sighed.

On went the lights again. This time it was Rachel.

"Look at my teeth! I can see fine cracks. They're going to fall out for sure." I was given close scrutiny of her front teeth.

"You're crazy. There's nothing wrong with them. Go back to bed." I lay down again.

"Well thanks very much. You're as bad as Paul. You're supposed to be here to support me – not say things like that to me."

"I'm sorry Rachel, but you're pushing yourself too hard and probably grinding your teeth in your sleep. Settle down or *you'll* crack!"

I woke after dreaming I was back home. Home was a very rickety old house. I opened the cutlery drawer in the kitchen. It was full of red earth. The teaspoons had moss growing in them and they were all cracking.

I went to the bathroom. As I leant on the basin, my eyes squinted back at me from the little mirror. I called out to Rachel or to anyone who was vaguely interested in my plight: "Guys, I think the prime minister uses Softymo Super Cleanser on his eyes!"

Discovering new places.

Today, heavily rugged up, woollen scarf and all, I find Place Igor Stravinsky on the south side of the Pompidou Centre. I am amazed that I find it without any difficulty and am the first to arrive along with Claude who greets me with his handsome smiling face.

Interesting place. A large raised square pool of water on which sits a treble clef spraying water and modern mechanical sculptures, a pair of huge red lips and a colourful piece in polyester, all created by husband and wife Jean Tinguely and Niki de Saint Phalle, the pieces representing the music of Igor Stravinsky. A huge image of Salvador Dali painted on a side wall contrasts with a backdrop of an 18th Century church which overshadows the water. This is in the Beaubourg and Les Halles area just across the Seine from where I am staying in the Latin Quarter.

Claude seems very pleased with my efforts at sketching in water-colour pencils and says he will photograph it. He shakes his head, tut-tutting me – "Before you ruin it Julie, by putting water on it as you insist on doing."

Many people stand around in groups and take photos and one American woman makes me feel good when she says as she passes "That's fantastic!"

Lunch at a gorgeous little restaurant. I have salmon which is served in a little stack of morsels and seems a bit too much like a tidy little pile of flesh for my liking. One of the girls who is from Chicago is a strict vegetarian and is disappointed at my ordering salmon I think.

I laugh with the group a lot and Claude makes use of my plans to go to the Versailles area for the second half of my stay, as the joke of the day. He feels he can laugh at me as we are old friends from last year. I have mistakenly booked a hotel somewhere off Avenue Versailles which I feel must be near Versailles itself. It has been paid for in advance, before I have had a chance to re-book elsewhere. Oh well, this will be a new experience but I can't ignore my slight irritation at having to leave central Paris for ten days.

Claude says that for starters I should shoot my travel agent and that he feels he must now put out an ad in Paris for a man for me "Because you will be bored to death with nothing to do and nowhere to go Julie.

"Educated woman alone and bored in Versailles – needs man!" He roars and everyone is amused.

From there we go on to Musee de la Chasse et de la Nature which is a collection of art on the theme of mediaeval hunting up to the 19th Century. This museum is situated on the corner of Rue des Archives and Rue des Fils, still in the Beaubourg and Les Halles area. There are hundreds of stuffed animals with that smell about them. I'm sure they got the animals from Jardin les Plantes. They were all zoo animals, horribly dead, old and stuffed.

During the Prussian siege of Paris I have read that zoo animals were slaughtered to feed the hungry Parisians. I have also heard that the eating of exotic zoo animals was the rage amongst the rich for a time and when I question Claude on this he doesn't believe it. There are paintings of boars and rabbits and deer being hunted and killed. Not the place for two vegetarians to spend the afternoon and Claude expects us to paint them – ugh! Glass eyes with no life in them. You'd have to be joking Claude!

I sketch in my water-colour pencils the only acceptable subject I can find – a doorway with curtains opening into another room where a lion is sitting, large and dead. Claude urges me to include the lion – bizarre!

A painting of a bitch with pups makes me sad as some printed information on the wall says that up until 1750 it was believed that animals felt no pain and had no feelings and that the artist had painted the bitch and her protectiveness towards her pups as a statement of the inaccuracy of this old belief.

I read that stags were the supreme animal of the forest as they were symbolic of new life in Christ with the replenishing of their antlers and the ten branches of the antler symbolic of the Ten Commandments.

I've had enough by 5 pm and leave with the aroma of taxidermy in my nostrils.

Expecting a long walk home, surprisingly I find my way without any slip-ups.

My oldest friends Penny and Mark arrived in Paris today and are staying in an apartment in The Marais quite close by. However I will not pursue them yet, knowing what it feels like when you have just arrived from that agonizing flight from Australia. Penny and I were next door neighbours in East Ivanhoe when she was five and I was seven. We have been looking forward to meeting in Paris, although the timing of our plans was quite co-incidental and they will be going off in a few days on a cave tour around France. I am really excited for us to be meeting in Paris of all places. Penny has been enthusiastically encouraging me in my idea of moving over here since last year's trip.

Susan from Oregon who is about my age is mad on animals too and her dog is all that keeps her from moving to Paris or another European city. Ideally I'd like to live half the year here and half the year in Melbourne but I could never consider leaving my furry children for that much time. Susan is wanting a new direction and challenge in life just as I do. It must be our age.

I have been so cold again today. The wind is chilling and sitting drawing out in the open is the last thing to be doing in this weather. I don't have enough warm clothes and it is getting colder by the minute.

Rachel stepped out of the shower, wrapped herself in a towel and said crossly. "Someone flushed the toilet when I was in the shower."

"You've inherited that from your grandfather Rachel. He freaked out every time anyone touched a tap while he was in the shower. Next thing you'll be lining up the saucepans and giving them marching orders."

My father, who should have remained an army man, was obsessive in his daily routine and the butt of jokes with the children when he got older and more obsessive, as he tried to hang on to a shred of power in the grown up and straying family.

"There's nothing wrong with that" she said laughing.

"Get ready for school or you'll be late" I ordered.

She poked out her tongue at me and the children laughed at this change in role-playing. I strode over to her and smacked her soundly on the bare back-side. The children in shocked amusement watched the back of their naked mother twisting to look behind her.

"Red hand-prints! I haven't had those for years."

"Yes more's the pity," and we were all laughing. Thank goodness.

Gosh, I remember my mother on one occasion, armed with an Aboriginal "wife-beater" from Arnhem Land, chasing me around the house when she was trying to make her point. I was laughing at the time and it was done to illustrate that she meant business. No wonder I had an innate interest in Aboriginal rights.

Red hand-prints were old-hat and boring back in the 1950's. Everyone had them.

Dad had brought a small collection of Aboriginal artifacts back with him in 1934 from a six-month driving trip with his mate, to Darwin in a baby Austin, cross country where there were no roads. An old newspaper clipping reads "*...they went off to wage war on crocodiles and other big game.*" He wore jodhpurs and a pith helmet (given him by a magician in Melbourne) in the photos of him lined up with the remote Aborigines of Arnhemland, a linear art-form with their multitude of tall spears. He looked very much like he was going off to hunt tigers in India. He had not flinched at the weapons threateningly waved in his face during a corroboree put on in their honour and from this act of courage, he and his mate were invited to witness a very secret initiation ceremony of boys entering manhood. These Aborigines had little or no contact with whites and were living in their natural tribal state, fit and healthy, away from European interference. However the Mission on Thursday Island protected many and I wonder what number of smiling black faces in his photos he took of them thrived because of their placement there as children. How unjust it was that the First Fleet and their criminal cargo got in to their home country like illegal immigrants, not even needing to present a passport or a working visa.

When my Dad boarded a pearling lugger on Thursday Island sporting a beard, the native crew all greeted the young kind eyed 30 year-old with a revered "*Good morning Jesus,*" and probably to avoid blasphemy with such an idea, (being the *son of a preacher man*) he immediately shaved it off.

I had tried to get him to recall his memories with me but by that time he was well in to his eighties. We should have gone over it together years earlier as he could only remember a little and was no longer interested. His travelling partner had been the one to keep a diary and he had died a long time before. It would have made for interesting television had it happened half a century later.

I don't remember my father ever actually hitting me. He just used to tell us in his most severe Army voice, on a very regular basis if we misbehaved, that my brother and I would be sent off on the "training-ship." I had this dreaded sepia picture in my mind of all these poor kids, one looking a lot like me, lined up in short pants doing star-jumps for the rest of their lives, towered over by a hulking great brute with a whip on something Fletcher Christian would have sailed on.

Forty years after those threats I went with a party from the hospital in Perth where I worked, to spend the day on the "training-ship" Leeuwin. We sailed around the Fremantle area. It was all wine-sipping, lobster and salad, sun-tanning and laughter. If only I'd known.

"There's an email from Carrie."
"Angela's teeth are better."
"Don't let's start on teeth again."
"It's been raining all week but she's walking the dogs and Levi's been giving her horror nights of no sleep.

I wondered why to myself, does anyone have children? You risk your life giving birth to them and never get a night's sleep again, because if they're not waking you up with colic or teeth or getting into your bed, they're keeping you awake watching the clock because they're now driving your car. You clean up their messes, taxi them around, and suddenly they turn in to big strangers who can't stand you and blame you for all *your* decisions and all *their* mistakes.

Carrie had commented on the child labour situation that I'd told her about with Rosy scrubbing floors at the school and reminded me of the time she'd been asked to clean the toilets in primary school and how angry I had been about it. I didn't remember that at all.

"I hope you will find enough to keep you busy during the day Mum." She was always concerned for me, but then she was the psychologist and I was a bit uncertain of whether I was the loved problem mother or the problem patient. A bit of both probably.

Tonight we were watching a show on TV while I confided in my diary, where there was a fierce but elaborate cake and confectionery making contest. The food was almost pornographic to the taste senses. So utterly extravagant, a thousand strawberries, rivers of custard cream, Van Gogh's Sunflowers graphically reproduced in pineapple and orange jelly-topped cake, chocolate and swirls of cream. It was quite disgusting but wonderful at the same time. After the creative preparation ended, it was tested out on tiny children with hidden cameras, watching their reactions and then tested on adults. This seemed to be the most popular type of program. Not cooking really, but tasting and the reactions to it.

"That's what I'm going to do when I grow up. I'm going to make cakes" said Rosy wringing her hands with intensity.

"Last night you were going to produce TV shows and the night before you were going to be a vet."

"Well, I can't decide."

And how absolutely wonderful to have the choices and opportunities like this, and those her mother's generation had I thought.

My father's well thought out career advice was "I'm not having you go to art school with a lot of poofters. My boundaries were set by my father with what "*his sisters might think.*" This included very obviously the dismissal of "art school" and later of course, heaven help us, knowing "a divorced man."

"I want you to be a secretary – like your cousin."

Maybe then I'd become a nun, after seeing Audrey Hepburn's portrayal of one in "The Nun's Story." I'd also read a book on the life of Ida Scudda, medical missionary and believed that a life of philanthropy would be a lot more meaningful than secretarial work.

"You just want to be a hero" said Mum in a disbelieving voice. "And why don't you join the tennis club at the Methodist Church dear." But she had more sympathy for my predicament than Dad and suggested I talk to the art teacher at school.

I could tell I was an annoyance interrupting his conversation when I timidly knocked at the door and began whispering "Mr Robinson, I just wanted to know what you thought about commercial art as a career…."

"Oh, it's very competitive, very, very competitive." I knew by the raised eyebrows and the long pause, that there was to be no further information available and he couldn't care less anyway. Why didn't he discuss the options of the film industry, advertising, illustration, art gallery curator or even teaching? He was more interested in the Geography teacher's weekend. His back was turned to me.

Life was surely meant to be more than the mundane order of middle-class suburbia, catching the train every morning at 7.27 and sitting all day staring at a shorthand book. Mine was a highly decorated one of course, embossed with lips, eyes and snorting horses which I doodled away at while waiting for the Manager of the Debt Collection Agency to get off the telephone. This was the post that the Business College had me fill and Ida and Audrey would have been very disappointed in me.

Dad's ambitions hadn't played out the way he dreamed either. He had wanted to be a surgeon and I think he would have made an excellent one, but his father was a fire and brimstone Baptist preacher with a Viking background and a large family to support, so extravagant pursuits were out of the question. Dad turned out to be a perfectionist with a will of iron and as an engineer he performed like a surgeon.

He demanded good and honest principles that had been laid down by his father who wouldn't hesitate to lean down the length of the table, grab him by the scruff of the neck and wave the carving knife in his face if he spoke out of turn. Dad adored his father but it seemed to me that he saw women as fools and if a woman was worthy of praise it was because she did whatever she did *"like a man."* My cousin Felicity, who was on Mum's side of the family was beautiful, capable and had fifteen years ahead of me of proven success. According to Dad, she was the only woman driver who deserved to be on the road because *"she drove like a man."*

I remember well, my first and last driving lesson with Dad. From the moment I turned the key in the ignition he yelled and this continued while I hopped helplessly along the street, whereupon he roared at me hysterically to get out and he took over the wheel. I slammed the door "I don't *ever* want to drive!" He drove back into the garage, mission accomplished. No wonder Mum never drove and I didn't attempt to drive after that episode until I was in my mid-thirties, my first brave act of liberation after my divorce.

Ed said he was closer to my Dad than to his own father. He admired and respected him and had been wowed by the adventurous tales he had told him, some that he had never shared with me. I had heard many times the story of him playing two-up in the desert with Arabs and stamping on the hand of one who was trying to cheat him, only to be surrounded by a knife-wielding mob. Drawing his pistol, he had held them at bay, backed off and climbed in to a taxi that his mate had grabbed. The typical Aussie Digger's story.

He looked like Errol Flynn in those days and I wonder if he believed he was. He kept any unpleasant stories about shooting the enemy to himself, or evidently only shared these with Ed. He referred to himself as "the black-sheep of the family." I suppose that was the term that was used for "one who dances to his own drum" back then. He'd been given that title by a visiting preacher who pointed Dad out, while he stood in a line-up with his two brothers and three sisters. "There's your black-sheep. He'll be the stone-breaker."

He was very proud of that title. He never became a stone-breaker, but he was known as a bit of a heartbreaker. He was also known to break the family's rigid rules by coming home late on a Sunday night after racing cars on the Sabbath. He would climb through his bedroom window and leap into bed fully clothed, boots and all, the bedclothes up around his chin before his father came in to bid him goodnight and query his absence at Evening Service.

Half of me was like him and half of me was like Mum, who should have married someone a bit bohemian. In her later years she went to art classes and was quite skilled at drawing but as a young girl she had wanted passionately to be a dancer which was out of the question for a respectable Methodist girl and would have been seen by her family as a quick-step to the street.

Mum's artistic talent on a few occasions led her to angrily gouging a particularly nasty image of Dad with horns, but they weren't Viking horns. Funny, but I found myself producing similar images of Nick when he was around.

I think my brother Bruce inherited the calmer more talented and workable halves of our parents.

Paris – 2013

5 am. Woke up and began working with water on my pencil sketches. I am beginning to get the hang of this. Quite pleased with my "Stravinsky Fountain."

8 am. Just returned from breakfast where a very nice Californian woman struck up a conversation. She is travelling with her daughter, who she said gets a little impatient with her – fancy that. Was nice to chat at breakfast with a friendly face.

10 am. I'm now near Hotel Invalides, where Napoleon's remains are entombed. I stayed a few doors down from here back in 2002. This is a wonderfully central and fashionable area with the Military Academy across the road where Napoleon spent his early career. The Musee Rodin is just around the corner housing many of the sculptor's wonderful works (The Kiss, The Thinker among my favourites) and only a 10 minute walk to the Eiffel Tower. Wish now I had booked the second stage of my Paris reunion here instead of going to Versailles.

Having a *café crème* (not as good as Le Rostand). I have been walking an hour and will stay here for a 20 minute rest. I am wearing black jumper under black and grey striped top and grey jeans, black cardigan and corduroy jacket with mauve woollen scarf wound heavily around my neck, and sneakers. Had to stop at Musee Cluny and remove my cardigan as I began to warm up walking and I'm now miles too hot. It's supposed to rain today so the group are meeting at the wet weather venue at Trocadero.

I'm finishing my coffee and in another fifteen minutes I'll be on my way again. Have enjoyed the walk down Boulevard St Michel and St Germaine and on to Rue du Bac, which is an area I've never seen before – gorgeous, and into Rue de Varenne to Invalides. I was intending to try the bus this morning but decided it looked a walkable distance on the map and really, it's the only way to see Paris. Lots of people exercising and toileting overweight dogs. Men here wear colourful, quite feminine looking scarves, and as the women do, wear them over their jackets.

Today is my first sighting of the Eiffel Tower since I've arrived back in Paris. It gives me a rush to see it still here in its elegance. It hasn't moved.

Funny to think that today Penny and Mark will be lunching in the restaurant in the Tower. I can't wait to see them, not today though.

I find the Institute of Architecture with a bit of help and a lot of back-tracking and we start sketching the Eiffel Tower from the windows that look down over Champ de Mars.

This building is full of hundreds of replicas of famous sculptures, practically all with biblical references from all over the world. Ancient European sculpture, Romanesque, Gothic etc. Claude explains the significance of it all. Lots of religiously symbolic work. Jesus a huge figure, the disciples much smaller and other figures incidental and tiny. Claude says they depicted the important figures as larger than life and the size became smaller as they were less important.

Susan arrives really late, having passed her stop on the bus and then had to get a taxi back. She is flustered. We both decide to quit at 12.30 and go for lunch and a drink. Had lovely *omelette au fromage*. The waiter commented on my good *Francaise*. We thought we might go on to Musee Rodin but rain came down in buckets and my umbrella was blown inside out several times as I struggled against the weather along the Champ de Mars. We decided to go our own ways and I was not sorry as I've already seen Musee Rodin in 2002 and don't want to spend money unnecessarily.

Was taken by surprise from behind my umbrella while walking along near the Eiffel Tower, by a swarthy young woman, waving what I thought was some kind of petition to sign about the plight of handicapped children. I signed it rather illegibly at her insistence with my country of origin and postcode which aroused my uneasiness somewhat, but I gave her two euros. She chased after me, ranting and raving. "Two euros is not acceptable! You have signed a form that promises a minimum of five euros donation!"

I said against the biting wind that whipped my words away "Well give me back my two euros then."

She got very excited and loud. "You have to give me a minimum of five euros!" I told her to go away and walked off, hoping there wouldn't be a group of them waiting on my doorstep in Healesville when I got home, as I was approached instantly by another girl waving the same paper. This time I just said "Get lost!" I can't believe I gave that girl two euros. Beggars try different scenarios from year to year. Last year it was the puppies.

4.30 pm. Weary and footsore I arrive back at my hotel having walked all the way back from Trocadero. It was much warmer today just because I had extra layers on and didn't need them after all.

I exclaim to the man at the desk as I collect my key quite exhausted. "I have walked all the way to Trocadero and back. What a walk!"

"Yes Madame – that must be *at least* two kilometres. It would be far for me too" he adds.

What! – Where's my map? That can't be right. It does only look a couple of kilometres. I walk at least five kilometres every day with my dogs up and down mountainsides. It must be the cobblestones.

I have had a shower and taken all my sweaty clothes off and put these in a bag to wash and finally disclose the day's doings to my dampened diary.

The man at the desk says there is no laundry in this hotel, only a *laverie* down the side street, past an old church. I am too tired.

In clean clothes I go across to the shop and get mineral water. Can't get used to the fact that it's not possible just to come in and put the kettle on, and I don't fancy drinking water out of bathroom taps for some reason.

The Sorbonne area and St Michel now have my "homiest" feel.

It's funny to see Miranda Kerr on TV ads for fashion followed by Cate Blanchett doing perfume ads – both Australians.

I slept until 6 am which is a change. Woke to a pool of water in the bathroom and thought it was from my wet items hanging over the shower, but no, it is dripping from above through the light-fitting. It's always plumbing problems in Paris – why is it so?

Last year, the very day I arrived at my hotel I had slept for half the day. When I awoke I showered and dressed with hair done to my liking, was about to go out to lunch and for some reason I checked the tap in the shower and suddenly the entire bathroom was being sprayed and I couldn't adjust the taps. Luckily there were still five unused fluffy white towels at hand and I managed to throw them to the spot where the bathroom floor met the carpet in the bedroom. I managed to mop it all up on my hands and knees but my hair was wet and plastered to my face and so I began my toilette again and another wardrobe change.

2004 – Welcome Mummy

Tonight is Friday and it's Megumi and Miko's "Welcome Mummy to Japan Night" in my honour. This is to be in our apartment and Kotone who works at the Post Office is invited too. A special "girls-only night."

Maddie-Rose dressed herself in a scarlet kimono and looked most unconvincing with her golden hair tumbling in a tangle around her shoulders. This followed changing from a lavender fairy dress, wings and all which was much more her personality. She was a show-girl at heart and liked to make a show-stopping entrance in her get-ups, but as soon as she got the desired attention from everyone in the room, became embarrassed and surly and collapsed in a heap on the floor turning purple in the face, genes inherited from both her maternal grandparents.

Megumi arrived first, busying herself with the food, then Kotone arrived. I had not met her before and she gasped and said "Obachan oh, so *beautifor*. So young."

I saw Kotone as very attractive in the Japanese way, broad-faced, glossy smart hair-style and large spectacles with a lovely smile. There was a lot of chatter between the three of them and I asked when would Miko be arriving.

"When her husband lets her out" said Rachel. "He's really weird." That didn't surprise me as they kept poor "Long" tied to the front doorknob.

"We need some music." I suggested. "What have you got Rachel?"

"Only traditional music and Megumi hates anything traditional. I only have Maddie's *Barbie's Night Out* otherwise."

"Oh Rachel haven't you got any Bee Gees or Dire Straits? Anything?"

We sat on the floor around the table. Kotone had brought chicken sticks and kebabs. Megumi opened a bottle of California fruity red. It was very good. I had bought soy-flavoured rice crackers, individually wrapped wedges of "Camembert cheese" which turned out to be just a soft soapy sort of tasteless stuff and some sesame covered crackers which were OK.

Megumi and Rachel chatted and Kotone stared at me. When I smiled at her she clasped her hands over her face and shook her head from side to side. The others laughed at her. "*Beautifor. Beautifor.*" I felt uncomfortable. I looked at her wide jawline. "It's my wide face. I look like them with my wide face."

"You don't have a wide face. It's just your eyes they're fascinated with. They'd *kill* to have blue eyes."

Miko arrived with a warm exchange of greetings. They were such warm people. There was much excited chatter. Kotone sat cross-legged on the floor and occasionally fell over sideways pointing to me and going into waves of flowing Japanese to Miko. I was feeling somewhat embarrassed. This was really becoming ridiculous. "Tell them Rachel that I am embarrassed now. I am not used to being called *"beautifor* like this." I laughed. "It's all very strange. I see I should have come to Japan to live years ago - (me with the negative body image). My life may have been quite different."

Rachel laughed and repeated what I had said to the three women who were now pouring beers and they all laughed together and Kotone rolled over on to her side again, still quite overcome, obviously because I was the only one in the room with blue eyes.

Rosy had a yukitori (chicken kebab) in one hand and a fistful of popcorn in the other. Megumi uncorked a bottle of white Japanese "Happy Wine." We clinked glasses. Rachel found some taped music at last and I turned up the track of "Stand by Me" with the volume I enjoyed at home. Four pairs of eyes widened soberingly. "You can't *do* that here. Now you have disturbed the neighbours."

Rachel said she would have to go upstairs and invite the young American teacher down. "Now that she *knows* we're having a party – and she's sick."

Sandy from North Carolina was as fluent as Rachel in Japanese. She was recovering from an infection that she couldn't shake. It seemed antibiotics were eked out in a short supply here for only a few days at a time instead of a full course and so they never had the desired effect.

We opened the bottle of Australian red which was really dry after the sweet wine we'd been drinking. Megumi, Miko and Kotone grimaced at the taste but pretended diplomatically because there was a kangaroo on the label, to like it. They talked together and Rachel was telling Sandy about my surprise at all the family members sleeping in the same room together. We laughed and I said "I don't know how anyone has a sex life here."

"Mum reckons that's why the men have affairs."

"No" Sandy assured me. "Women are second-class citizens here. It's all romance and love and then they get married and the husband plays around." I looked at Sandy thinking "You've got a lot to learn yet little twenty-three year-old girl from North Carolina." I tried to remember my Japanese man's face.

"Mum doesn't believe me about the vending machines and the used high-school-girls' undies" either.

Sandy laughed. "I've seen them with my own eyes in alleyways in Tokyo. You can buy *anything* here."

####

Saturday again and we cycled to a supermarket to buy something to take for afternoon tea at the house of one of Rosy's school friends, Ami, in the next town.

I still can't find any nail polish remover.

Ami's father arrived in his eight-seater people mover. He was in his thirties, nice looking, hair lightened to Western brown too. He seemed a little shy.

Rachel had told me I *must* remember to say *"Ita dakimasu"* before I ate food or received food. It sounded like "Eat a ducky mouse." That's what the kids said. "I can't" I said.

"You *have* to. *Ita dakimas*. You don't need to sound the "u" on the end. Ita *dakimas*. *Ita dakimas…ita dakimas….ita dakimas…* and *Konichiwa*. Don't forget. That's easier than good morning. *Ohiu gozamaisu*. Again, you don't need to sound the 'u'."

"Yes Rachel."

It was afternoon and I could remember *"Konichiwa"* and as Anthony reminded me, *kapochya* (pumpkin) and *futon* too." My vocab was improving. Hopefully we might be discussing sleeping arrangements and vegetables. Natsubi greeted us at the front of the house, bowing and smiling. *"Konichiwa."* Much bowing and more bowing.

There was a Dalmation, a strange dirty white one with faded black spots tied up on a short rope at the entrance to the house. He had the Bali dog look. I found dogs in Bali all to look part dingo. I saw this in a lot of the dogs in Japan too. Dingoes had obviously been crossing the line here as well. I said "Hello" to him and he leaped up at me with a throaty bark, straining on his rope.

"His name is *Kunta* - pronounced K*ooo*nta" Rachel emphasized.

"*Long* is not such a bad name after all."

This was the first Japanese house I had been in, quite different to the apartment. There was a quaint coziness, a bit like a doll's house. The hall, the *genkan*, where the family removed their shoes smelled of sandalwood and there was a lot of timber and steep stairs that I would have loved to climb, but we were ushered in to the living room, all shyness and smiles from everyone.

This was a small room; everything was compact, practical and space-saving. There was a kitchen sink and cooking facilities at one end, a computer, TV, books, CD player, fish tank all down the side wall and at the far wall that faced the kitchen there was a window with a large flower arrangement and a piano sitting in the corner snuggly beside it. I indicated to the piano with a questioning gesture and Natsubi said that her daughter

Ami played. Ami sat down and performed a slow beginner's piece to which we applauded enthusiastically.

Natsubi enquired about my opinion of Japan. She was very slight, feminine and refined, her hair worn up and I imagined her sitting on her knees at a table in a kimono, serving tea. We all communicated quite easily with Rachel as interpreter.

The drinks, iced black coffee and iced lemon tea arrived with cake. *"Ita Dakimas"* was tossed back and forth reverently before I had time to contribute a squeak. I was a poor last with a whispered "*..dakimas.*"

I learned that the speed limit in Japan was 30 – 40 km around the streets and 50 km on the main highways, but on toll roads it was 90 km. You don't drink and drive at all. The alcohol limit was zero. The fine was around $3000 if you were stopped and tested positive to even a trace. Your front seat passenger was fined $3000 too and the back seat passengers $2000 each whether they'd been drinking or not. That's the way to do it. I couldn't imagine any political party trying to push that one in Australia.

We discussed pets. What names did I have for my dogs and cat. "Coco, big chocolate coloured dog, Lillie - Maltese, little and white." They know what Maltese are like and they are popular with the Japanese.

"Where do animals sleep?"

"Cat on bed. Big dog and little dog" – I pointed to the corner of the room."

Natsubi looked quite amazed and Rachel repeated to me in English what she had said to her in Japanese. "I told her that you sleep with your dogs and cat but you won't sleep with your grandchildren!"

Conversation was made about Rosy's missing front teeth and the Japanese customs in that regard. The tooth fairy doesn't exist in Japan. The child throws the lower teeth up on to the roof to encourage the new ones up. The top teeth are put into the ground to encourage the teeth to grow down.

We waved goodbye to Natsubi's husband as he drove off from our apartment having driven us home. "Well, I don't believe *he's* having affairs. They seem a very nice happy family." Rachel agreed and was pleased that I liked them.

Tonight at 5 pm Rachel and Anthony had taiko drum lessons. We walked there with Rosy having one of her special tantrums because she had lost interest in taiko earlier and had given it up, but now of course, because I was there she wanted to play too. There was a wretched performance of pleading and screaming protests all the way, and when the Yakuba's music echoed down the streets at 5 pm I wished they might come and arrest her.

We slipped into our indoor "srippers" and bowed to Sensu (the teacher).

I now knew why Rachel didn't seem bothered by the kids' snoring at night. She probably couldn't hear them. She would probably suffer from tinnitus for the rest of her life. There were about a dozen drummers. The smaller drums vibrated into my chest and made me feel almost nauseous. Sensu pounded a larger, louder drum and then moved on to a huge drum as big as a cannibal's cooking pot, and my eardrums shuddered painfully. I pressed my left ear-lobe into my ear.

Rosy had squeezed her way in to the group and on to one of the smaller drums and Anthony, his huge blue eyes staring vacantly into space, half-heartedly slapped his taiko, his mind in some other sphere. But Rachel, as usual, attacked her drum with a passion, swinging the *bachi* over her head, crashing them down in perfect time as if this were an Olympic event or she was beating someone to death. She was giving her all and I would not have expected anything less than a dramatic performance from her. There were six huge drums together with the smaller ones, some that were played horizontally whilst lying on one's back, the taiko supported by one's knees and one that was played against the wall at shoulder height which I imagined caused a great strain on the shoulder and abdominal muscles.

The drummers called out "*SO-RE*", a cry for help (which is pronounced like "sorry!") which made me smile painfully. It was so appropriately fitting that they should apologize continually. The room was an explosion of continuous and quite alarming sound as I watched the old faded pre-World War 2 clock on the wall slowly crawl around to 7pm with the final dramatic effect of Sensu striking the huge gong which shuddered waves of sound through me long after the connection.

Eat your heart out J. Arthur Rank! What an experience.

There were some wonderful travel programs on Japanese TV.

I was sitting looking at old Kyoto on a travel program.

"I wish I could see some of these places."

"We don't have time and we're not on holiday."

Rachel set the computer up. We had managed to get the children to bed by 9 pm with the usual struggle and I was now very sleepy. "Who are you contacting Rachel?" I yawned.

"Nobody. We're going to watch "The Last Samurai."

"On that? It's too small."

"Do you want to watch it or not?"

"Put it on. Just put it on!"

"By the way," she added, "Megumi wants to know when we can all go to the bath-house together."

"The bath-house – all of us!?"

"Yes. You really can't say you've experienced Japanese culture if you haven't been to the bath-house."

"You don't mean in the nude?"

"Well of *course* in the nude. We'd all be in the nude. I've been a few times."

"No way Jose! Take my gear off and hop into a bath with your *neighbours*? I don't think so!"

"It's not mixed bathing…it's just with women."

"Well I'm relieved to hear *that* – but I think *not* Rachel. Are we going to watch the Samurai or have you changed your mind?"

"Gosh you're boring. You're not going to go to sleep now are you?"

"No."

She said that it was filmed in New Zealand.

"Yes, it looks like New Zealand. It doesn't look like Japan. The light is not right."

She agreed.

"Yes, it is too bright." I emphasized, trying to sound as if I was being impressed aesthetically at least. "Japan has a soft light, not too different to Europe and there is a golden glow to the scenery which is getting closer to the light in Australia. I think they've filmed late in the afternoon. The shadows are long and it is afternoon sun. They've set up some cherry blossoms there too to make it look like here…"

"Oh… just watch the movie and don't spoil it Mother. You're not going to go to sleep now are you?"

"No" I reassured her, realizing I was fighting to keep my eyes open. It was too blood-thirsty for me and I closed my eyes. And I had stopped finding Tom Cruise appealing years ago. At 10.30 she switched it off.

"You're asleep!"

"I am not."

"*And* you're snoring. Do you want me to switch this off now and we'll watch the rest tomorrow?"

"I'm sorry. We had a late night last night. Let's watch it earlier tomorrow."

2013 – A morning at Montmartre.

Last night I dreamt my Dad came in to kiss me goodnight. He shuffled as he used to in his slippers, over to the bed and bent down and kissed me and turned and looked at my paintings laid out on the table next to the bed. He said nothing. He was very pensive. He looked at them then he just wandered off again, as I last remembered him, an almost 93 year-old. It was very real. Did he really visit me?

I'm doing a bit more work on my Eiffel Tower and will go down at 7 am for breakfast and report the leaking lights.

This morning buying a ticket on the Metro proves a bit of a trial and after a Middle Eastern teenage boy who has about as much knowledge of the system as I do shrugs and walks off, a young American couple who look like students come to my aid and say they'll make sure that I get on to the right train.

I was in plenty of time but because Claude insists we telephone him no earlier than 9 am to check his recorded message saying whether it is to be a "wet weather or fine weather" venue, I have had to hang around waiting all this time and now I am running late.

Get to the meeting place in Jules Joffrin Metro too late to meet him, but with the aid of helpful Parisians, walk in the direction of Sacre-Coeur and the Utrillo Escalier staircase which is our other option to meet, but again miss them. Claude's instructions of "between Rue Lamarck and Rue Paul Albert" are not helpful. A French woman with a little dog doesn't know Rue Paul Albert at all and a young businessman even stops in the street and checks on Google with his smart phone and can't find it either. Don't let me ever hear anyone say Parisians aren't helpful!

Wander on around Sacre-Coeur. I decide I'll forget Claude today and just be a tourist. I stop at the first café I find and sit outside changing out of ankle boots into sneakers again. No-one comes out to serve me. I am very annoyed at Claude for not coming to find me.

I continue on lost and suddenly the girl from Chicago's bright aqua coloured sweater catches my eye. It takes me a while for my anger to settle down (of which I make Claude very aware in an attempt at French haughtiness) and start on sketch of steps leading up to Sacre-Coeur.

We go to lunch very close by—gorgeous waiter. I tell him he looks like a movie star. Looks like a Moroccan version of George Clooney. We all agree on his beauty and Claude questions him on his heritage and he is Egyptian.

I raise my eyebrows. "Susan – Maybe Egypt for next holiday."

Quiche and salad, bread, wine and coffee, very good.

David from California has a terrible cold and is sneezing and coughing everywhere. Hope I don't catch it. He says he must go up to Sacre-Coeur and check out the artists who paint there in their hundreds.

"Does anyone want to come?" He asks.

"It's a circus up there" I say, remembering each year fighting my way through artists of many nationalities with easels, all painting the church. "And they chase you down the street doing a portrait of you. I've had that happen on two occasions" I add.

Claude waves a baguette in my direction. "You mean to say Julie, they are chasing you down the street while doing your portrait?" He smirks. Our table roars laughing.

"Yes – and then they want seventy-five dollars."

"And how did the portrait turn out - ?" he smiles.

"I just looked like – a – a *French* woman!" Everyone at our table roars again.

"So" says Claude, "He makes you look like a movie star and you don't like it? What did you pay him?"

"Nothing. They were only charcoal sketches Claude, not oil paintings for goodness sake."

"Julie, seventy-five dollars is very cheap. And show me that address you are going to next week." I rummage through my bag for the receipt.

"Julie, this is in the 15th arrondissement, not Versailles, and it is very definitely still Paris. I won't need to put an ad in paper after all."

I find my way to the toilet and a man pushes the door open as I haven't locked it securely enough evidently and I am exposed!

"Sorry, sorry" he cries and much laughter back at the bar. A first time for everything. I'm toughening up.

After lunch back to the same spot between a series of stairs which is the unique charm of Montmartre.

Claude looks over my shoulder at what I begin sketching. He sighs. "Do you think I'd like Australia?"

"It depends on what you want to see."

"But - it's all beaches."

"Well, I would have thought you would like to see all the girls in their bikinis Claude." He smiles coyly.

"There's a lot to see. You could go to the Red Centre maybe."

"What! That's the desert. You must be joking Julie. I die of boredom in *Paris*!"

I continue sketching. "How come you don't look Australian?"

"What do you mean?"

"Well, the Australians I have met are huge and rough and loud. Australian girls come up to me in nightclubs and shove me and say "Howya goin' mate!"

"Does that describe me does it?"

"No. But you don't *look* Australian. You don't *sound* Australian."

"Well what *do* I look?"

"I don't know. You are something - *different*!"

I'm not exactly sure how to take this, and I assure him that neither of my daughters would greet him with a shove and say "Howya goin' mate?" nor are they huge and rough either.

I am surprised to see groups of armed soldiers wandering the streets around Sacre-Coeur in full army fatigue. Claude says they are a permanent installation and bored out of their minds too, and we should think about asking them to pose for us.

There has been a young man and woman spending hours on the stairs below us, inflating heart-shaped white, red and purple balloons. Claude finds out from them that they are a Russian couple and this is part of the decorations for a wedding this afternoon. Some of their balloons burst and some fly away in the direction of the Eiffel Tower and some escape, bouncing down the stairs and riding off on the wind like Aubrey Beasley the indoor cat manages to do sometimes. I add them in to the sketch I am doing of the steep stairs and Claude sits down and joins me in this pursuit. I see by his smile to me that I have pleased him at last.

Susan and I leave at 4 pm intending to catch a train together, but I get us very lost trying to find my way through to Abbesses and instead we arrive at Pigalle which I haven't seen before and which I don't like the look of at all. It is very crowded and it feels alien to me. (Was told later that this is a red-light area.) There are endless stalls of fabrics on sale but Susan is in too much of a hurry to get out of Pigalle to let me browse. I so want to get some old faded French fabric to drape over a chair at home or something. Maybe it is all made in China anyway.

Before I can pacify her anxiety and annoyance at my sense of direction and deplorable map-reading, she turns a desperate request to a couple of young obviously British men and implores them with "How do we get back to Paris from *here*?"

One sprawls back on his chair, a glass in one hand and a joint in the other and looking her up and down says very condescendingly, "Madam this *is* Paris."

Manage to cope with the Metro. It's really only the buying of the ticket that is complicated. There is very little help behind counters these days, but of course it has been non-existent in Melbourne for years where the public transport system must be a nightmare for tourists and I don't even attempt train travel there.

2004 – The Funpark.

Anthony's teacher has given him three free passes to an animal park and we were on foot headed to the railway station at 10 am next morning. I had been telling Rachel about the Aboriginal Reconciliation church service I'd been to with the Aboriginal Elder whose portrait I'd been painting over the summer. I had asked her to sit for me.

I recalled the first time she sat, aggravated by the heat, bribed with cigarettes and sticky chocolate éclairs. We had been talking about the upcoming Labour Day weekend and the Moomba procession (Melbourne's cultural event) which I feel usually heralds the end of summer. She had licked the remains of the éclair from her lips, wiped her chin with her hanky and flapped it at the persistent flies.
"…. you know," she went on in a serious tone, "I thought at the time – and this was many years ago mind you – I should really tell one of the organizers. Don't they know Moom means…backside….and ba….is up, in

or on." She chuckled, "but I never got around to it "she confessed.

Aunty Dot Peters is one of the proudest Australians one could meet. She had lost her father Vincent in the Second World War as a prisoner at the hands of the Japanese working on the Burma Railway. Talking about this horror is the only time I see a sadness cloud her eyes. Otherwise at 85 she has an amazing zest for life, a delightful sense of humour and holds no grudges as she fights for recognition of her people who gave their lives for her beloved country and I am proud to be her friend.

That Reconciliation church service had been quite beautiful with a story from the Dreamtime as the children's message with a portrait I had done of a famous Aboriginal elder from the past, William Barak, which leant against the pulpit. My Elder friend had chosen some beautiful old songs from her childhood: "The Old Rugged Cross"; "Shall We Gather at the River"; and "One Day at a Time", which Aunty Dot tells me she wants played at her funeral when her time comes.

Now as we skipped along behind Rachel, who was striding out as usual, like Joan of Arc going to war, the children and I followed along hand in hand singing together, "Shall we gather at the river, the beautiful the beautifulla river", laughing, swinging our arms, looking down at the filthy Argebori dyke crawling beside us, occasionally an escaped lavender or hydrangea trying to dress it up here and there but not succeeding in hiding its murkiness.

"Are we going to have this all day?" Rachel called over her shoulder.

I repeated the two first lines of the song again as that's all I knew and Rosy piped up with "Australians all eat ostriches for we are young and free" which I had been teaching them earlier. We three laughed and sang it again and again adding silly verses to our national anthem. We were led up the stairs to the platform to take the train to our destination. I was an outrageous child!

The scenery during the trip was ugly. It was very grey with power lines and electricity towers everywhere, grey shabby houses, the only green being occasional rice fields. We went about four stations and then had to walk a fair way at the other end. My feet were hurting by the time we reached the entrance and I began to limp.

There was a mountainous roller-coaster ride at the entrance bearing down on us, an ancient looking timber construction which Rachel said Paul rode and referred to as the "Mother of all roller-coasters." I definitely wasn't one for rides.

Rosy was pleading for every cheap curio her eyes landed on. This was not where I wanted to be. Why come all the way to Japan to see this.

It was fiercely hot and crowded and dusty. There was a vertical ride, a display of hydraulics where the seat was lifted a hundred feet into the air and then dropped like a stone. "That's probably the way they get rid of unwanted pregnancies here" I whispered to Rachel.

"That's not very nice Mother."

"Where are the animals?" I asked tentatively.

"Come and see the koi."

I'd not seen these funny fish before and they gathered in a writhing, boiling mass around a landing where people tossed morsels of food and cigarette butts. As the food hit the surface of the water they climbed across each other's backs to get to the offerings. They were just oversized goldfish, big and orange, yellow, white, khaki and black, their toothless-looking hungry mouths forming large gaping circular caves. The water was very dirty.

All the big cats were in tiny enclosures, the big apes too. The poor old lion sat quietly staring, in a cage of very small proportions with a crazed look in his eyes. Rachel was obviously really pressed for something to do on the weekends.

I had just come from months of petitioning, protest marches and writing of letters to Government Departments including the Prime Minister's, to try to ban the export of live sheep and cattle from Australia which involved hideous torture of livestock. Why couldn't they process cattle in northern Australia humanely for the overseas trade, and why was this a world where the continuation of species depended on the suffering and death of another species and here I was……..

"Nanny come and see the bunnies." They disappeared in to an old rusty and derelict bus. It stank of human sweat and rancid air and was unbearable in the humidity and heat. There were several children crowded in there, sitting wrestling with baby rabbits. I was aghast. There were boxes on one side, where baby bunnies trembled and cringed, having been dumped in there by kids who had tired of them and run off to look at something else, only to be dragged out and forcibly nursed, examined, squeezed and chased again and there was no sort of supervision of them. Rosy and Anthony sat quietly stroking one each, wondering why their grandmother was staring at them in such a horrified way.

"Let me out of here!" I rushed out into the fresh air and began breathing oxygen again.

It was so hot. There was no shade and no sign of water for the bigger rabbits outside with no escape for those being chased mercilessly. They were dragged out of their hidey holes in bits of drain-pipe, forced to sit on laps, dropped and chased again. I stopped Rosy and

Anthony as they attempted to rush past me, delighted to join the tormentors.

"You're not going to chase those poor little things now are you?"

"Yes, it's great fun" they both cried and shook me off.

"Oh Mum, you're ruining their day. They love coming here. The rabbits don't mind."

"*The rabbits don't mind!?*" Did the rabbits speak Japanese or English? If I spoke Japanese like Rachel I'd be off to see the manager with my protests.

I was really fed up but we trudged along all day in the unrelenting heat.

"When are we going home?"

"We haven't seen everything yet."

"Oh come on! We've been here five hours. My feet are killing me."

Rachel disappeared into a souvenir shop and after waiting outside on one foot and then another for fifteen minutes, I followed. Rosy was wheedling and morose, begging at Rachel's elbow for a white toy tiger. I could see a scene from "Who's Afraid of Virginia Woolf" about to break out again. Rosy screamed and pleaded all the way behind us as we left the shop tiger-less.

Anthony wanted a swan boat-ride.

"It will cost us 1000 yen Anthony."

"They're just common old pedallo boats we had in Melbourne fifty years ago."

My feet were so sore I didn't have any interest in pedaling anything. I just wanted to get out that gate and start the painful trek home. I saw an ice-cream van. "Let's get some ice-cream." We bowed low to the ice-cream man and departed with one each, the most pleasant exercise so far. As we got to the gates Rachel said over her shoulder "You realize we could have gone on the boat rides for less than what you paid for these." I limped off, glaring at my daughter's back, licking up the melting ice-cream as it ran down my hands.

We watched the second half of the "Last Samurai" after dinner and I was not, moved, but then I was boring.

At bed-time Rosy complained of itchy backs of her knees, "Itchy back, *itchy everywhere!*" When I suggested she may have caught mites from the rabbits and imagine having to wash all our bedding if it's scabies or something, Rachel roared at me. "That's right…. Why not imagine the very worst scenario!"

"The rabbits' revenge!" I yelled back as I stalked out of the tatami room.

Megumi came to the rescue with some soothing cream and the itching stopped thank goodness.

I was tossing and turning till after midnight. I was filled with sadness for that lion, pacing back and forth. The rabbits were easily expendable to the zoo, but the big cats would remain prisoners long after I returned to Australia. I would always remember them – pacing and hopeless.

In 1954 Grade 3 at East Ivanhoe Primary were practising for our performance at the Melbourne Cricket Ground for the arrival of the young Queen Elizabeth. Our class was doing a "Toy Box" theme (I still wonder why to this day.) There were some girls lucky enough to be chosen to be dolls. (I would have probably preferred to have been a cowgirl.) There were also toy soldiers, spinning tops, very inappropriate golliwogs and rabbits. I was a rabbit of course. Mum was not too pleased with the overall affect at dress rehearsal because apart from the fact that she would rather have seen me dressed as a doll, she was quite upset by the tail. She eyed it and winced. I knew it didn't really resemble a tail. It was cotton-wool stuffed in to a gauze covering, in almost hospital bandage mode, designed to wobble and bounce like a rabbit's tail. I twisted to look at what it was she was wincing at. It was a bit like one of those oversized, very misshapen things I'd seen in Mum's "forbidden" drawer in her bedroom. In other words, a scrunched up sanitary pad. (They weren't streamlined and/or with wings in the 1950's.) I had no idea what those strange things were and dared not ask. In the same vein, I remembered opening a tin once that Bruce handed me when I was five and screaming "worms!" and dropping it again. He bent double with laughter and it was not until twenty years later that he enlightened me about the time I had found a tin of condoms.

The display at the Melbourne Cricket Ground was for the audience before the actual arrival of the Queen, so Mum decided instead of me returning to school on the bus with the others we would wait with the crowd that lined the route of the Queen's cavalcade so we could catch a glimpse of her. Mum was very excited that the Queen had indeed caught sight of a large white rabbit in the front row of the crowd along the road, (bearing a striking resemblance to James Stewart's pooka friend "Harvey") and raised her eyebrows and laughed in my direction. Who wouldn't? And then I had to have insult added to injury and travel home in a crowded train at peak hour. Squirming on the great lump of a tail, shrinking beneath the unwanted spotlight and the amused stares of the commuters, it was all just to make Mum happy with my huge pink-lined ears, one now limp on my shoulder.

….I chuckled remembering the dismayed response from Caroline as a toddler to the commercial for an airline on television advertising the appeal of an exotic Eastern destination

"Sail, go fishing, shoot the rapids…!"

"Oh" she cried sitting bolt upright on Ed's knee. "The poor little bunnies!"

Now I echoed her.

####

I flew home to Melbourne in my dreams and confronted Angela who said "Yes, your dogs and cat are too much for me. You'll have to arrange to put them in kennels before you return to Japan."

It is 5 am and I am exhausted, still stiff and sore from yesterday's zoo visit. I wonder if it would have been better to put the dogs in kennels after all.

I emailed Carrie and asked her if she thought the dogs were beyond Angela who was trying to get on with saving her marriage. Carrie emailed back:

"Don't start inventing problems. Everything's fine. The dogs are fine. I went and walked them myself today anyway."

Today Rachel has the day off and is very thrilled to be taking me to "a very traditional Japanese restaurant." We were all ready and about to ride off on our bikes, when the phone rang. "Maddie-Rose has a fever. Please come and collect her!"

Rachel rode off on her bike and returned with Rosy, really annoyed. She didn't believe Rosy had a temperature at all. She took it and it was half a degree up from her usual reading.

"Can I have peanut butter on toast Mummy? I'm hungry."

Rachel was cross. "Our day is ruined. I've specially taken this day off to take you to lunch."

"Can she come with us? Let her lie down for a while, take her temperature and we can still go maybe." I was sorry for Rachel who had had her plans mucked up, but sorry for Rosy who probably knew we would be going out together and wanted to be included instead of being dressed for surgery and serving squid to a crowd of Japanese kids and a grumpy woman with a toothbrush rolling around in her mouth poking her. I marveled at the hurdles this little pint-sized girl had coped with.

There was obviously nothing physically wrong with her.

"We'll have to call a taxi now. I've never had to use one before but because Rosy's with us we'll have to." She rang the company and explained where we lived. This was a local taxi but they were very unsure of where we were situated. I was curious too to see a taxi come to an address that wasn't an address at all. We went outside and waited.

Half an hour later Rachel rang them again. They were "*still rooking on the map.*"

"I'm glad you're not going into the last stages of labour Rachel."

"Were we near the park?"

"Yes."

We waited. The post-lady came by on her bike and Rachel asked her for help. Smiling and bowing she took Rachel's mobile and rang the taxi company herself. The conversation went on for some time with arm-waving gesticulations and directions and nodding. Eventually they arrived and the back door of the cab swung open.

The journey took a long time and when I saw the ugly highway loaded with cars and trucks I felt God had given Rosy a temperature to save me from certain death riding the bike down the highway. The area was like the busiest and greyest parts of industrial Melbourne and there was the traditional Japanese restaurant stranded in the middle of the ugliness and it had closed at 1 pm!

Rachel wailed.

"This is your fault Maddie-Rose! If we'd left earlier like Nanny and I intended to, we would have been on time instead of waiting all that time for the wretched taxi. Oh I'm so disappointed." I felt sad for her disappointment.

"Don't worry Rachel. We can go to another one."

The taxi took us to another one. Everyone was wearing work clothes and work-boots. They were all workmen. "Do I have to take my shoes off?"

This was a "cheap noodle restaurant" according to Rachel. "No *of course* you don't have to take your shoes off!"

The stewed meal was very large, very salty and although she stressed "vegetarian" on my behalf, the meat had been cooked with mine and then the body parts removed.

"This is not what I wanted to bring you to." Rachel almost sobbed. "I'm *soooo* disappointed."

Rosy ordered a huge meal of chicken and corn soup with noodles, a bag of tiny teddy-bear biscuits, a blue jelly and a roll. Their processed food was "very processed" and over-loaded with sugar and salt.

"Eat the soup and the noodles and take the rest home to share with Anthony. I'm *really* cross with you Maddie-Rose. You're not sick at all."

Back at the apartment, day turned to dusk and it began to rain. The TV had talked of nothing but the typhoon all day. It was over Hiroshima early that morning but it looked like its direction was well north of Tokyo and our apartment. Nagoya, where my Japanese man lived was mentioned a lot on the news linked to the typhoon and I wondered if he was safe. There had been three deaths due to tidal waves (my greatest fear). Would we feel any effects?

I heard the approaching cries of a vendor as he drove around the shiny wet back streets. The wailing voice cut through the heavy night air. It made me think of Elvis Presley's "King Creole" and the calling out of "Crawfish." There were always vendors coming by, some selling food, others clothes line poles or some begging for old bikes, furniture and CD players.

Megumi was sitting on the floor of our apartment drinking tea with us and when I showed curiosity about the caller outside she said something to Rachel and ran off to get her purse. We followed her down the street in the rain and the van came to a halt.

It was warm and very muggy with light but steady rain. The smiling old face greeted us bowing and he began to shake frying pans over a gas stove in the back of his van. He was the "Gyoza man." I ran back to the apartment for my camera and took a couple of photos of him. He smiled at the camera and gave the usual peace sign. It was just their form of "G'day mate" I suppose but I found it silly and so seventies. Were they reassuring us all was forgotten, their armies' cruelties towards our prisoners of war, or our allies dropping the biggest bomb on their parents and grandparents.

We waited ten minutes in the rain, half under cover from his van, while he cooked and packed the Gyoza into little containers and we thanked him, bowing, bowing, and ran back through the rain to the shelter of the apartment.

Gyoza is bite-sized rice and vegetables and has the flavour of a Chiko roll but is not greasy.

Megumi ran off again, returning with a small bowl of cooked green beans and a sauce to dip in.

The wind began roaring and the rain was heavy.

I realized then that it must have been a typhoon we experienced in Bali when Carrie and I were there nine years earlier. It had rained incessantly and the wind blew like nothing I'd ever experienced for several days and for a while I had feared we might end up statistics in the river with the rest of the straw roofed huts sliding down the hill on top of us.

We had gone to Obud in Bali for my 50th birthday. I was given a pink-coloured drink with ice in it on arrival and was vomiting in the first half an hour. I had managed to stumble around on Carrie's arm for the next four days before Bali belly declared war on my nether regions for the rest of our holiday.

I spent the actual big "50" in bed reading a copy of "Gone with the Wind" which I'd discovered in a local book-shop, another of my life's cruel ironies and another thing I'd picked up locally, the title describing one of the symptoms of my illness. It was there lying in my bed watching the thrashing about of the tall trees across the river that I made the decision to leave Perth where we were living at the time and return to the Yarra River and Warrandyte.

2013 – Surprise!

7.30 am – Breakfast as usual in Paris. "*Non juice – no baguette.* Just *thé et deux croissants s'il vous plait Madame.*" We say it in unison - she knows it off by heart now.

She waits, head tilted on the side "*Numbre….?*"

"*Quarante …cinq.*"

I get the little encouraging smile of "Well done!" And a nod.

I leave a two euro tip for the first time today as this particular dark-skinned waitress takes care of me. She ran out into the street yesterday morning while I was standing with the maitre d' who is a charming gentleman, outside the hotel. He was very helpfully giving me directions of which Metro I could choose to get to Montmartre. "…and you must take your time when you leave the Metro at Jules Joffrin to look at the area between there and Sacre-Coeur because my mother lived there until just last year and it is very nice…." He had sung to me in his French-accented English.

She had fussed around me "Madame, your coat - *it is not right!*" and both she and he tried to adjust the back of my jacket which was caught up in the strap of my shoulder bag. I wondered if this was what it was like to have a maid and a butler. I could cope with this kind of attention. Maybe it was the fact of me walking out of their hotel looking dishevelled. I would rather think they just cared. I love the French.

9.30. I'm sipping *café crème*, the way I like it. A half a cup of strong black and a jug of hot creamy milk. So far I can't seem to get it anywhere but at Le Rostand.

I took a different route for a change this morning and went around Pantheon Place – big cobble-stoned area. The Pantheon (inspired by the Rome Pantheon) has also become an icon to guide me home. It can be seen from afar and its dome is very distinctive. In 1744 Louis XV decided to build this church to honour St Genevieve, the patron saint of France.

I feel most "at home" here on the Left Bank more than anywhere in Paris as I look across at Luxembourg Gardens. I don't find it quite as frantic with tourists as some other very popular spots. From here to Musee Cluny and Boulevard St Michel are my "homey" areas. This includes the Sorbonne and my hotel area up to Jussieu Metro.

I am to meet the group at St Sulpice Square this morning.

Got a bit lost after coffee but a Frenchman catches up to me and smilingly asks "Are you lost Madame?" Would you believe I couldn't find my way into Rue du Vaugirard? I thought I had worn a track down that street last year. Anyway I find it but then cannot find St Sulpice Avenue. He almost takes me by the arm right to it. *"Merci beaucoup Monsieur."*

The others begin arriving and Claude points up to an apartment that looks over the Square. I notice through a window, a black cat leap from the floor and perch on a table.

"That's where Catherine Deneuve lives – where that cat is...." Claude informs us. "And the café de la Mairie beside the square which is where many movies have been filmed."

Several people have a peep at what I am doing as they pass. I have chosen to paint the lion at the fountain as he reminds me of my cat Aubrey Beardsley when he is angry.

A couple of hours dissolve and we take note of the crowd of young people with masks and goggles, almost naked, jumping in to the fountain shrieking with laughter in the freezing cold water.

I see the legs of two people out of the corner of my eye approaching, maybe another two Americans? And I look up to smile.

"Penny and Mark!" – What! I can't believe it! I struggle out of the collapsible chair Susan had leant me.

"Out of all of Paris – unplanned and here we meet!"

Penny is looking at my hair. "Yes, what a surprise."

I fiddle with a strand. I thought I'd brought her up to date with the hair drama in Melbourne. "I know.

I only asked for a few streaks – and while you're at it – look at my tooth!" I point – "First morning in Paris. But this is amazing. We couldn't have planned to meet here like this. What are you doing here?"

"We were in the Luxembourg Gardens and just wandered on up here and saw people sketching and we thought you might be one of them."

There is a little more idle chatter as I tell them how I had braved the Metro and went to Montmarte and back. "And don't bother to go to Pigalle" I add. I didn't like it. Have you been?"

"No we haven't. The Metro? You're gamer than we are then" said Mark making to leave, with "Come on Pen. We'd better be off."

Penny gives me the security number to press on the entrance gate to their apartment on Sunday and with that they both hurry off with a "See you on Sunday."

I've had enough of sketching and feel I've finished anyway. I am tempted to call out to them "Hey guys, can we do another take - that was a bit low-key." But instead I close my sketch book and gather up my pencils and Claude strolls over.

"If you're bored come and have a look at the painting in the Church."

"I'm not bored but have gone as far as I can with my sketch."

The painting in the St Sulpice church is by Delacroix "Jacob Wrestling with the Angel."

Claude says he thinks there is a funeral taking place inside as a hearse has pulled up a while earlier. He laughs about a time he'd wanted to paint in a church amongst mourners while a funeral was taking place, but the people in the class had been horrified at his suggestion and left in a hurry.

He leads the way to a restaurant in a lovely little area with very old shops in the 7th arrondissement and he suggests we book lunch for all of us at this very traditional Italian restaurant. Their salmon pasta and cream is beautiful.

None of the group had been to the Luxembourg Gardens yet and Claude makes that our next destination for the afternoon. I can't believe a couple of my group haven't bothered going there because they "aren't really interested in gardens."

The palace was built in 1631 for Marie de Medicis. There are miles of gardens and Claude says they plant the flowers while in bloom and then replace with new flowers again in different colour schemes, "…which they must do overnight because the maintenance is huge and there's never a sign of anyone working on planting during the day" Claude adds.

I choose to paint a large urn of tumbling hot pink geraniums with a statue of a woman with a serpent wrapping itself around her body in the background. Claude says my effort is "cartoon-like." I am wounded and Carla's (she works in a bank in Madrid) is "obviously painted by a banker." David's "painting is all wrong," but I think he is the best artist in the group. The girl from Chicago snaps at him as she storms off "There's no pleasing you Claude" as he comments on her work.

It's the end of the season for him and I think he is at screaming point with boredom now, finding it hard to keep such a small group entertained, whereas when it is a large group they entertain each other and him as well. Our class ends tomorrow and his year comes to an end which he says he looks forward to.

He wanders over to where I am packing up and says paintbrush in hand "There's the best ice-cream shop just near here. Would you be interested in going there tonight?"

"Do you mean with the group – all of us?"

"You can go on your own if you want to" he mumbles and walks off to continue arguing with David over his work. Have I offended him? I have unintentionally turned down an invitation with a Parisian? Unforgivable.

I walk on back to my hotel and work on my two paintings from St Sulpice Square and Luxembourg Gardens after my dinner of bananas and grapes and am quite pleased with the effect and Luxembourg doesn't look "cartoon-like" at all.

2004 – The Map.

This morning the typhoon passed over Japan and we really only felt the edge of it. A temperature of 35°C has been predicted which means a very humid day after last night's heavy rain.

Rachel went off to work grudgingly and for some reason it was a day off for the kids. Rosy was in an extremely irritable mood and I realized the humidity must knock her around awfully after Perth with its dry heat.

I decided to humour her and I asked her for some coloured paper, pencils and scissors. I drew some gum leaves in pale green, a koala in grey and a tree in brown.

She cut them out carefully and we glued a picture together on a dark green background.

"Why are you doing this Nanny?"

"Because I thought you might like to do this."

"I'm having lots of fun doing this Nanny" she said in the deepest and the gloomiest voice she could muster, obviously making every effort to humour her grandmother.

Anthony's two friends telephoned and asked if they could come over.

"Yes fine."

They brought their computer games and the tiny apartment was taken over all day with noise and chatter and the sound of the computerized world in Japanese.

I cut some oranges into segments and offered them to the girls together with drinks and biscuits. I drew faces with a marking pen on the remaining oranges, a round-eyed one and a slant-eyed one. Anthony was delighted at the art work on the oranges. The visiting girls seemed delighted too.

Rachel had been emailing reams of instructions to the twenty-one year-old English girl who would be her replacement when she left. She drew her a map of the local area, showing her how to get to the shops and the schools and the points of interest to make life easier for her. It was coloured beautifully, together with cherry trees in pink blossom.

"I would have been really grateful for something like that. I hope you don't expect me to eat curried beef and rice tonight."

"Well, yes I do. You won't have any meat in yours. I'll take it out after it's cooked."

The Noodle Bar might have got away with it but I would not be fooled. I'd just have cucumbers.

After dinner was cleared away Anthony told Rachel, "Nanny dropped a whole potato down the sink when she was peeling them tonight Mum."

I had discovered, due to this incident, that the sink had a large plug-hole with a mesh "catcher" beyond it. You could put a rabbit down the plughole and still retrieve it. Strange place Japan!

"I got it out again Anthony. What a *dobber*!"

"Well I hope you didn't put it in the dinner Nanny."

"It was washed and peeled and cut up and cooked and you ate it Anthony."

His mouth dropped open and he screwed his nose up.

"Nanny is acting very strangely."

"I'll take you to the cheap shop Mum, before it's too dark." (Was this a means of my disposal?)

"Good, I might be able to buy some post-cards or a writing-pad—or nail polish remover!" I was still touching-up the chipped off areas and I felt they were looking quite gross. We mounted our bikes once again.

"Now, take note of where we're going Mum. We're going down the road the Shrine's in."

"Well I know how to get there" I said, pleased with myself, "down to the corner where there's two rocks painted yellow and turn right."

She took me a different way. Turning abruptly, a few yards short of the yellow rocks we went down an alleyway. We arrived at the chemists where I had dropped in looking for cold-cream my first day there.

"I know how to get *here* Rachel."

Then we crossed the road. It was almost dark. Another turn and we arrived at a supermarket. "I thought we were going to the "cheap shop."

"No, I meant the cheaper supermarket in case you need to buy anything. You're spending far too much money."

Further on we came to a large chemist shop which also stocked all kinds of food. I picked up a bottle that said *"Nail remover"* in English. The check-out girl was vague and sing-song. The women all seemed to speak that way.

Dreaming in Paris.

4.10 am Saturday. Woke from a funny dream. I was working at a kindergarten in a church in Paris and was amused to hear one of the little boys as he was arriving say to his father "I think that painting is of Jesus shampooing his hair." His father answered "If that is Jesus he would *not* be shampooing his hair." This tickled my fancy and I chuckled aloud which woke me. Strange dreams I'm having.

5.00 am – Did some work on my St Sulpice fountain and some more painting of the background which I checked on the photo I took yesterday. Claude said not to put the background in, but I think it looks better.

9.20 am – I'm sitting opposite Notre Dame in Café Panis waiting for my *café crème*. We're going to meet in Place Viviani where we began the week and had to leave because of the rain. Huge crowds outside. I thought I saw Susan wandering past and I picked up my things and hurried after her in to a souvenir shop. I called out "Susan" and when she turned around it was not Susan at all so I returned to my seat by the window in the café again.

I'm more lightly dressed today in blue jeans and top that Madeleine gave me last year, the olive green cardigan made in Morocco and bought on Boulevard St Michel, and a bright blue scarf. Madeleine was a charming Parisienne woman who joined our group at the chateau in the Loire Valley. We had been sitting down to lunch with our crowd outside in the sun when I commented on the top she was wearing just to make conversation.

"That's a lovely top you are wearing Madeleine."

"Thank you. You must have it!"

"Oh no, no. It looks lovely on you."

"I want *you* to have it Julie."

The next morning she handed me a brown paper bag containing the top which was in aqua and light browns. "You must have!"

What could I say but *"Merci beaucoup Madeleine."*

I love that top and wore it often in the following summer in Melbourne to many compliments. Souvenirs like that are priceless.

Caught a snippet of Australian news on TV before I left this morning – football in Melbourne. Might have been the semi-final with Carlton thrashing Richmond. Girls being interviewed were dubbed in French of course. Tom Hurley's very Aussie accented voice stood out, not dubbed. I actually felt a patriotic pang. I was surprised to see this on French TV. Last year when I commented on how I cringed to think what the rest of the world must think of our politics, Ralph and the others said that there is never any news of Australia on TV in the U.S., except when someone is attacked by a shark or there is a major bushfire. We must obviously be of more interest to the French than the U.S.

9.50. Coffee not hot enough. That's a first.
There are people heading for Notre Dame by the hundreds and just as many filing past the window in the other direction. It's like a wildebeest migration across the plains of Africa. I really don't think I could live with all this tourist population – but I am just a tourist. It gives me the same feeling I had when I lived at the beach as a kid and felt really put out by seeing total strangers lying on beach towels, lapping up the sun on my favourite spot, which I had staked out for myself emotionally, years before. They had no right!

This is our final meeting of the group today. Saturday *(Samedi)* already. And Susan didn't turn up at all.
A young woman approached me to sign and donate to their beggar's fund and I told her in a loud voice to "go away or I'll call the gendarme!"
Claude called out to me "You tell 'em Julie!"
A group of these girls hung around in the park approaching all the tourists and yelling abuse at each other and at someone on the end of their mobile phones,

probably their husbands, sitting back in a pub somewhere giving their women-folk orders and drinking the funds. I was enlightened of this by a Parisian man when I came to Paris in 1993 and had been taking pity on every beggar I saw and parting with my money on every street corner.

Carla and the girl from Chicago suggested lunch at a vegetarian restaurant "Le Grenier De Notre Dame" and I had a wonderful salad with tomatoes, olives, walnuts, corn and lots of cheese. They laughed loudly at my dream about "Jesus shampooing his hair." They invited me along with them tonight to a wine-bar at Montmartre but they are staying on the other side of Paris and the thought of me travelling home alone in the early hours of Sunday morning via the Metro from Montmartre was not pleasant, so I declined, saying I had to go out early tomorrow. Anyway, I am not of their generation and I think they really only asked me out of politeness.

3 pm. Back at Le Rostand opposite Luxembourg Gardens. Feel a bit jaded so have come here to get a red wine and some mineral water. Disappointed I'm finishing on such a low as Claude was quite unimpressed with my efforts for the week – said my water-colour effects "look like they've been rained on – should be clearly defined and detailed." Yet the other day when

we were painting the Eiffel Tower from the Institute of Architecture, he was really pushing for minimalist, blurred effects which I've been trying to achieve.

The same coloured young waiter who was here last year is still waiting tables but I haven't seen the young charming English boy from last year who was studying Philosophy at the Sorbonne.

Gosh, you only get a little sample of Vin Rouge for five Euros 30 here. Mineral water four Euros. The wine I chose is a cheap one and not surprisingly, it's not too good. I am at a seat inside by the window and the only noise is the waiters yelling orders and the clang of plates. But it's bedlam outside. I suddenly feel cut loose from my moorings. Snap out of it! After all, I AM IN PARIS!! I draw three love hearts next to these words.

A pretty white cat with a tabby tail is wandering around the café.

4 pm. Into Luxembourg Gardens. There are signs on seats warning that they have just been painted. They are shiny and black. Musicians wearing bright red play popular classics. I've never seen the Gardens so crowded. The afternoon sun is gentle and the area under the trees where the orchestra is set up looks like a Renoir painting – all dappled and sunlit.

Strong smell of cigar smoke. I savour the memory of romance in days gone by. They are playing "Beat out that rhythm on the Drum" to great applause. Find myself a chair in the shade under an oleander. My spirits have lifted. Quite a few "mixed" couples in Paris, young black men and white girls. Lovers everywhere of course. The "William Tell Overture" now ruffles the leaves on the plane trees, followed by "Stand Up and Fight" in a medley. There are quite a few people on their own. The orchestra packs up. Another band in black is tuning up. Then applause for a brisk march.

The Parisians once more stand out in the crowd, classic, well-cut immaculate, linen suits on the men and elegant women match them. And more drifting aroma of cigars. The younger people look more casual and very touristy. Maybe they are tourists. But they chat in French, and I spot a Billabong T-shirt!

I don't think my stomach cares for that red I had, any more than my taste buds did.

I smile to myself when I recall last night's dream again that woke me up chuckling. We *were* in St Sulpice Church yesterday looking at Delacroix and I *did* buy hair conditioner on the way home. Funny how the subconscious randomly puts bits and pieces together.

The band in black attire are now playing very solemn music. The sun is fading a little along with my mood as the time draws towards 5 pm. Wonder if the fruit shops are still open. Don't want to return to my tiny room just yet. Coloured bubbles float by, chased by a little girl in sun-frock and blue leggings. One pigeon struts in and out bravely, pecking the dust for morsels with not much luck. Think I'll go.

Strolled very leisurely, unhappy to see my little park near Musee Cluny, full of angry Africans and Middle Easterners arguing. Their poor little kids howling. I feel sad for those children.

6 pm. I'm back in my room and happy to be "home" again. As I devour my black grapes and banana for dinner, see on TV there's been terrorist attack in Kenya.

7.30. Water leaking through the light-fitting again. Have put a waste bin in the sink to catch it. It drops on to my hair as I try to see myself in the mirror. Tried working on my drawing of Place Viviani from today, but it's a bit of a dead loss and I scrunch it up. I'm feeling very disenchanted tonight – most of all with myself.

9 pm. Water has stopped dripping thank goodness.

2004 – Japan

I wandered on down along the same route Rachel took us the night before. There was a group of gardeners with clippers, re-shaping the very ornamental trees in the corner house just down from us. There was the Post Office and there was the supermarket and down further was the chemist that also sold food. I was making headway.

I enjoyed looking at all the different food. I didn't have a clue what most things were with everything labeled in Kanji. I found the soy milk easily and took two packs. I found envelopes. I went to the check-out and said *"Ohayou Gozaimasu"* and she straight away asked me an involved question in rapid Japanese.

"Sorry, no Japanese."

"That's OK."

Then I found my way to Rosy's old Buddhist kindergarten. I could hear the children. I walked around in the grounds of the temple, taking several photos of the peaceful garden and returned home. My horizon was widening.

When Rachel came home she took me to the *Takowen* "$2 shop" at last, after asking for eleven days where I could get a birthday card to send to Levi, my other grandson. I'd be lucky if it got there for his *next* birthday. I wished I could buy heaps of stuff in the *Takowen* shop but it would have been too difficult to take home. I bought some small dishes and two cups for green tea each only 100 yen and post cards each 100 yen too. We went on to the supermarket and Rachel bought a bottle of champagne and some chocolates to give Miko, seeing it was her birthday. She was turning thirty-nine. If I didn't look in the mirror I could believe I was still thirty-nine.

Megumi rushed in with a bowl of what looked like coleslaw. I peered into it when she had gone.

"What's that pile of stuff on the top?"

"It's fish."

"It looks like maggots."

"Oh Mother, really! I thought you were more adventurous."

We went to wish Miko happy birthday.

Later I was presented with my own photo-copy of *The Map*. Maybe I would frame it when I returned home.

2013 – St Martin's Canal, Paris

7.00 am - Slept til nearly five o'clock. Went through entire wardrobe, such as it is, and finally at 7 am decided on black leggings, black light-weight top, grey tunic and black/white coin spot scarf with black lowish high-heels (my tap-shoes? I think they look like comfy shoes for elderly matrons rather than dancing. What possessed me to buy these?) I'll take higher heels to change perhaps along the way, because they are loose and comfy and still holding together, and there's no way I'm wearing those sneakers with this outfit. I plan to just have a *café/vin rouge* day, just lounging around with my oldest friends, talking and laughing and watching Paris go by, so I won't be needing walking-shoes.

I ponder over the decorative effect of my Paris scenes sitting up around my small room, yet I feel I've wasted my week's painting. I should have used acrylics again like last year. We couldn't drag paintings with thick wet oil paints on them through crowded restaurants, so we put our oils aside until we got to the chateau. Instead of acrylics, I have been sketching in watercolour pencils and later "raining" on it (as Claude says) with a brush that contains water inside its stem and then trying to capture it from there. Caroline had given me some black ink pens to use for detail and they're back in a drawer at home I found to my disgust. The brown pen I brought doesn't work, so it's been a failure on my part. I have paid for a tour of Paris art spots, museums and restaurants and had company, but art-wise, I've screwed up. I seem to have been just mucking around, not taking anything but lunch seriously. Off to breakfast.

7.45 Breakfast over. Heard Australian accent and conversed with nice woman from South Sydney, agreeing on the significant amount of English spoken here now.

There's a funny ad running on TV for "Help for pre-ejaculation!" Two match-sticks in bed entwined around each other and suddenly one match-head ignites, but wilts. Then two match-sticks in bed entwined and suddenly both light up and collapse happily together. Hugh Jackman is in a Lipton tea ad and Miranda Kerr, one for perfume as well as fashion. Turn TV off.

9.00 am – Set off for the Marais. Find it after couple of wrong turns which take me 45 minutes to correct and I have to stop and ask a barman in Rue du Temple for directions.

Penny comes to meet me outside their apartment in the tiny narrow Rue *Vielle* du Temple. Mark is leaning out over the balcony gazing across the cobblestone courtyard, with a lazy "Hi there."

They have a lovely apartment. Upstairs bedroom and bathroom, downstairs bathroom and lounge, kitchen and laundry. What luxury. Would be quite easy living here with two dogs and maybe even the cat. I have the feeling that I wouldn't really want to live here in the Marais though. There are too many tourists and I prefer the Left Bank anyway.

I take photos.

We go for coffee. I fall into a chair outside as usual, happy for the waiter to come and take my order.

"I'm not having anyone waiting on me" Penny announces and goes to the counter to order the coffees.

"But Penny *this is Paris - relax!*"

I take a *"selfie"* (with my camera) of the three of us, looking for the moment our old riotous selves of thirty years ago, when a champagne cork would pop and we would revive our childhood memories again to the rather bored amusement of Mark. I am now content to just sit back here and absorb another corner of Paris for the rest of the day and catch up on what my friends have been up to and do a lot of laughing as we usually do together, but it is decided that we are walking to Canal St. Martin to watch the boats in the locks. I don't feel the need for an excursion just now even though this is a part of Paris I have not yet explored and Canal St. Martin is reputed to *"exude Parisian atmosphere."*

I struggle along behind them along cobble-stone streets in unsuitable shoes that pinch, and lean against the bridge looking down into the murky water. Water rising, falling and rising again - slap slap slap slap. Boats rising and falling.

"Do you find this even slightly entertaining?" queries Mark behind his hand, leaning on the bridge beside me as I stare down into the ever-changing depths.

"My little Grandson certainly would." I need a glass of red.

I laughingly relate the ad with the two match-sticks to Penny but she is already disappearing in the direction of a group of musicians with a lot of brass instruments. "Oom-papa-oom-papa." Am I still in Paris? I could swear I'd been whisked away to Amsterdam.

Off to Hotel du Nord for lunch. Penny orders. I manage to slip in *"C'est vegetarian?"* as I catch the eye of the waitress and point to the menu before she retreats.

We return to the apartment. My feet feel as if a horse has walked on them as I trip over the cobblestones. We sit down and kick our shoes off, resting our feet on the coffee table.

"Penny, you looked like you didn't know me when we met the other day – why?"

"I wasn't expecting to meet a *blonde*."

Rather than bore Mark with more girl-talk of hairdressing disasters, the talk turns abruptly to dreams and I relate my dream of Dad coming in to my room and kissing me goodnight. We all laugh about the kindergarten in the church and Jesus shampooing his hair.

Mark relates his dream of the night before. "I had a sore throat" he says "and I dreamt that I went to see a friend who is a doctor." Mark is also a doctor and continues on - "He looked down my throat and said that I needed to have my tonsils out. When I protested that I had already had my tonsils out, he said he'd never speak to me again!" We laugh.

We resort to discussing Paris' weather and Penny recalls the amazing storm they watched come sweeping across the Champ du Mars while they were having lunch in the restaurant in the Eiffel Tower.

"I know. I was out in it, under the Eiffel Tower, fighting with an inside-out umbrella - and gypsies" I tell them.

I change into my comfy high heels. They go over the map of the area and point out how I could have been here in half the time had I just gone down Rue de Jussieu and across the river. Well, I'm not very good at following maps, especially French maps where not all the rabbit warrens are marked. Instead I had circled the Hotel de Ville a couple of times. "I must have got confused with *Rue de Temple* and *Rue Veille de Temple*.

"You'd better take our travel book with you then. We don't need it now."

It weighs as much as my cat but I take it.

Our conversation dwindles. We are all tired and our fuel gauges seem to have been on empty all afternoon. I feel it is time I left. Penny sees me out to the heavy timber gates that groan with age and history. I turn to wave but she has already closed them quietly behind me.

9 pm. Not feeling well at all. My legs and ankles have been aching again and cramping so much that I have taken two Panadol (and given orders to shoot that horse.)

It's very noisy tonight with people struggling with the locks on their doors just as I did when I first arrived. There must be a horde of new tourists arriving and there is the crazy loud laughter of a woman outside. I don't know if she is down in the street or in the hotel—drunk or mad. Maybe it's me.

Has there been a full moon this week I wonder?

Feel a bit feverish and unwell. Hope it's not David's cold. The weather is warmer tonight and tomorrow is supposed to be 24 degrees.

The Black Van

This morning Rachel said just as she was leaving. "I was able to keep this place in a much better state before you arrived. I can't believe I'm so disorganized."

"Maybe I shouldn't have come" I replied, closing the door after her.

Today I would write a letter to my aunt, a postcard to Angela and send Levi his birthday card.

I was dripping wet from the heat already but decided to leave the house at 10 am and went straight to the Post Office. There was no sign of Kotone who was at our drinks night last Friday. The female postal worker was charming however and I struck no problems. I mailed my letters.

I walked on to the supermarket Rachel told me not to go to *"because they're dearer"* rather than the one she took me to the night before. I liked this one much better.

It was very clean, very cool and spacious. Everything looked immaculate, but trays and trays of the tiny maggoty fish looked up at me almost like sperm, their little silver eyes staring. Yuk! I found some eggs for Anthony. He liked the toasted egg sandwiches I had been making. It was nice to be good at something in that household.

The phone rang when I returned. It was Rachel checking the day I had to go to Rosy's school in her place and learn *"How to brush teeth."*
"I just want you to check the calendar. I thought it might have been today. I *was* going to include you in the talk I have to give tomorrow afternoon to the sixty year-olds at the Community Centre." I shrank at the suggestion. *Not the Yakuba!*
"It's on Australian lifestyle and I thought you might be interesting for them, and you could have spoken too."
Well, it looked like I'd be walking around with Rosy's teacher the next day, possibly with toothbrushes protruding out of our mouths. I had no intentions of being looked over by the Yakuba as *"something that might be interesting"* with my daughter holding the microscope. Nor did this little pumpkin want to do "Show and Tell" for the Yakuba.
There was a black van patrolling the maze of streets, announcing clearly and slowly and persistently in Japanese with a hint of urgency I noted. There was no sign of any equipment or bikes being sold off. This sounded like instructions. For all I knew they could be instructing me to stand in the front doorway because of an impending earthquake! I looked out at the sky and

listened for rumbles but there was nothing – only the echoing sound of the speaker.

I thought I'd make something for lunch that might be regarded as Japanese and actually I wanted to use up at least one of the eggplants that I'd bought and that Rachel had made a point of ignoring in the fridge all week. I peeled it and sliced it and tasted the contents of several bottles under the sink before I found some cooking oil. One was cooking sake. That could be interesting. I pan-fried the sliced eggplant in ginger and oil, defrosted some rice from the freezer and then poured sake and soy sauce over it all.

I sat down on the floor at the table with my chopsticks. I thought I might watch a "Travelling in Japan" show to feel really like a Japanese house-wife.

The TV refused to come on. The food was too greasy to be Japanese and quite disgusting. I ate a dry sesame biscuit and poured a cold lemon tea to wash down the greasy eggplant. Well, I didn't think I'd try to impress Rachel with anything Japanese for dinner tonight.

I had spent two afternoons watching a soapy, starring the most handsome young Japanese man. It was a really romantic tear-jerker and I understood the story and even felt teary at times although it was all in Japanese with no sub-titles of course. It ended tragically. The acting was excellent.

Megumi and Miko came in when Rachel arrived. She'd been shopping and they very suspiciously checked everything she'd bought, unloading it all onto the kitchen bench and holding up each item to each other as though they questioned the legitimacy of each one.

"By the way, they want to let you know, that at this time of year there is often a warning broadcast to keep children indoors because of photochemical smog!"

"Thanks for the warning" I gulped, placing my hand on my chest and suppressing an involuntary cough, remembering the mystery black van and its broadcasting. "Photo chemical smog" - too late!

They left and Rachel wandered back in.

"I've just spoken to Sandy. She says she saw "Lost in Translation" and it's just *soooo cliché* and really pathetic and the only funny part is when Bill Murray does a commercial."

"Well, everyone I know that has seen it loved it. It's not just about Japan. It's a very subtle unpredictable love story that happens to be set in Japan and it's hilarious."

"Well, Sandy said it's *pathetic*."

"Sandy's only twenty-three. What would she know about subtlety?"

Miko wanted to know what Australian kids ate for breakfast as her friend was going to have two baseball players from a Melbourne team staying in their house in a few weeks and "she must prepare." She made notes and spelled out the word *"Cornfrakes"* and I was curious to see what it looked like in Kana.

Anthony was pleased that I had at last learned a new Japanese board game and he now had someone to play it with.

I had emailed Carrie that morning and was able to report successfully this time, the story of our failed attempt at lunch the other day, describing the bleak area the restaurant was in. She emailed back tonight, saying it seemed a shame I wasn't doing some touristy things and seeing the beautiful places while I was there.

Carrie said her eyes felt "gritty" for lack of sleep with Levi lately. She'd given him a little birthday party with her Mothers' group and their one-year-olds and had enjoyed icing overalls on teddy-bear biscuits and decorating them with hundreds and thousands (sprinkles) as I had done for Rachel and Caroline when they were little kids.

2013 – Au revoir Latin Quarter.

2.30 am. Woke with bit of a sore throat. Spray nasal spray up nose and back of throat.

7.00 am. After trying on many outfits I decide on grey jumper, grey smock, black stockings, blue/black/grey long scarf and ankle boots. Have re-packed totally and am ready to head off on part two of my holiday, but will leave it until late as possible so I can have 10 am coffee at my second-favourite "Royal Jussieu" café a few doors down.

Have just discovered an English news channel at 6.55 am. A bit late as I am about to check out.

Have my final breakfast at the hotel. Order taxi (glad the very nice man is on desk to finalize account.) Yes, breakfast was included in my bill. Phew! My euro card works and all up plus phone 1,039 euros for ten days. I have 1,050 euros on my card, so 11 euros left. (Of course I am still carrying quite an amount of cash on my person.)

Will stay in room and watch TV for a couple of hours and go for coffee down the street and return for my 11 am taxi. All good.

Russia intends sending troops to intervene in chemical weapons problem in Syria. Angela Merkel, German PM wins majority and she represents "Christian Democrats." Greece not happy – "Europe becoming market land." Greek economy is the lowest in Europe. More trouble continuing in Kenya. Ten hostages being held. Death toll 68 and rising. In Somalia Al-Shabaab have claimed responsibility and will kill hostages if force is used. Pakistan's attack was against Christian community by suicide bombers. Worst typhoon in China in thirty years and Liz (my sister-in-law) is travelling alone in China! Hong Kong airport affected. Flights backed up from Sunday. Wonder how and if that will affect my flight home. Hope Liz is OK.

9.30. I'm back in my little corner of my second favourite little "Royal Jussieu." Still, Café Rostand is the only place that does *café crème* with the special little jug of milk the way I like it. Penny said they do it like that at the Eiffel Tower. Coffee is always really hot in Paris which she and I agreed on. Everyone is rugged up and it's quite cold and I don't have enough clothes on. I am fighting off a head cold with the aid of my nasal spray.

Very busy here as usual, being Monday morning. Just over four euros seems to be the standard price for *café*.

A young blonde man with whippet strides past. Well dressed couple, she with silver blonde coiffure cycle past and ease in to the threatening traffic. Don't know how they do it!

I have spilled some sugar. Mum used to say that spilling sugar predicted "joy." Well I'm in Paris aren't I? Group of four pass with dozens of pink toilet rolls, bottles of mineral water and doonas. Wonder where they intend to sleep tonight. Window boxes full of red and pink geraniums prevalent throughout Paris and they hang from window boxes across the way.

I told the charming man on the desk after breakfast that I found everything very good at the hotel. The staff so helpful and polite and I would stay there next time. Next time? I wonder when that will be. This time last year I was checking properties for sale in Paris and all over France on the Internet. I had every intention of coming back here to live. I even got a quote for transporting two dogs and a cat.

A beautifully groomed white-haired woman stops at a corner post while her black and white King Charles spaniel urinates for some time. She and I acknowledge each other with an understanding smile, fellow dog lovers. My windows are open to the street this morning. That is why it is breezier and chaotically noisier than usual, but so very "Paris."

A crowd of excited school children, eight-year-olds maybe, collect outside on the street and head up the hill chattering happily.

With the windows open the fumes are beginning to get to me. A bus to Champs Elysees, a truck with "Passionfroid" written on its side, motor-bikes, cyclists, Parisians, so noticeable with their style and American tourists so typical in shorts, with bare arms, cameras around necks. More doona (or duvet) and toilet roll carriers (maybe there is a toilet-roll and doona convention?). A bus to Saint Germaine des Prix and one to St Francis de Xavier. A priest stops to post letters and I wonder if his arm is stuck in the yellow post-box or is he trying to remove letter again. Heavy green rubbish truck turns at corner, toots car side-swiping him and he throws hands in air. An overweight, obviously American couple, grey-haired, baggy cargo pants, sneakers and bright blue T-shirts survey the street anxiously for some time, before they cross hand in hand.

10.15. Think I'll return to the Hotel and await taxi.

2004 – Stag Beetles with teeth.

I have been given my copy of the big artistic map Rachel made, even with the blossom trees coloured in pink. It is beautiful. She has marked the area where I can walk in my indoor shoes and where I have to wear my outdoor shoes and where the gym is for the lesson on "Toothcare."

"You look sort of sad. What's wrong?" Rachel asked.

I felt my eyes filling.

"Oh, I just don't feel a hundred percent, and I'm so hot."

Actually it was much cooler outside but the apartment was not cooling down and I had really lost my punch. I didn't dare try and re-vitalize my hair with any colour as they used different hair colouring products to back home. I didn't want to use something I wasn't sure about and go bald. They bleached their hair and then coloured it and I didn't want to do anything extreme when I couldn't understand Kana let alone Katakana, so I was going to age a little for the rest of my time there.

There was a message from Carrie first thing. I was overdrawn on my credit card. "That was strange. I paid it off before I left Melbourne." I emailed back in alarm.

"Can you call in at the Bank and see what's happening and thank the girl who gave me the ready reckoner and all the info on Japan." But I told her not to worry if she couldn't get there as she had enough on her plate already.

Rachel rang to tell me it was raining. I knew it was raining and I'd done a lot of washing and all the bed sheets and pillow cases were out in it! She said she was bringing home a huge stag beetle for the kids in a jar.

"Why don't you let it go free on the way home?"

"No. Kids keep them as pets here."

"How long do you intend keeping it in a jar?"

"Oh, I don't know." She went on to say that it had bitten a man at the school quite savagely and she would bring it home for the kids. How strange of you Rachel.

Megumi brought over a "special stag beetle box" and "special stag beetle food" and it was put on the steps outside, right at the door, behind where I slept. I might have guessed, after it "bit the man savagely at school." The door was always open with the screen door gaping at the sides very inadequately.

"We'll take it to the shrine tomorrow and let it go, OK?"

"That's a good idea." After it's made a meal of me tonight.

I sat down with a mug of boiled water with sugar and salt added – a tip I had learned in Bali to re-hydrate me. This was the strong flavour that was in all the processed food here, sugar and salt. In a climate other than a humid one it would be very unhealthy.

There was an interesting program on TV. I liked their Japanese TV. It was about the pruning of hydrangeas which were in bloom at that moment, growing wild as well as hanging over fences everywhere. I would always think of Japan when I saw them. I actually picked up some gardening tips although it was all in Japanese.

Then there was a cooking show on. Black seaweed shredded and added to a chopped celery stick, stirred with chopsticks and …

There was an empty utility truck cruising slowly down the street doing a broadcast. He went past again. Probably collecting old bikes and used CD players, maybe used high-school girls' undies? Or maybe broadcasting more warnings of toxic fumes I should have a mask on for.

Time to head off to Rosy's school. I went the wrong way. I had to get out my huge scroll with the cherry blossom trees and the Argebori River marked on it out and re-trace my steps. I couldn't believe I was not able to follow Rachel's map.

Across the river, down the road and then the children's voices led me the rest of the way. Now Rachel's art work was all creased and bent. It no longer looked like a crisp page out of the adventures of "Milly Molly Mandy."

I carefully walked at the side of the *indoor shoe path* until I arrived at the gym. Then I changed my shoes and waited for two young women to give me my cue as to when we should go in. We were the first there.

The gym slowly filled with young mums in jeans and t-shirts and western brown hair. The school nurse was at the front of the room with an overhead projector and several gleaming kettles. Were we going to have a tea ceremony? She introduced herself but nobody was listening.

In walked the Headmaster. Gregory Peck's double again! I knew it was him because of the dramatic and proud way he strode in, taking rather unnecessarily giant steps just as he did to get from his car to the front window of the apartment on the Monday before last. Good, he would recognize me and see me in a different light now that I was not wearing my nightclothes. He took the microphone, his voice staccato, his face smiling with approval at the collection of mums. I let my glasses slide down my perspiring nose and stared at him with my pale Western eyes. He would recognize me for sure because I was the only non-Japanese person there, but his speech went on while I blinked slowly at him. He showed no recognition though he seemed to be looking straight at me. Wouldn't I get even a little nod or inclination of a knowing smile? Didn't he see the colour of my eyes? I was the only one listening to him and there was a hum of voices blanketing his words and I had no idea what he was saying at all. He eventually bowed, twirled around and strode out of the gym. I turned slowly, keeping my Western eyes fixed on him but he was gone. I wondered what that was all about.

After about thirty minutes of what I supposed to be information on the importance of cleaning one's teeth from the school nurse, Rosy filed in with her tiny classmates carrying their tiny chairs and mugs, toothbrushes and milk cartons cut in half.

The small child sitting in front of me on her mother's lap laughed showing a row of broken lower teeth. Rachel said their teeth were a real problem (she must have caught the teeth obsession from the Japanese). Maybe it was the sugar in everything.

Rosy didn't see me. Her eyes swept across me. If she couldn't see me in this crowd of Japanese women, how would the Headmaster. It must have been my western brown hair, wide face and glasses. I looked like one of them. I thought I was going to stand out.

The nurse held up a huge plastic model of teeth and gums and with an enormous brush the size of one that you would clean your toilet with, indicated brushing left to right. Was she saying to do it this way, or *not* to do it this way?

We went through a long and tedious lesson and I watched the clock. Out came the shiny kettles. How intriguing. The teachers filled the children's mugs from them. Maybe they would have soup and then clean their teeth. But no, they used their cups to rinse and then spat into the half milk cartons.

Some mothers raised their hands up in the air. They had been asked a question. What had I missed out on? What should I have been owning up to? Maybe they were asking who had their own teeth or who cleaned their teeth or who had a secret lover they were going to spend the afternoon with. My hand found its way into the air uncertainly. The mums hopped up from their chairs and went down to the front to their kids. I did the same. The woman who had been sitting next to me didn't quite come up to my shoulder. I felt conspicuous.

Rosy was pleased to see me and opened her gummy six year-old mouth to show me the hot pink colour it had become along with her tongue.

I stared. "What's that?!"

"I dunno."

They all had bright pink mouths and tongues. I didn't feel well at all.

Rosy filed out calling across the room to me "I can't come home with you. I have to go home in my line."

"I'll see you at home then" I called back and hurried off, changing my shoes along the way.

I thought how easy it would be to find my way home but I actually missed the turn-off. The roads were so narrow I kept mistaking them for driveways. I retraced my steps. This was so much harder than finding my way around Paris although I got lost in Paris every day but it wasn't scary. I didn't mind wandering lost in Paris; that was how one discovered the treasures of the city. Here I felt like I'd be swallowed up in the ugly landscape if I made a wrong turn.

After dinner we watched the first Harry Potter movie. He's as popular in Japan as he is everywhere else but the books or the movies have never appealed to me. Witches and spells I've never had any fascination for and I disgraced myself again by sleeping through the second half of it.

I could have brought up the incident in Amsterdam back in 1993 when I was travelling with Caroline (but I thought better of it and managed to bite my tongue.) I had stopped to look for a postcard to send back home to my Dad. I searched for one that wasn't depicting a crash course in gynaecology, which to my embarrassment, most of them seemed to be. I was approached by a gentleman in a suit. He spoke English with a heavy Dutch accent and after a brief introduction on his part, asked me how long I would be in

Amsterdam. He seemed disappointed with my reply of "only a few days."

His answer was a little cryptic:

"Oh, that's a shame. If you were staying longer in Amsterdam I could have taken you to a town far away from here and proved you to be a witch."

I was aghast! What had given him that idea?

I smiled to myself then at the memory but had no intention of giving this choice bit of ammunition to Rachel or Anthony to fire at me for the rest of my stay.

2013 – Port de St Cloud.

11.30 am I arrive at my Hotel in Port de St Cloud in the 15th arrondissement. The taxi seemed to "stall" at every set of lights or hold-up in the traffic. Was it a clever economic strategy or was I a jinx, a carrier of a faulty engine virus? I started thinking back to my little car at home suffering with an unknown complaint.

I would estimate this to be a half an hour's very fast walk, or maybe a run to the Eiffel Tower which we passed on our way here. Probably further than that, as I recall Bonnie's exhausted comment last July when she and I set off to walk to the Tower which seemed to be getting further away all the time instead of closer. She was very flushed and hyperventilating quite dangerously and I tried to reassure her continuously with "We're nearly there. It's looks much closer now. We're nearly there," to which she panted an answer in her Southern accent: "Just because you can see it – don't mean shit!"

Have left luggage at desk (struggled to lock it – hope I can unlock it again!)

"Your room is not ready til 1.30 Madame."

I am in totally unfamiliar territory and I could be swallowed up and lost here in a few minutes. Sit down in smoking area at "Le Cardinal" which I quite like the look of, but with ashtrays on all the tables and lots of smokers. I decide to take a table outside where I can sit and get my bearings and wait out the time, probably having lunch here or somewhere close by. Coffee here is three euros 60 – that's not bad. Taxi was only twenty-two euros too.

Mix of modern and old architecture surrounds me. Unbelievably busy traffic. I'm still in Paris. It's believable.

11.45. Church bells ring out.

Little African boy races by on a scooter. Woman with pusher but no baby, instead half a dozen baguettes where the baby should be and a Jack Russell on lead. Taxis lined up on curb three-deep in a long queue.

Well-dressed Parisians walk by and the obviously local residents with babies in pushers and shoppers with definite destinations, not wandering. (They seem to buy toilet rolls in enormous bulk here I notice.)

Young French teenagers – untidy and smoking.

A Middle Eastern woman a few tables away calls out to me "Excuse moi Madame...?" I smile and answer my well-worn phrase *"je n'comprehend pas Francais Madame."* But she is not threatening, dressed in white, sipping coffee and using her smart phone as she smokes. It will be an interesting exercise seeing how I entertain myself for one whole week here.

12.00. Another bell strikes continually with an urgency in its "clang." There is a long line of buses – no shortage of transport. The bell continues for about two minutes, eventually fading to a reluctant murmured defeat.

I decide to go inside and eat. Staff are very welcoming, the interior smart and spotless. Friendly waiters/waitresses rush to show me to a table.
"*Table for one Madame?*"
"*Oui monsieur. Merci beaucoup.*"
I order *salade Nicoise* and *rosé*. The bread arrives. The wine and water arrive. The *salade Nicoise* arrives but the "tuna" looks like meat!
"*Excuse moi Madame - salade Nicoise?*" I venture.
«*Oui Madame.*"
"*Ce'st Tuna?*" (Looks and tastes like beef but I haven't tasted beef for thirty odd years.)
"*Ce'st tuna Madame.*"
Actually now I know for sure it is indeed tuna it is a beautiful meal, with olives, green beans, hard-boiled eggs, tomatoes and lettuce and very well presented.
"*The sky is out - the sun is blue*" and things are looking up half way through the *rosé*.
Young blonde woman at next table eats alone and a tiny black and white dog sits on the chair opposite her – only in Paris. He watches her, looking a little embarrassed as she nibbles on her bread. He looks

around him as she takes her eyes away from him to her phone.

I comment to the waitress "*Ah - petite chien!*"

"Yes, he comes here every day."

I smile as he accepts a mouthful of bread and I wonder how Lillie would behave in here, let alone Coco with the voracious appetite!

He stretches in the handbag that is his throne and looks around. The boyfriend arrives – big, overweight. The *petite chien* stands up, tail wagging and leans towards him, grinning, paws on the table. He looks like he might make one enormous bound for the boyfriend – or the bread – which will it be?

Have I finished my *salade Nicoise*? No not quite. The oil at the centre of the plate is now swimming in delicious flavours and that is what beautiful bread is for.

The boyfriend butters his bread – almost too much for the *petite chien* who watches closely as it moves to boyfriend's mouth. His tail gives a couple of flops and looking from one to the other "*Remember me?*"

Woman gives boyfriend's hand a smacking kiss! "*C'est sanglant fin!*" (My interpretation of French speaking dogs is rough I know.)

The waitress places a whole basket of bread in front of *petite chien*. He sniffs it closely and glances back at his mistress – "I'll have mine buttered *s'il vous plait.*"

"Le Cardinal" buzzes with activity. Business lunches mostly I think. Dinner arrives at *petite chien's* table. Lots of lip-smacking (from the dog), but then yawning, he resignedly settles back in to handbag with a disappointed *"Non pour moi."*

Mama mia – Four Euros 90 for a cappuccino!

1.30 pm – off to my room.

Well this is a nice surprise. Lovely and spacious with fridge, TV, huge desk on which to write and a view! And all paid for in advance. There are two fruiterers across the street. I'm very happy! Kick off my ankle boots and settle in for eight nights. Lunch was superb for under 22 euros, *and* I managed the combination lock on my luggage – *tout de suite*! – and there is even a laundry bag! Breakfast 7 am to 10 am.

A lot of abusive car horns out there challenging and competing while I lie on my huge bed and glance through the travel guide that Penny insisted I take off their hands.

4 pm. Third café today. Think my intake of caffeine will be high this week. Nothing much else to do. Have walked the length of Rue de Murat one way. There are schools, which seem to be discreetly hidden amongst apartment buildings in France, hospitals, laundry and the choice of a few restaurants and no fashion anywhere to look at so far.

I'm in Avenue Versailles having a not-so-great café. Anyway there are lots of boulangerie and fruit shops in this area.

ABBA pumps out "Gimme Gimme Gimme."

The waiter grunts at euro card with 11 euros still on it. I thought I'd try it, but "No. No cards." Didn't like this café much anyway. Won't come here again.

5 pm. Back in my Hotel after exploring further to Salle St Jean Catholic and English Church. No antiquity about this one. Took photos of the area and found Metro Porte de St Cloud.

Well I don't think much of it at all but a Number 10 train will take me "back home" for a visit. St Michel/Luxembourg area tomorrow. Can't spend a week here, and half these grapes I bought are rotten. TV won't stay on! Banana and *poir* OK.

The man on reception seemed stunned when I asked about laundry (seeing as "Welcome" brochure in room says "leave laundry to be done within 24 hours.")

"No, but there is a *laverie* (laundromat) down the street Madame."

At least I have a selection of pillows here to choose from instead of a door draught-stopper.

7 pm. Yay! I've got on to CNN in English. But it's all about the Kenya terrorist attack.

The Trip to Tokyo

Saturday and it is very overcast.

We set off for a long walk through the mixture of ugly and exotic areas surrounding us, Rachel with an eagle eye retrieving broken bits of blue and white china that peeped out of trodden-down earth all the way. This is quite an interest of hers and she keeps these treasures in a large decorative jar on show. I wondered about the antiquity and history of the pieces and had they been dropped there just last week or lifetimes ago. What wars had they lived through sleeping in the brown earth crushed by millions of Japanese feet?

We stopped while she called out in Japanese to some kids bashing a ball around the tennis court at the high school. The junior-high kids have to go to school on Saturdays. They grinned and waved and called back in struggling English to her.

After lunch Megumi offered us a drive to Kuki. There was a store there called "Hard-Off" that sold recycled home goods, jewelry and clothing. Rachel said that all second-hand stores, which she knows I have a weakness for, are called "Hard-Off." She reprimanded me when I asked what they called the brothels in the area. Maybe then "Hard-Off" was their interpretation of "hard-up." The messages on the T-shirts in shop windows were often of an unintended crude but hilarious nature because they were American sayings translated into Japanese and then back into English by non-English-speaking translators. Anyway I was not going to bring up the subject of "Lost in Translation" again.

I was fascinated by the second-hand goods and bought a pretty blue and white noodle bowl for a dollar.

We moved on to a big department store and I found a little T-shirt for my grandson back home. I was now feeling quite ill and in a bit of a daze with the heat and humidity.

When we got home Rachel and Anthony raced off to their taiko drum lesson and I waved them out the door not feeling up to another of those episodes. Rosy was forbidden to go with them and cried bitterly outside, comforted by Megumi's husband. I went and retrieved her from the neighbours and slumped down on the couch and she extracted no reaction from me when she announced angrily that she was going back to Megumi's apartment again.

####

Last night I didn't believe that I'd be well enough to go to Tokyo this morning, especially as we have to leave at 7.30 am but Rachel has every intention of doing so.

We left home at 8.15. I had searched through my luggage for what attire would be suitable for an obachan in Tokyo. It was fairly limited. But I felt very optimistic about the day and I lent Rachel my new red blouse. She suggested I wear my long pink and mauve sheer coat dress over my white cotton trousers and I put with this some rather ornate beaded mauve fabric scuffs.

I felt quite glamorous as we strode off to the station but had to ask her to slow down her pace as my rather ornate scuffs weren't for track work. We all seemed very happy and light-hearted anyway.

It was an hour's journey to Asakusa and I felt a bit conspicuous in my outfit. Everyone else was wearing jeans and t-shirts. The trip was quite boring and uninspiring with ugly built-up areas drawing us in to Tokyo. The children were busy with their heads buried in the usual supply of Japanese comics all in Kana and Kanji and occasionally a chuckle would emanate from behind the pages.

Rachel insisted on buying all our tickets and we left the train at Asakusa. She collected them and we put them through the machine. She then returned them to each of us three children, six, ten, and fifty-nine.

We arrived at Nakami Se-dori at morning-tea time, but I was too overwhelmed by the colour and crowds of old Tokyo to hurry to a coffee house as Rachel suggested. I just wanted to stand and take in being part of this "event."

A couple of rickshaws flashed by which brought a comment from Rachel on how, when she was in Singapore as a teenager, (the prize for being the winner of a beach-girl contest on Scarborough Beach in Perth), she went for a ride in a rickshaw and felt so worried about the welfare of the rickshaw boy that she swore she'd never do it again. So I didn't suggest a rickshaw ride. I decided myself that although this was their livelihood, I rather agreed with Rachel's thinking and instead was drawn down the long street of colour noting many women wearing kimonos.

I wanted to find a "happy-coat" among the stalls for me and maybe one for Angela and Caroline. There was food and more food, clothing, jewelry, wigs, woodblock prints, postcards and chopsticks. I decided on two "happy coats", one in mauve, pink, and gold, with a pattern of peacocks for me, and a sky blue one for Carrie, with pale pink cherry blossoms and geisha women.

As I inspected what Rachel said were "work-clothes" a navy jacket that wrapped around the waist with pants in a pattern of pale blue butterflies, I heard Anthony's voice calling out to Rosy. She had been right beside us up until that moment. We both spun around, abandoning the stall and darted in and out of the crowds with Rachel going back in the direction we had come.

"Maddie-Rose....Rosy" she screamed.

A tiny sour-faced old woman stopped me, tugged on my arm and stiffly pointed back over her shoulder. Anthony charged off in that direction, disappearing into the crowd that stared at us curiously as though we might possibly be making a movie. He reached the spot where the woman had indicated, but Rosy had disappeared into old Tokyo. He looked back disbelievingly at me and shrugged and another woman pointed up ahead and there at last we saw our lanky skinny little Western girl standing, mopping her eyes. Anthony pounced on her, giving her a severe tongue-lashing which was followed by a tongue-lashing from Rachel. We continued on, Rosy clutching at our knees, red-eyed and sniffing in fright and relief.

We headed back towards the Senso-ji temple and stopped at a big incense cauldron. Crowds wandered around it, encouraging the smoke up towards their faces and clothing with their hands. This was said to bestow good health. I got Rachel to photograph my experience of the "cleansing." We walked on up the steps to the temple entrance. Inside it was decked with flowers and the smell of strong sweet incense rained down on us as people knelt and worshipped.

Stone steps outside led towards a garden and an old stone bridge, reminiscent of the willow pattern design. An old, rather stooped Japanese man approaching us in the street stopped and took my photo. We stood and looked over the bridge at the koi, huge and molten gold in colour, red, orange, apricot and black. How much happier their condition was here than the writhing mass at the fun-park living in muck. The old man with the camera was in front of me again and I turned and smiled and he took another photo and bowed. Rachel asked him if she could take a photo of both of us together. I stood beside him and could feel him searching for my fingers, which he squeezed gently. He turned and smiled quietly and bowed low and formally, then he was gone and we wandered on with the thought of coffee on our minds.

Rachel found a little upstairs coffee house, its floorlength windows looking down on to the busy street below. She ordered iced koki. I ordered cappuccino and the children had jelly and ice-cream. They protested about the size of the tiny biscuits on the side and Anthony made a loud public announcement about the annoying smokers around us, then sat down shaking his head in irritation and said grace.

Rachel paid the bill and I slipped some money into her purse as we left. On the way out she photographed me with the waiter, and Anthony went searching for the bathroom.

We stopped to let Rosy pet a cute little dog travelling in the basket on the handlebars of a bicycle. We finally tore her away and came upon a shop selling classic Japanese motifs on fabric. I bought one for Rachel that she liked and chose one with a design of cats for Carrie.

The children were *starving* again and demanded we find a McDonalds and on the way we discovered a market stall that had some second hand jackets. I bought a mauve and white printed summer kimono, as Rachel referred to it, which was rather like a cape with the underarms open, a sensible design for Japan's climate. I paid about seven dollars for it. Rachel tried on a new black jacket with a subtle decorative print and fell in love with it so I bought that for her. I wanted to buy Rosy a dress but I had seen nothing but kimonos for kids.

We found a McDonalds. Fancy coming to Tokyo and choosing to lunch at a take-away. The kids ordered their hamburgers and Anthony looked around him complaining loudly about the smoking before saying grace again.

"We'll look for somewhere more authentic to eat afterwards Mum."

The kids finished their burgers and we followed Rachel down to the Sumidagawa River and then on to the Hama Rikyu-teien garden. This had been in use since the days of the Samurai and now the shaped trees, ponds, streams and bridges sat with a backdrop of skyscrapers looming over them. There were domestic cats everywhere, resting under the trees in the long grass but there was only the sound of the infernal crows. I didn't imagine any other birds would survive there, being easy prey to the numerous cats. I took lots of photos and we found our way to the tea-house, walking in single file across the stepping stones of large smooth rocks.

"Shoes off Nanny!" Anthony ordered and I slipped out of my scuffs and put them on a shelf beside many different designs of footwear and we were led barefoot into some open, glassed rooms that looked over a lake. We knelt, sitting on our heels on tatami mats with the children kneeling beside us.

A girl in a work suit similar to the one I'd seen with the butterfly design brought Rachel a tray with a bowl of frothy green liquid and a tiny pink confection. They bowed to each other. I wondered if Rachel would say "Eat a ducky mouse" but I didn't hear it.

There were quite a few people lining up waiting their turn. It was almost like a communion service. We rose and tiptoed around silently to collect our shoes. My thought processes must still have been switched off because I heard the noisy clatter of my mauve rather ornate sandals as I knocked them from the shelf tumbling to the floor. Everyone in the room looked up with startled faces and gasped at me as though I had farted.

"Nanny!"

"Not here Mum! Wait until you get outside to put your shoes on!"

I bowed apologetically to the roomful of people. "Sorry, sorry."

"Where to Rachel?"

"We'll walk to Ginza."

The children and I followed her out of the park. There was a constant roar of traffic which we could hear but could not see.

"That sounds like Paris."

"Oh don't keep comparing everything to Paris. You're in Tokyo. Just enjoy Tokyo."

"That was the worst thing about Paris" I continued "the traffic."

"Oh *Mother*."

Actually, not daring to say it aloud, it sounded different in Paris because they have cobblestones everywhere. But I kept this comparison to myself.

"I'm starving," said Anthony.

"You couldn't be, you've just had McDonalds, and Nanny and I are going to find somewhere to have a *proper* lunch."

"McDonalds was hours ago," he whined.

We were now in modern Tokyo. Several streets became a mall on Sundays. I imagined the stores there must be very classy but it didn't look as though I was going to get a look inside any of them at Rachel's rapid walking pace.

The road was filled with people walking in every direction. I felt that this could definitely be the area where Bill Murray got out of the taxi and chased after the girl. I related this to Rachel and she said there were several areas similar but busier than this that they may have used. I could almost *see* Scarlett walking away from Bill through the crowd and I stopped and stared down the long wide street that hummed with colour, just to make sure he was not really there and I had missed him. We took some more photos and passed some showy wine bars that also reminded me of somewhere in Paris.

We stopped for the kids to watch a street performer hurling something that looked like a huge cotton reel in to the air on a string.

Rachel chose a restaurant and we waited for a table. Anthony pushed in front of me and grabbed the seat behind the table we were taken to.

"I'll have anything that doesn't have meat in it" as I glared at my grandson.

"Just order whatever and I'll take the meat out."

Rachel asked the waitress if we could have the egg sandwiches, mine without the meat. The girl shook her head in a concerned manner and rattled a reply at us.

"No, you *must* have the meat" Rachel said. "They're always like this. You *have* to have it as it says on the menu, and put your legs down Maddie-Rose! You're wearing a dress remember!"

Rachel ate half my ham and put two slices on Anthony's plate and with the ham hanging out each side of his mouth he placed his hands together underneath his chin and very solemnly murmured thanks.

Rachel rolled her eyes. "You don't need to do that *every* time you put something into your mouth Anthony. And put that ham in to your mouth *properly!*"

"Just grace before meal-times Anthony" I added and he looked from one to the other of us, offended. "He's either going to be a priest or it's a nervous tic."

We were soon off again which was a relief to all those around us and heading to the subway. Rachel handed us our tickets and we put them through the machine and back to her for safe-keeping.

"Can we slow down a bit Rachel?"

We were now headed to Shinjuku, the area I had always imagined I would not want to see, with huge video screens on high at every angle and neon flashing. The place was jumping with street performers and a group playing Japanese music entertaining the crowd. Amazing. A girl across the street with long cerise coloured hair and a long hippy style dress caught my eye reminding me of Cherry, an artist friend back home. She nodded to me in a bowing gesture. I bowed back. The bowing was becoming a natural response. She laughed with her friend and I laughed as we Westerners realized we were getting very used to this custom and doing it automatically.

We moved on and I heard familiar music, this time from Peru. I didn't tell Rachel that the first time I heard this particular tune was on the St Michel station in Paris, when a whole group of Peruvians tumbled out of a train and entertained the early morning commuters with "El Pituco." Hearing it again gave me goose-bumps like I had that frosty morning in April as they bounced their music off the walls of the Metro.

We caught the 6.40 pm train from Asakusa. Rachel wanted to go on to Harajuka *"where all the crazy young Japanese people hang out"* so Sandy had said and that "if she had just one hour to show someone Tokyo, she would take them to Harajuka."

I'd been hanging out with crazy young people all day anyway, who were now whining miserably and I felt I'd been satisfactorily filled with all the Tokyo culture I could hope to digest in one day. We had three different trains to catch to get home and it was dark. We also had a long walk to the apartment from the station during which time we stopped and watched some boys playing taiko drums in a quiet little moonlit park. I guess after all, you could possibly call the area around the apartment *rural* after Tokyo.

2013 – Back to visit my favourite haunts.

Tuesday. Slept well but woke before 5 am. Throat worse than ever – really sore. Gargled with some Dettol hand-wash in water. Feels a bit better. I've had a really sore throat for 24 hours. I think it's the exhaust fumes of the cars. The fumes were really strong while taxiing over here and the traffic has been unrelenting.

Am watching hilarious send-up of politicians from European and Arab countries in Wallace & Gromit type animation. Such French faces. Characters so recognizable but with very explicit and gory scenes.

Off to breakfast at 7.25. Breakfast the same as at my hotel in Rue des Ecoles but feels more formal and I don't dare say "*Non baguette.*" I break the baguette up in to tiny pieces, butter and honey them and quickly sip on the tea with each mouthful.

There is a Parisian business-woman breakfasting, and a honeymoon couple (well – a very young couple) two English-speaking women together and an older Parisian business man and a young girl on her own.

Bee Gees "Staying Alive" playing. I need to get up and dance. Kitchen-help very black, friendly and smiling.

"*Tea Madame*" pointing, responding to my query.

Back in my room it is very warm. Open window to a blast of icy cold air and traffic sounds. Penny and Mark will be leaving Paris now for their Tour of France for the next three weeks.

I venture to the Metro and am helped by very charming French gentleman to purchase my tickets.

10 am – Back in central Paris. No fashion shops are open for business yet as I pass on my way up Boulevard St Michel.

Here I am back at Café Rostand, sipping the best *café creme* in Paris. All is forgiven! As soon as I came up the steps of the Cluny de la Sorbonne Metro the ruins of the Roman baths at Cluny welcomed me home again. This is *my* Paris! No longer feel let-down. Am reading detailed information from Penny's book on the Latin Quarter/ Cluny/Luxembourg areas which are home to me.

A jogger crosses road from Gardens, weaving through bumper to bumper traffic. Police and Ambulance sirens clash and truck unloading crates of bottles all add to the cacophony of noise. Two silver-haired gentlemen stand beside me and shake hands graciously, farewelling each other in musical *Francaise*. One returns to the café and the other struts off into the Gardens. A blonde woman waving a tiny French flag leads twenty tourists in to the Gardens. The trees are taking on gold and russet tones. Some are bare. Today is predicted to be 23 but it is still very cool. The weather is similar to that of Melbourne if this is the start of autumn.

12.45. I have walked back down Boulevard St Michel looking for something to buy Caroline but everything is "Made in China" or Vietnam. Disappointing but this is of course the "cheaper fashion area."

I call in to Musee Cluny to finally see inside but "Shut on Tuesdays." Thought it about time I did a proper tour of my favourite place from the inside.

Finally find a little boutique actually selling "French" brands of clothing. I decide on ear-rings "Made by craftswoman somewhere on the coast in France" the charming woman explains. The pair of earrings have a slightly different flower design on each one. They look like Caroline and are very pretty. Then up to the top of St Michel where the old woman shook her fist at me last week. No sign of her.

The trees in Luxembourg Gardens have turned the same colour as my *crepe fromage*. The sun is out, the sky is blue, and it's lovely under the oleanders with pigeons begging for protein – now there are four. Too much *fromage* in this *crepe* for one person anyway. Six more land. What a wonderful escape this place provides.

The clock has chimed 1 pm and I am surrounded by the local pigeon society. One flutters off with a piece of cheese and sits on the balustrade gagging on the mozzarella. Some have missed the bus entirely but continue to peck amidst the cigarette butts.

Everyone is sunbathing, even the statues! The crowds flow in and out. Kids are trying out brightly coloured cheap curios at a stall.

I have escaped to the shade. I'm hot. Think I have developed David's cold finally. Nose beginning to leak. Have moved back in to the sun. I need it. I'm chilly.

2.30. Am enjoying having this book to read on the history and development of Paris. I'd be lost without it frankly. Now I've sneezed three times ! ! !

3.45. Man playing sadly on violin "La Vie en Rose" as I leave the Gardens early to avoid work crowds on the train. Wish I only had to walk to my "homey" La Familia hotel.

Train goes via a different station on the way home which I thought I'd find a bit tricky, but I change trains and get my bearings with no problems.

Back in St Cloud I feel the ground shudder as I wait for the lights to change at the crossing. There is another world of busy commuters beneath my feet. Walk on to *fruitier* and buy my two bananas and some black grapes and mineral eau and the boy there asks me where I am from. He was "Made in Morocco" and he says he welcomes me to France. He seems a nice boy wearing heavy framed spectacles (A Moroccan Woody Allen in a white apron.)

Now resting on my bed and drinking mineral eau and actually have TV going OK. I open the window for some fresh air and can no longer hear the TV for the incredible noise! Shut out the fumes again. Put myself to sleep early. Not feeling well at all. TV really annoying me. I'm tired of rapid French language that I can't understand when I desperately need some solid conversation with someone.

Geri shiteimasu! – Bless you.

It's 5 am and I'm so thirsty. I crept out quietly and put the kettle on so that I'd have some boiled water to drink. I think I'm really in for it with my stomach. I was yet to learn that I am fructose intolerant with spring onions at the top of my gut irritants list, of which I'd been fed substantial daily amounts by the well-meaning Megumi.

Rachel called out in a very irritable voice "What are you doing up at 5 am? I have hardly slept all night for you getting up and down and I've got to go to work soon. I'll be a wreck!"

"I've been up and down to the bathroom and Rosy's kept me awake anyway, gasping for oxygen in that stupid tatami room that you keep all closed up. You're depriving them of oxygen by making them sleep in that shoe-box for the sake of the bloody Japanese culture. It's like a tomb in there in the morning, all shut up."

"Well, I don't want people climbing in the window at night ….and you swear too much and it was Anthony who was doing the snoring, not Rosy."

"I think Rosy's amazing the way she's had to fit in to all this change and cope with so much and don't forget she was quite ill last November. She's probably still not over it by the sound of her lungs."

"I tell you, it was Anthony. He's always been a snorer and children are adaptable. I mean, we were dragged *all over* the country at their age."

"If you mean our two years in Sydney, at least you were able to speak English there Rachel."

I thought how like her father she was in the mornings and it was *he* who insisted we go to Sydney for his career.

We went once more through the horrible routine of getting the children off to school. I said to Rosy "When I go back to Melbourne I will find a pretty dress for you. What colour would you like?

She scowled. "I don't want a dress. I want a kimono."

"But you've already got a red kimono."

"I want a kimono."

I was so glad to have the place to myself once they'd gone. Rachel had only one class that day at the school she was at and for the rest of the time she would be catching up on the adventures of Harry Potter. I was sure she'd cope.

The phone rang a little later and it was Rachel, sounding teary.

"I'm really worried about Rosy. I'm sorry about this morning, but I need my sleep and I didn't realize you were sick. I noticed this morning how thin Rosy has become. I'm really worried. What if there's something *seriously* wrong with her?"

"I'm sorry about this morning too. I just think she's been expected to cope with so much. She amazes me but it might all be a bit much for her you know. But then, she could have this tummy bug I've got. She did have a headache and a temperature when she was sent home last week."

"She wasn't sick last week."

"But she could have been. You forget how Anthony had very different beginnings to Rosy because he was your first."

"Well, I know he had me all to himself."

"...and Rosy's been expected to keep up with all of you ever since..." I continued carefully, "Going to a Buddhist kindergarten and then starting school in a foreign country and everything... with a different climate and nowhere near enough sleep either."

"Well, that's the way of life here. They can't believe that our kids were in bed at 7.30 pm in Australia."

I heard her voice beginning to break at the other end. "What if she's got something *seriously* wrong with her?"

"You'll be going home in less than four weeks now. Wait and get her checked out in Perth with her own doctor. You'll probably find she picks up once she gets back into familiar surroundings, although you'll be in a different house, a new house. Her grandparents are there, and she loves the beach and probably misses all that. She's not used to this humidity either. It would knock anyone. Perth is such a dry heat."

She started to cry.

"You seem to be very tired yourself Rachel - and I'm sorry I disturbed you this morning."

"I'd better go."

"OK. See you tonight. Try not to worry. I'm sure Rosy will be OK" and with that I picked up the Japanese phrase book and headed off down the street to the chemist's.

The woman at the counter spoke no English.

"*Kusuri*" (medicine)" I said while pointing to the line in my book in Kana that said "I've got diarrhoea." She understood the Kana and I didn't attempt to pronounce the Japanese "Geri *shit*eimasu" which amused me all the same.

She began to play charades indicating "Do you have a temperature or nausea or stomach pains?"

I nodded and shook my head from side to side appropriately. She handed me some tablets and held up two fingers in the peace sign. I hoped she was meaning two tablets. She looked concerned.

"My daughter...at school...teaching English....very good Japanese." She looked a bit more confident that I would understand the instructions and we bowed and I paid the girl waiting at the cash register and headed off again into the heat.

I felt lousy as the afternoon wore on and wondered if the tablets were making me woozy or clashing with the other medication I took. I had to get well before the weekend as it had been arranged that we were to go out with a group of Rachel's Japanese friends and they would be picking us up at 7 am on Sunday. I had to shake this off.

I got another call from Rachel, showing some concern for my health and then: "I'm beside myself with worry. I went down to the school in my lunch-hour to talk to Rosy's teacher. They weigh and check the children at regular intervals, so I got them to check the average weights on the Internet and she's only on the 5th percentile!"

Rachel arrived home later laden up with an assortment of extras for Rosy as the teacher said they would allow her to take additional food and as soon as Rosy arrived home Rachel began lecturing her on the importance of putting weight on.

"I wouldn't make it too much of an issue in front of her Rachel."

She said to me quietly "If I find out she's got something *seriously* wrong with her…I mean *really* serious, that would have been diagnosed if we'd been in Australia and not come to Japan...I'll...*I'll cut my wrists!*"

Megumi came in and Rachel burst into tears but Megumi comforted her with "the *right* kind of advice" as I was told later. Megumi had a "special rice" for my stomach too. I was to eat it with some seaweed. She'd also brought me some eggplant, tofu and green beans. I settled for the rice and seaweed.

I noticed she had painted her toenails.

Rosy was force-fed a dinner of hamburgers rice and seaweed washed down with "You're not going home looking like you've been in a refugee camp for twelve months." This and the subject of sleep went on as Rosy gulped her food tearily. We got her in to bed by 7 pm but Paul rang and Rachel, who was in the middle of reading a story to her, kept her waiting while Rosy sat, staring into space. Forty-five minutes later she was still pouring out her fears to Paul and itemizing every morsel of food that Rosy had eaten over the past twenty- four hours and what she actually should be eating in the future.

"You sound distant Paul. What's the matter?"

The house was full of kids, Anthony the loudest of all. He never stopped talking and yelling nonsense. Again I thought I had been blessed with two quiet little girls.

I went in to the "dressing-room" and curled up on the floor in the foetal position by the window to get some air and some quiet. There were noisy kids outside too but they weren't related to me. I was used to a silent empty house with two dogs and a cat. To put it mildly, this was a real trial.

2013

This morning the TV predicts 24 degrees again. After several wardrobe rehearsals I settle for black leggings, black short cotton dress and long olive cardigan over it which clashes with the red nose.

I enquire to the man at the desk (not as charming as at my other hotel but still helpful) seeing as I haven't been able to find a phone in my room, could I please send email via the computer I spied in the corner of the breakfast room. He makes hand-signals to indicate it is a bit "iffy" and I say "I need to make phone call and where can I find phone?"

"In your room Madame."

"I don't have phone in room."

"Yes, beside your bed."

"Well, I will go up and look *under* the bed and if not I will return." He laughs.

I looked under the bed. No sign of phone. Then, hidden behind the desk lamp – "*voila la phone!*"

It will be 4.30 pm in Melbourne. For some stupid reason I have not recorded the code for Australia. Now I have to go downstairs again. Hope he won't freak at my intention to call Oz.

And after all that I can only leave a message as there's no-one home, just the recording on their message machine. I forgot to leave them my room number here – damn. That will be a wasted overseas call I'll be charged for.

Opening the window I see my young Moroccan boy stacking fresh fruit and vegetables on his display stall.

TV weather says 24 tomorrow and 26 *Vendredi*.

Can't believe it – I'm trying to get CNN news and what comes on but *"La Jours de la Vivres."* Days of Our Lives! Where is "The Bold & the Beautiful" I wonder? I'm sneezing my head off. I won't be walking miles today. Wish someone would make me a cup of tea.

I take my laundry bag 100 yards down Boulevard de Murat to the *"Laverie."* A waste of time. Have phrase book out and cannot make head nor tail of bloody machines. There are about three rattling away in action but nobody around. I don't want a machine permanently devouring or cremating my clothes. Will have to wash what I can by hand and hope they have time to dry.

Turn TV on again as I can't stand silence and there's Bill, Hope, Brooke and "Stiffi," The B&B!! All *parlez en Francaise*. Damn it – just in time for the final scene of the long lingering stare.

I wash my blue jeans in bathroom basin. Well that makes three disappointments for the morning – failed phone call to Caroline, failed attempt at laundry and missed the "Bold and the Beautiful!" Will go and drown my sorrows in a *café crème*. I'm just going to have a day of rest now the cold has established itself. Wonder if Penny and Mark will come down with this too. Well, he's a doctor so I'm sure he'll be prepared and now I think of it, he did say he had a sore throat which led to that funny dream of his. I could blame him.

There is a panel show on TV. A beautiful woman and old bald man with "Mr Magoo"- type spectacles and a cobalt blue jacket. They discuss the merits of yoghurt. He has just dipped his finger in the yoghurt and put his finger in his mouth, leaving a glob of yoghurt on his lips. The hostess after an uncomfortable pause, attempts to wipe his lips with her finger but he continues to promote the benefits of yoghurt while dodging her hand. Now they discuss *jambon*. I think he is complaining about preservatives and the date on the packet of sliced pork. The word "polyphosphates" is being tossed around in the conversation. Now on to poultry and *"grande oeufs."* He obviously has a book out on these subjects. Now they turn to something lighter and not edible – a twenty-two year-old opera singer.

TV has gone mad and switched itself off. Time for coffee!

Back to "Le Cardinal" for *café crème*. Hard to know whether to sit at a smoker's table in the shade with my cold or at outside table behind the glass screen with the smokers. Too cool outside and I choose a table as far from the smokers as I can get.

Church bell clanging 10.00 am loudly and urgently, continues to ring for ten minutes.

My voice is croaky and deep as I ask for *"Un café crème s'il vous plait Madame."* I sound like an old out of work actress. Maybe I am.

"Un croissant?"

"Non - ce tu."

I'm thirsty – I drink the water she brings me. (In Melbourne, you are rarely given water with your coffee, automatically like they do in Paris.)

A man has come and sat just in front of me. After much shuffling through his bag he produces his cigarettes and I watch the smoke rising above his bald patch. The coffee is good. A woman passes by with a Chihuahua and the tiniest terrier on leads.

Ridge was in the B&B scenes on the TV this morning. He was written out of the series months ago. Are they months behind us in France, or does he return?

Taxis are banked up three abreast again. Won't be hard to find one next Tuesday to take me to the airport.

I feel like I'm settling here at St Cloud. It is still Paris after all as Claude said. I am no longer feeling threatened with the unfamiliarity of it all or isolated, (or so I tell myself.) It is just an extended area of Paris, now I have found the Metro gets me anywhere in central

Paris that I want to go to. I have no intention of walking miles today and am content just to sit here.

11 am as church bells ring out. I settle down into my chair in the corner of "Le Cardinal." My eyes are watering. I blow my nose and empty the last of the bottled water.

A squad of pigeons drinks from the gutter outside. A jogger runs past, a cyclist and women with shopping bags and women pushing double pushers. It's Wednesday and the half-day at school for most children and several kids walk and ride scooters beside Mums and occasional Dads. A lot of taxis have dispersed only to be replaced by more just as quickly. A driver walks in, adjusting the belt on his trousers. He'll grab a *cafe noir* no doubt. Bread sticks pass by again and again, leaning out of shopping bags.

The bell chimes the quarter hour. I reach for one of the many serviettes in my bag that I have souvenired for handkerchiefs. My eyes swim behind my dark glasses. Mr Baldpatch is enjoying his third cigarette. The other smoker is engrossed in his Smartphone. A dark-skinned woman, slim with perfectly braided raven-black hair sits down with a cigarette and answers her phone. She wears black off-the-shoulder top with her jeans.

The sun is out and the sky is blue and Mr Baldpatch picks up his phone and his Marlboros, puts on his jacket and leaves. I wonder if the dark-skinned women pushing children in strollers are nannies. It's hard to tell as the children look dark-skinned too.

The waitress who served me my *salade Nicoise* yesterday has arrived for work and I feel more at home.

"Bonjour Madame." I am happy in my little corner.

The boyfriend has joined the raven-haired woman. She has draped a scarf of terra cotta shades around her shoulders. He doesn't smoke.

Several children walk past. A boy about eight years struggles with the breadstick he carries, tearing off a chunk and cramming it in to his already full mouth. His sister strides ahead, blonde curls bouncing, one arm attached to Mum, the other laden with baguettes.

The bell chimes the half hour.

11.30. A man at outside table reads Arabic, or is it a Turkish paper, which is rested on his enormous stomach. His wife looks Jewish. I hear her address him in French. The headlines depict the Stars and Stripes with a bold caption in Arabic or maybe Turkish. I wonder what that's about.

The fish section of the café is opening for lunch. There is a mural of oysters in shells covering the wall behind the fishmonger. He rips a red rag up into four pieces.

A lot of mothers and kids outside could easily be arriving at any Melbourne Primary School by the way they dress – sweaters tied around waists, jeans and sneakers and T-shirts. Many of them pushing prams.

The clock chimes another quarter hour.

Oysters are shovelled in to plastic bags along with a joke shared with the customer.

The middle-aged Parisienne women here are well-dressed and skinny (like me – the skinny bit anyway). One older woman with a dog on lead wears ocelot pants, orange top, scarf and sneakers to match. Smart, but a bit loud for me maybe.

Just noticed a McDonald's facing me two streets away.

A very merry waiter arrives to do his "watch" greeting everyone with "*Ca va?*" He asks me turning on his heel, a tray in his hand "Is it paid?"

"*Oui.*"

The clock strikes midi. Much clanging of bells! I leave to wander.

There is a Portuguese *Boulangerie* called "Eugènie's." There are several hair salons in the area and chemists and fruiterers/small markets where I was able to get packet of tissues for 50c. Took a couple of photos of flower shop and "Le Cardinal" Restaurant. Walked back again. It's actually a very nice suburb.

Back to "Le Cardinal." Asked for "*table pour un*" and "*Ou est la toilette?*"

Tables full of smart-looking businessmen. Four of them at next table pass around a small bottle of hand disinfectant. The bread arrives – beautiful and with it a dish of olives. I order "*oefs et mayo.*" They arrive and my olives are whisked away. Damn.

I noted on my wanderings a No. 72 bus goes to Hotel de Ville at about 12.15, right opposite my hotel.

The meal is delicious. Two organic eggs on a bed of "white greens" in mayonnaise and a mustard-based dressing on top.

I am suddenly aware that my nail polish is looking worn as I hold my wine glass. Searched high and low for my nail polish this morning and it's disappeared. Memories of Japan.

Some good looking men walking around here today. The baguettes are all so viciously crusty I will be lucky to avoid dental extractions. I'm trying to keep water and *Bordeaux* going with each timid bite. No sign of the *petite chien* yet. The waitresses walk rapidly back and forth. They fly by so efficiently. My plate is empty, but for extra hard crusts and is whisked away as I comment "*superb!*" She was pleased. "*Je voudrais un cappuccino s'il vous plait.*"

1.30. What am I to do with remainder of day? I am enjoying my rest here. Some extra time over the coffee. Eyes swimming again. Trying hard not to sneeze. My cappuccino arrives in tall glass. That's new. I mean a *really* tall glass with four very sweet biscuits and it's not hot. Maybe it's classified as a dessert.

My money pouch has worked its way up under my clothes making me look very well endowed. Pity I'm not naturally that way.

"L'addition s'il vous plait!"

Back in my room and sneezing, sneezing. My room is not made up and only one towel. I'll be resting for the remainder of the day to try and get on top of this damn cold. TV doesn't want to come on of course.

Today is September 25th. My maternal grandmother's birthday. She would have been 145.

African cleaner has done my room, providing new box of tissues (like gold) and will return with towels hopefully.

Tomorrow, if feeling better: No. 9 train to Marie de Montrieul, go eight stations to Trocadero and change to No. 6 train. Then travel three stations to Charles de Gaulle-Etoile. I'll have coffee and walk on to Arc de Triomphe and back down Champ Elysees to Tuileries for lunch. Then I'll walk back to Franklin D. Roosevelt Metro on Champs Elysees and get No. 9 train. My destination being Pont de Sevres. Go eleven stations to Porte de St Cloud. I've got it sorted.

I washed my blue jeans out earlier and they are now hanging on the handle of an open window. Hopefully they'll dry over the next six days. The noise outside is the usual chaos and there is a movie on TV which is set in Paris. I don't know whether the police siren is on TV or in street below.

4.30. I'm still sneezing. TV on and Gerard Depardieu is absurd! He has red hair in plaits and a Viking helmet and a sort of Tweedledum Tweedledee striped strapless outfit with his fat chest and bare back hanging over it. Totally insane but totally French. (Still sneezing!) Roman soldier picks up a pigeon and holds it to his ear like a phone *"Ello Ello!!"* The pigeon is dead and limp so he slams it down again.

This has actually entertained me for an hour or so and I laugh at the pigeon and a Miss McIntosh speaking French like all foreigners *"Mersee Bow Koo."* She gives long tirades of this "tourist-French" and I can relate to this - *"tray bee yen."* From Vikings to Roman soldiers. It's now become a soccer game. The soccer ball lands on a Viking ship. The Roman soldiers arrive. Catherine Deneuve appears wearing at one moment a tartan cape and tartan crown. Now she wears the British flag! I don't know what this film is called but it seems more like one of my disjointed dreams than a movie.

6.15. Dinner tonight was very sweet black grapes, banana and a kiwi fruit.

Now in bed and still sneezing!

I wake in the early hours from a dream from which I am crying and in a sweat. I lie there recalling 12 months ago when I occupied a bed in the Emergency Room of a public Hospital back home, Caroline standing at my side. I felt the insertion of something in to the right side of my neck above the collar-bone which stung. The young woman doctor said something to her male colleague standing behind my semi-conscious body. They didn't think I could hear them obviously. I heard him say "I don't really think it's wise to go in to the jugular – take it out and go in to the groin!" He turned to Caroline and said "You'd better leave. This can be difficult." Caroline told me later that he looked so young, longish hair and dressed in jeans and a jacket as though he'd just come from the pub! She returned later to me lying on a pillow saturated in blood. This time had been like a nightmare for me. After every test and antibiotic and antiviral known to science I was released nine days later still none the wiser about what had given me "blood poisoning." They covered every possibility "Could have been picked up on the streets of Paris" two months earlier when I was painting with Claude and the crew of fifteen internationals – or in my garden. I was certainly questioned on my intimate relations while in Paris of which I'd had *none* or "have you been taking recreational drugs? Be honest now."

Well, I thought through the fog, not since that first and last time I puffed a few times on something that was handed around in the group I was with and spent the rest of the evening in the washroom, unable to do anything but stare at the grubby ceiling hoping I might die - and that was thirty-odd years ago.

"No, certainly not!" I answered.

"You may have just picked it up walking down the street when you returned home" I was told. I was discharged with "*sepsis of unknown aetiology.*"

Now I lie in my damp sheets feeling a little insecure. This *is* just a cold isn't it?

Tuesday morning the 29th of June 2004 and it is Levi's first birthday and I'm trying to email Carrie in Melbourne but I can't get through. Then the phone rang. It was Rachel. The school had rung her.

"Rosy has swimming today. Do you think you could find your way to the school with her swimming gear? She didn't take it. You've got to be there before 8.30."

I left the computer and rushed to the school realizing I didn't have my inside shoes with me and hoped bare feet would not be too informal at school. I pattered down the corridor and found the room marked "1-1." Rosy's teacher didn't have a toothbrush in her mouth but she bowed, looking decidedly irritated and she asked Rosy to translate for us. I bowed back.

"You have to give permission for me to swim" scowled Rosy.

"Yes. Yes." I said to her teacher, nodding and bowing and scooting away again.

Once back at the flat, I began writing some postcards and had another try at emailing Carrie again. I left a message wishing Levi a happy birthday and told

Carrie briefly about our trip to Tokyo, but didn't mention Rachel's worries about Rosy. I said I really wished we could get on to the chat line together but I didn't know how to do it. I so needed to talk to her.

I returned to my postcards, all photos of Tokyo. I checked for a reply from Carrie a couple of times but there was nothing. On the third try she popped onto the screen to chat.

"How amazing! We got on at the same time" she said.

She was able to let me see Levi via the camera as he tottered around all rugged up in winter clothing in the study.

"Why is he dressed in all that?" The sweat was trickling like wandering flies down my legs and my back.

"It's the middle of winter here remember Mum. Oh, and Jamie's father gave him an old guitar to play with and he adores it and strums it all the time."

"You know who'll be giving him lessons soon then."

"No he won't. I used to beg Dad to give me lessons and he wouldn't."

"I didn't realize you wanted to play guitar. Oh well, you had piano lessons for years and you've got Nanny's beautiful old piano now. Who needs a guitar?"

"I *hated* piano lessons with that terrifying Mrs Sargent."

And at the mention of "guitars and trickling" - I thought back to when Carrie was only a toddler and together with Rachel, we accompanied Ed on a trip to the country for a gig. He and I still laugh about it. It began with a stop at Channel 7 where he was doing a number on the Telethon for the Children's Hospital Good Friday Appeal first. Patiently, we three sat in the car-park for an hour surrounded by all the paraphernalia one took along on trips with small children. We were "lucky to be included" on this trip.

We arrived at the motel in time for Ed to have a quick nap before going up to the restaurant for band rehearsal. It was a very hot day. I thought I was being helpful and picked up the shirt he had taken off and thrown down, putting it in the bathroom basin to soak.

He jumped up, looking at his watch and said "Where's my shirt? I have to go to band rehearsal! No I'm not wearing bloody sequins to rehearsal" as I hurriedly thrust his fancy shirt at him.

"I'll have to iron it dry then" I gulped, edging towards the bathroom. "I'll go up to Reception and borrow an iron."

"There's no time for that. I'll have to wear it wet!"

He stormed out the door, buttoning the shirt up as he went. It was indeed very wet, sopping wet and dripping in fact.

"It's quite warm out there. No-one will notice, Ed."

He burst back in an hour later. "No-one will notice eh? There were three women waiting at reception with autograph books. It was bloody embarrassing to be signing an autograph book, having water trickling down the fucking pen and making big blue puddles on the fucking page."

I couldn't stifle my laughter. At this point his sense of humour won too and he took the wet shirt off and threw it at me, angry but grinning "….and it's nearly dry now, silly – *bloomin'* woman."

At twenty my folk-singing love and I believed we had rescued each other. Now, decades later, we call each other up on our birthdays and apologize yet again for our failure to do so. Then we share the latest on the wonderful achievements of our daughters.

I thought of poor Ed's back and the old player piano we had bought for Rachel when she was five years old. She had given it away to a friend in Perth before leaving for Japan which I was sad to learn. She had wanted "a better piece of furniture, a good piano" to go in their new house in Perth and had no memory of the fact that Ed had nearly broken his back moving it out to the furniture van we had hired to move to Sydney all those years ago. This had been so she could continue her lessons and I was "not moving to Sydney without it." We'd bought it second-hand in the music store and paid it off. It had signs of earlier wood-worm but the gold lettering said "Made in New York" and that was enough for me to believe it was the most precious thing we owned, and it was, apart from Ed's back which was never quite the same again.

This afternoon Rachel was on her way to the doctors down the road because Anthony had what I believed was heat rash. I didn't dare bring up the subject of *rabbits' revenge* again. Megumi had intercepted them and insisted she would call Miko and then she would drive them to a "better doctor" in the next town. I didn't know why she would think he needed "specialist" treatment. Anyway, Miko got lost in the next town and by the time they reached the doctor's he had left for the day, so they had to come back again to the doctor just down the street from home. On the way back to the apartment Miko saw a friend with her kids who went to school with Anthony and she wound down the window and screamed out across the street in Japanese "I've taken Rachel and Anthony to see the doctor. Anthony has a rash… ON HIS BOTTOM!"

"That's how they are here" said Rachel as Anthony stormed in past me scowling fiercely. "They don't seem to have heard of discretion."

"But they are all so kind and they mean well." I reminded her. Rachel began preparing another huge meal for Rosy who was sitting quietly but wide-eyed, obviously planning her best line of stony resistance. Miko and her daughter, Megumi and her three boys,

Anthony, Maddie-Rose, Rachel and myself were crowded into the tiny apartment and Rachel was cooking ginger pork with the aid of Megumi who was giving instructions, pouring iced lemon tea for all of us and rushing back and forth to her flat, setting me up with a choice of various dinners to choose from. I was sticking to just rice and seaweed with a piece of tofu.

Anthony's rash thankfully turned out to be "just heat rash."
After they all left Rachel began discussing with me Rosy's "anorexic" condition and seemed willing to hear my opinions. She had never really asked for my advice before. It looked like we were gaining ground in our relationship and I felt a bit more confident that things might be progressing between us.

2013 – Paris

After my continental breakfast and two cups of tea plus the polite greetings of *"Bonjour Madame"* and *"Au revoir"* of the older immaculately dressed Parisian businessmen who shared the dining-room with me this morning, I feel quite a bit better.

Back in my room there is the sound of a little girl sobbing on the street. I open the window to see three number 72 buses draw up and she and her mother no doubt are on one of them going in the direction of Hotel de Ville.

9.00 am - "The Days of Our Lives" returns. I think the characters I watched forty-six years ago when I was pregnant with Rachel are most likely dead and gone. People still thrive on tragedy, with multiple weddings to the same person, mystery pregnancies and intriguing unfulfilled romances. It's nearly as absurd as the farce I watched last night with Gerard Depardieu.

Now it's *"Amoir Gloire et Beaute"* – The B & B with "Stiffy." They are about a year behind Australia with their episodes.

I didn't realize there were so many exits and entrances to each Metro. It's very confusing. I had to ask for help again at the ticket machine. I got stuck, but *"Excuse moi Madame,"* got me the help I needed.

A young woman gets on the train with a huge parcel, mostly hidden by green garbage bag all taped up. Gradually a plump leg escapes and what emerges is an inflatable woman. Eek!

St Cloud is well placed as a residential area really, only eight stations which pass so quickly, to the Eiffel Tower.

I'm now sitting in Place du Trocadero, facing the Eiffel Tower in Le Malahoff café. I am wearing my black and grey striped dress with black cardigan over it, and don't know whether I feel happy about my appearance or not and black high heels. My cold is drying up a little. Coffee here is six euros!

The noise is incredible! The clothing is varied. The older Parisians as usual, stand out in the crowd with that certain elegance and quality. The sun is trying to break through the smog, or is it just the usual early grey skies of a Paris autumn?

Some of the street crossings here don't have any lights and you take your life in your hands crossing the roads.

I am almost feeling dizzy watching the circular stream of traffic. Red double-decker tourist buses full of gaping faces whiz by. This is *their* Paris experience. A bus with a promo photo of Naomi Watts as Diana on its behind passes. This is a controversial subject here I think, from what I could gather from TV this morning. Although she is beautiful, I don't think she represents Princess Diana nor does she do much in that role for a lot of Parisians it would seem.

It's just after 11 am and I'm sipping my tap water. I wonder where Brad Pitt and Angelina are right now.

King Charles spaniels seem popular in Paris. I put my legs to one side for some red patent flats to sit beside me. She looks Spanish. Her partner with spectacles and silver hair, looks a lot older and doesn't sound French and he is all over her. He seems to have a problem with the waiter. He kisses the woman as if to leave and walks off. I'm curious.

A man with a beagle on lead trots past. The affectionate boyfriend returns with a bag of croissants and his companion sips her orange juice and stirs her café noir. They speak in English with a strong accent. Evidently the waiter refused to serve them croissants at 11.15 in the morning and he has picked them up elsewhere. The boyfriend is saying "I think *seexty* to seventy percent *ees* good. One hundred percent *very good!*" He fondles her shoulders, his arms around her. Is he discussing her body, or the croissants or some international intrigue? A police siren wails and they giggle together.

My waiter is handsome. He takes the money from me *"Merci, merci."* I squeeze past the red patent flats and brave the two crossings without lights, almost tripping to keep up with the other brave tourists who cross. Large shiny limousines wait patiently for me. I am curling my toes to hang on to my shoes which have become suddenly very loose and I almost jump out of them. I didn't dress for this. I had intended to go to the Arc de Triomphe but settled for Trocadero, the ticket machine deciding my choice of destination.

I hobble past the Institute of Architecture, where I was with Claude last week, which now seems like weeks ago, and dodge the Africans offering hideous black miniature Eiffel Towers for one euro.

I have found a quiet seat amongst the pigeons on the Parc de Champ de Mars, the carousel and the Eiffel Tower on my right – the spot where I photographed a wedding party eleven years ago, the bride in white and the groom in powder blue. I wonder where they are now and if they are still married. Was it all they had hoped it would be?

I can see the dome of Invalides where Napoleon lies entombed and there is just a background roar of traffic. I don't think I could live in Paris now. I am disappointed with my feelings. Last year I returned to Melbourne hell-bent on making Paris my home. But I am finding Paris "done to death." The constant wildebeest migration is what gets to me. Could I cope with them every day? Am I coming down with *"Paris Syndrome"* the disease of the disillusioned?

I watch the lift descend the Tower and sky-writers scribble on the pearly faded sky above it. There is a mist everywhere, probably fumes I think, and the sun is trying its hardest to break through it. Children's voices are happy and shrill as they play on the climbing equipment in the park behind me. Lime yellow open tour buses crawl past the Tower and a persistent police siren drowns the children's voices out. Those police sirens are *really* the "sound of Paris."

I walk down to the merry-go-round/carousel, as it churns out typical old Parisian music. I feel fearful that those days might be gone. Is that the yesterday sound of Paris? Piaf's Paris?

An alarm goes off and the merry-go-round grinds in to action again – white horses, black horses, an old aeroplane, huge sea- shells, a big balloon and a rotating cup containing two hysterical teenagers.

It has gone 12 noon and I am waiting for bells or chimes but there is no sound of my favourite Parisian time-keeper, or are they drowned out by the continuous background roar of traffic and the worn-out carousel music playing "Tea for two."

I am now sitting almost under the Eiffel Tower. I have been interrupted by a strange little Frenchman jabbering at me – quite well-dressed so I don't think he is begging – maybe chatting me up with his pleading and smiling tones. I don't wait to find out. With a brisk *"Je n'comprehend Francaise"* I get up and quickly go on my way. He reminds me of the man who wanted to take me in to the countryside in Amsterdam and prove I was a witch twenty years ago. No thank you! History has shown that they burn witches here – no questions asked.

I see a bit of graffiti on a wall across the river in big red letters that just says "LOVE ME." That seems poignant and I stop in my tracks to absorb it as it speaks to me and I photograph it. A piano accordionist approaches and I take a picture of him, and his friend suggests he takes a photo of the musician and me together, with my camera.

I try to get a shot of the naked group in the relief sculpture, men and women laden with grapes, but can't get close enough. I really need to walk across the grass but I don't want a scene with the gendarmes.

Sit down on seat to eat the *crepe* I've bought. An African still tries to sell me a horrible Eiffel Tower. Do they really sell those? He can afford a phone so he must sell some. I throw a little bit of *crepe* to a pigeon and when I look up the same guy is looking miserably at me which I read as "You can give to the flying rats but you can't give to a poor African." I feel a pang of guilt. He's still hanging around.

My *crepe fromage* finished, I put a dash of lipstick on and am away. I need a cappuccino.

On the top level of Trocadero many more souvenir sellers converge on the stairs and then a policeman and a policewoman of the same race swiftly arrive on bikes and disperse the group who are beginning to appear a bit overwhelming to the tourists.

The cafes are packed. It is after all 1.30 pm, lunchtime. I find Café Kleber.

"Bonjour Madame!"

"Un cappuccino Monsier s'il vous plait."

"Oui Madame."

Six euros 90. Ouch! Wonder if Brad and Ange come here.

"Ou est la toilette?"

He points. One thing about Paris, there's always a toilet. I remember before I came with last year's group of painters, painting on the streets, I shuddered to think about the availability of toileting facilities. But every place you go for a coffee you can use the facilities, although it did just cross my mind, are there any hidden cameras? No, I think that happens in Melbourne not Paris. There are public cubicles on the street every so often of course, but I am too shy I think, to be seen walking into one. Or am I afraid I might lock myself in and how embarrassing that would be?

I am now resting on a seat in Avenue Kleber. There is a French couple beside me arguing hotly. She's wearing a Prussian blue top and looks Middle Eastern. Again he is a much older Parisian. Maybe she's his mistress. There is a line-up of motorbikes beside me, a red Ducati among them just like Caroline's husband rides. A lot of cigarette smoke. The sun is still having trouble penetrating the atmosphere. I don't want to go back to St Cloud yet. It's only 1.45 pm.

A motorbike roars off across the cobblestones in Place du Trocadero. The couple who were arguing rise. She towers over him. They walk to the Caretti Patisserie, but not satisfied with what the menu outside offers, go next door to Le Malahoff where I began my day. A very stylish young woman flies past on her motor bike.

Lucky I have my journal to talk to, isn't it?

A Police van pulls up. *"Prefecture de Police."* A sightseer's bus passes followed by a fire truck with its siren screaming. The flap of pigeon wings.

Two policewomen stand taking down notes of number plates of the parked cars right in front of me. Oh, the little red car has a ticket. So does the beige car, so does the black car. Stickers on windows and pink sheets and green slips. My face begins to burn in the sun. It's made it through finally at 2 pm.

A white-haired man in a red T-shirt has just returned to his car and a parking ticket. Was that extra drink with his mistress worth it? Another sporty red car gets booked. Two young girls return to first little red car. *Ahhh mon dieu!* She peels the sticker off and they discuss together the ticket under the windscreen wipers with alarmed faces - That's a nice end to *"dejeuner avec mon ami."* Then laughter and the tearing of tickets into many pieces. They *"au revoir"* each other with kisses and she backs out and drives away rather recklessly and the pink and green squares of paper fly away beneath her like a million butterflies.

"Excuse me Madame. How can I get to the Eiffel Tower?"

Someone is asking me! And in English! I point "there - crossing - crossing" and wave towards Trocadero. He smiles broadly.

"Thank you Madame – thank you."

A young woman flies out of the Caretti Patisserie to her parked car, horror on her face. Further horrors, the clampers have arrived. The little beige car is about to be towed away. A clamper in iridescent green worker's top and I exchange grimaces. Then he laughs and gabbles something in French to me as an explanation. I say and shrug *"Je n'comprehend Francaise."* His colleague also in iridescent green turns in my direction, giving me a suspicious glance and indicates me to his friend. I have been caught writing furiously and I think they suspect me of making a report. Better watch out or they may confiscate my best and only friend – my journal!

A young businessman has been watching with a look of fear on his face and not responding to my shrug of sympathy towards him. He makes a call on his phone and then disappears down the steps of Metro Trocadero which is right behind us. I suspect it is his car about to be towed away or maybe his boss's. Three young men pull up in a black Ferrari. They park it right on the spot where the beige car was and stroll into Café Kleber. I cannot watch! But someone has put them wise. They return at a run, back out and roar away.

I'm going home to my Moroccan *fruiterie* in Port de St Cloud and the quiet life.

I buy my *pomme rouge, poir* and *banan* and *eau minerale* and apologize for the 50 euro note.

"It does not matter *Madame*." No, we're old friends now.

The receptionist at the hotel gives me the key to 24 instead of 34 and after struggling with the lock in the dark hallway for some time I realize it is not the right key. Down again in the lift. *"Excuse moi Madame – je voudrais trente quatre,* not *vingt quatre."*

I have interrupted her interview with a charming black businessman in a beautiful pale suit who lounges comfortably in a Louis XV style chair, and he nods and smiles broadly at me. *"Bonjour Madame."*

"Bonjour Monsieur." I go up in the lift again.

I look like a more-than-middle-aged woman with a cold, not to mention the chipped tooth when I look in the mirror. How depressing! I kick my shoes off. Then

I pick them up again almost apologetically, stroke them with affection and say aloud "You have been very good shoes today. Very good – *tres bien* – trrraah trrraah trraah *be yen*, but I think you've had it."

I realize I miss my dogs. I'll have to take my shoes home though. Can't bear to abandon them to a Paris rubbish dump. I miss my dogs!

It's 7 pm and an alarm keeps going off outside. I hope it's not a fire alarm because I'm in my pjs and they're not flash enough to be out on Paris streets in, even the *suburban* streets of Porte de St Cloud.

2004 – Lavender Blue, Dilly Dilly.

"Mum. You're not pulling your weight!"

I was in trouble again and Rachel was yelling at the children for not getting ready for school and not eating their breakfast fast enough and Anthony was mucking around taking his temperature over and over and coming up with 67 degrees which he had written on his card for swimming.

I had dreamt last night that Ed was moving in with Caroline and Jamie back in Melbourne. I was helping him move house and loading up his car with basketloads of Rachel's washing together with English-language comics for Anthony and branches of an ornamental Japanese tree that protruded out the windows, and finally a Belgian Shepherd dog that I'd found that needed a home. My subconscious was frantically trying to pursue order in my life and that of those around me.

"Has anyone seen my nail polish?"

Rachel disappeared for a minute or two and then reappeared dragging a huge black plastic bag full of rubbish behind her. She struggled down the street with it. I wondered what on earth she was doing dragging the rubbish off down the street. When she came back inside puffing and panting I said "If you had told me where and when the rubbish went out I'd have put it out for you. Why did you take it down the street anyway? I could have helped you. And I thought you said the rubbish was Anthony's job."

"Well it *is* Anthony's job. The burnable rubbish goes out on Wednesdays and Saturdays and it *has* to be out before 8.30 am and you *have* to take it to the park. It *has* to go under the big nets and it *can't* go out the night before because the crows get into it. *That's* what the nets are for" she hyperventilated at me, "and how can I rely on *Anthony* to do it?"

She felt guilty she said, as the kids ran off to join the straggling line of children walking to school, because she'd been yelling at them and she was *"never* like this when Paul was here."

So the children's behaviour and Rachel's anger was my fault.

"He was able to put the futons away and I know you can't lift them and the children carry on so much *because* you're here."

"Maybe you should have got Hugh Grant's mother to come and stay here. She knows them better than I do and you know how she is when it comes to housekeeping, particularly yours," and I closed myself in the tiny bathroom, ending our conversation.

When they'd all gone I turned the computer on. It was now 10.30 and I left it to make a cup of tea. I heard a sound and came back and Carrie came on line. What timing!

"Hi. How are you? It's me again."

"I've been a bit sick but I'm feeling better now thank goodness."

She was going to the doctors herself with tonsillitis that day. Levi's laughing face appeared on the screen up close.

"Gorgeous boy" I wrote, wanting to hang on to them both. I briefed her on Rosy's weight problem and I heard the psychologist coming through.

"She shouldn't be *force*-fed. They need to get to the bottom of the problem of why she doesn't *want* to eat."

I wondered if "women in cess-pits in Colombo" or a "stint on the ol' training ship" would work better than psychology as it had worked for me.

"And talking of *bottoms*...." laughingly I related Anthony's rash incident."

Our chat was interrupted by Levi switching off the computer twice and *he* eventually ended our call, but it was nice just to reach out to them for a few minutes.

When Rosy came home from school I gave her some afternoon tea as her mother had rung and told me not to forget and make sure she ate it all. Then I suggested some water-colour painting and we rearranged the dolls-house furniture after she tired of that. Her mother arrived to a big welcome and hugs and we all sat down to watch Rosy's favourite TV show.

Anthony arrived "starving" and cheeky as usual, referring to me as "the *old pumpkin* ....Just joking Nan."

An English children's show began with the theme song being "Lavender Blue Dilly Dilly."

Do you remember when we used to sing that Mum?"

"Yes, and I used to sing along with that on the radio when I was younger than you Rosy, way back in the days when children didn't have television." I thought back.

When I was Rosy's age the only form of entertainment for pre-schoolers was Kindergarten of the Air on the ABC, the characters on "Sesame Street" not yet invented and the members of "The Wiggles" not having yet been conceived, but I had a preference for the ABC classical music program that preceded it anyway, and would dance until I fell in a heap, seeing myself transported off into the clouds by a prince on a snow white horse to the strains of Tchaikovsky.

Bruce was at school all day then and I think he only valued me as ballast for his billy-cart on the weekends as we roared down the street racing the Johnston kids.

He'd scare me with stories of two mysterious wandering characters, "Dirty Dick," who wore an old army coat and a handkerchief tied around his head, the uniform of a homeless and broken post-war man of the late 1940s and a slovenly woman whom Bruce referred to as "Metho Mary" his alcoholic "partner." The thought of meeting them on the street kept me behind the front gate for a while and then they suddenly disappeared.

We lived with our grandparents then and I'd sit on my grandfather's knee each night while he puffed away on his pipe in a soothing popping sort of a rhythm and made up stories about the black and white print on the wall titled "The Warning." The story he had built around it was always interrupted by the continual tamping down of his tobacco, then the re-lighting process would begin again after half a dozen matches had been struck. But I didn't show my impatience as this was all part of our ritual. I waited, staring into the glowing red of the crumbling briquettes in the fireplace, for him to begin once more the story of the 18th Century soldier on the white horse who was "Dad" and "Mum and Bruce and me" his brave but frightened family, warning him of impending danger.

My grandfather had a Scottish background and a fiery temper when roused which I never witnessed and the only curse I ever heard him utter was "Lord bless the Duke of Argyle!"

He had a habit which irritated my father immensely, especially when I attempted it once unsuccessfully, and that was to empty some of his scalding black tea from the cup onto the saucer where he would blow on it to cool it and sip quietly. I would watch fascinated. He was passionate about his garden, his chooks and his Collingwood football team. Sundays I would wake to the sound of him polishing all the brass door-knobs throughout the house before he toddled off to church alone in his best clothes; alone because my grandmother "Didn't like crowds." Sometimes I'd accompany him and marvel at his deep baritone voice and the rough but gentle hand that held mine.

My grandmother, the youngest of six had been born and raised on the goldfields of Warrandyte, home of the first gold discovery in Victoria. Her eldest brother born in 1858 was named Warrandyte. She was a gentlewoman who produced the most wonderful Christmases and brewed the best home-made ginger-beer. She would let me help her plant pumpkins, collect warm eggs from under the chickens, and never showed her dismay at my nearly stripping the apricot tree of its green fruit to play shops, with Timmy her cat as my only customer. Her distant memories of life on the goldfields were intermingled with the folklore and superstitions that grew out of them and she had a great fear of bushfires, but they shared an aura of quiet contentment and security around the pair. If only one could go back. The only real treasures I possess in my home sixty-five years later are the two beautifully carved Edwardian chairs they used to sit in, one which held my Pop and me, and where the tales from "The Warning" were kindled.

There was no kindergarten because Mum wanted me at home with her and in the mornings I'd sit on the front step in the hot sun, pressing the irresistible blisters of dark brown paint that swelled from the old timber door surrounds in the rising heat. I would be in wait for the baker's horse as it sauntered down the street that ran beside Darebin station, delivering fresh hot bread in a cart reminiscent of something associated with gypsies. The horse wasn't silver. It was brown and the baker didn't look like a prince as he ran in with a basket of shiny loaves, giving me a little salute as he passed, but it was magic.

I was seven years old when we moved away from my Nan and Pop to East Ivanhoe, a leafy eastern suburb of Melbourne where there was a street full of kids around my age. In the 1950's Penny and I and the gang held our own form of the '56 Olympics as a precursor to the Games in Melbourne. We would, in relay, sprint around the streets with her Dad's mechanic's torch held high, the lead still attached. We occasionally attempted to sell milk bottles of water and rose petals from door to door, with me as the creator and Penny enthusiastically taking the role of saleswoman. But our main occupation was cowboys and Indians all weekend on a vacant but prime piece of real estate in Outlook Drive, lovingly referred to by us as "Deadman's Canyon."

Friday night was the night Dad, Mum, Bruce and I went to the "pictures" and Dad's choice of entertainment was always westerns starring John Wayne, Rory Calhoun or Audie Murphy. My main creative outlet then was to direct a re-make of whatever I'd seen the night before and that became the weekend's theme for our little neighbourhood gang. In those days kids could disappear to the banks of the Yarra River unsupervised for the entire day, safely, climbing onto horses' backs over fences and returning home only when hunger eventually set in. I have often wondered what a different direction my life might have taken if Dad had taken us to the opera or the ballet on Friday nights.

"Lavender Blue Dilly Dilly ended and Rosy ran off to the dressing room and came out again dressed in her lavender fairy dress with wings. After some photos that pleased her no end she flitted off outside and then we heard a shriek, followed by:

"The stag beetle's escaped!"

Anthony pounced on him and returned him to his isolation ward.

"Thank goodness you found him or I wouldn't have been able to sleep tonight, seeing as his box is on the doorstep right outside my bed" I emphasized sternly.

It was decided that the poor stag beetle should be re-settled. He'd been in detention for days and Rachel and the two kids, with Rosy still wearing her fairy dress, walked off to the shrine for a suitable ceremony together under the maple trees. The little Westerner in her fairy dress evidently caused traffic to stop along the road and brought old ladies out of shops to gasp in Japanese "Oh how cute!"

Rosy was beaming as she stumbled back into the apartment, flushed and panting with her performance. Anthony's only comment to me as he burst back in the door was "*That* wasn't *my* stag beetle. *That* was a different one. Maybe that one ate mine." I would check my sleeping area thoroughly before going to bed.

Anthony and I had been laughing at dinner, re-living the story that always made me almost hysterical and the children too, of Paul and his last birthday present for Rachel. It was a very special blue and white bone china jar that he'd spent ages choosing and while walking back to the car, tripped and smashed into a million pieces on the pavement. It was more Anthony's hilarious athletic rendition of it that broke me up. He enjoyed being the comedian and actor in one. He mimicked beautifully the over-zealous bowling action of his overly tall father who, as he tripped on the gutter and brought the plastic shopping-bag containing the carefully gift-wrapped jar, shattering to the pavement. He achieved this with a circular arm motion that would have put any test cricketer to shame. Paul then spun around at Anthony who was trailing several metres behind him and roared:

"NOW SEE WHAT YOU MADE ME DO!"

I think this began Rachel's interest in collecting broken bits of blue and white china. This accident had given her a head start with her new hobby.

Anthony has the same sense of the ridiculous as I have and we seem to laugh quite out of control at the same absurdities. At that time he delighted in reenacting this incident for me over and over again, highly amused at his grandmother's response. But the mood for the evening changed again after his third trip to the toilet where he unraveled a whole roll of toilet paper around and across the apartment. We tried in vain to calm him down and get him to finally retire for the night, sending him off to get dressed for bed. Eventually he appeared once more, now stark naked, storming out of the dressing room and standing facing me, arms akimbo with the attitude of a Japanese warrior. All that was missing was a samurai sword at his side.

"Ever since you've been here I can't find anything on the chest of drawers for *ALL YOUR MAKE-UP!*"

It was obviously me he was addressing and I entered the tiny room shaking my head disbelievingly at his cheek.

"*What* do you mean, *all my makeup?* I've hardly got any." The top of the chest was covered in school-bags, books, papers, balloons, toys, a half-eaten banana, his dirty socks and one small bottle of nail varnish. This was the extent of my makeup.

"I've been looking for that" I said swooping on it. "And gosh, you're rude and ill-mannered Anthony" I added.

"Apologize to Nanny." And as he ran past me.
"*Sorry.*"

"That's not good enough. Come back here and apologize properly!" Rachel ordered.

"I'm sorry Nanny."

####

It was 9.30 last night by the time Rosy was settled into bed and this morning saw me trying to drag both of them into consciousness again. I so hated the mornings.

I'm so sorry Rosy, but it's time for school."

I dragged her into a sitting position, whereupon she slid onto the floor and rolled over snoring. Frail-looking and sleeping soundly she did not want to come out of her stupor. The act of getting the kids ready for school was my responsibility and I had to "pull my weight."

They were both in foul moods and Anthony sat like a thunder-cloud and slumped at the low table and Rosy had disappeared once more, curled up and asleep underneath it. Anthony then began walking back and forth in front of me in a trance-like state wearing only his underpants, toothbrush sticking out of his mouth and hands together under his chin. With his eyes closed, he mumbled a fervent prayer over the kitchen sink, his frothing lips still moving quietly, eyes still closed and then his prayer finished, spat out the mouthful of toothpaste. I sighed, watching him and wondered which one he was in touch with this time, Buddha, Jesus or Robin Williams.

Rachel said, as I watched her getting ready for school, dragging her long dark hair up at the sides and clasping handfuls in to combs, "Rosy wants me to take her to the ice-cream parlor we used to call into sometimes after kindergarten. She was just saying to me how she loved sitting with her chips and ice-cream, *just* the two of us... talking. So I'm going to take her to the shop down near the shrine after school today for an ice-cream...*just she and I.*"

"Well, that sounds like a lovely idea. She seems to need some exclusive time with you at the moment - a chance to relate *just* to you. You had three and a half years exclusively with me before Caroline arrived and then when we moved to Sydney you were at school" I continued. Picking up a comic, glancing at the Pokemon image that was representative of Japanese kids' passions and tossing it down again I went on ..."and then it was time for Caroline to have time *exclusively* with me – going painting together at Smoky Dawson's ranch in Sydney. Remember that?"

"What a wonderful time that had been. I was just thirty.

We had gone to Sydney for Ed's sake – for the club scene, *"because Melbourne didn't have poker machines and so failed to provide for entertainers' livelihoods."*

It was 1975. The weather was beautiful. There were horses, picnics and gossip at lunchtime under the trees with my artist friends and my three year-old daughter. We would watch the actors and stunt-men coming and going on the film set there and one day a rather well-known actor in full nineteenth century costume stepped backwards onto my palette in his long leather boots, just when I had squeezed a great dollop of chrome yellow onto it. I watched the flash of a sunflower from the sole of his boot as he walked away unaware.

And the Aboriginal actor who, I only learned later was a decorated veteran of the Korean War, who made us jump out of our skins one day when he suddenly popped up in front of us on a path in the bush, naked but for his loin-cloth, ceremonial paint, spear and a huge grin. He'd just come off the film-set. He happily agreed to pose for us high up on a huge rocky outcrop for hours, motionless, his right leg bent, his foot resting on his left knee and only speaking when he heard me query the time to my painter-friend. He turned his head, looking skyward, still balancing on one leg and called out "It's just gone 1.57." We put down our brushes to marvel at this highly tuned mysterious native skill as he wasn't wearing a watch of course – "Now, how does he know that?"

He shouted down to us, a smile and a flash of white teeth and pointed at the sky "That was the 1.57 to Brisbane that just flew over."

I loved Sydney and it almost broke my heart when two years after our arrival we left. I didn't have a car nor my driver's licence at the time and when we rode on the bus, every hill we climbed revealed the blue Pacific Ocean and that was magic to me and I would miss it. We agreed to accept Dad's generous help to get a house if we returned home. Ed was disillusioned with the "club scene" anyway and wanted to return to Melbourne.

He wasn't the only one disillusioned, as around that time our Prime Minister Gough Whitlam had lost leadership. His famous quote comes back to us often, "Well may we say God bless the queen, because *nothing* will save the Governor General." This was followed by another famous quote now commonly used in our country from the man who took over from him, Malcolm Fraser – "Life wasn't meant to be easy." I wonder who was originally responsible for "Lord bless the Duke of Argyle?"

I did feel that my Mum deserved to be closer to the kids. They were her life really and I felt they too were missing out on the relationship with her while they were in Sydney, but it was not easy sharing Mum and Dad's house in Melbourne while we began to house-hunt and little did we realize that my mother was developing Alzheimer's.

Today is the first of July, Mum's birthday. She often reminded me that she and Princess Diana shared the same birthday and that she too had married the "boy next door."

Mum and the boy next door had been neighbours since she was sixteen and in those days, if Dad thought any "competition" was coming to dinner he would slip in the back door and proceed to wait on table, a white tea towel folded over his arm to the embarrassment of my mother and her guest. But she was always "fascinated" by him.

Years later I would witness her standing behind the kitchen door, a large cake-tin held on high, ready and aimed. It was before refrigerators became a part of the kitchen and instead of Dad, who she was expecting to walk through the door, the ice-man burst in with a huge block of ice on his shoulder. Face to face with him, Mum lowered the tin to her side "Oh sorry – I thought you were my husband." Dad stood behind the iceman, thumbing his nose. He often laughed about this. They kept their senses of humour somehow, but I took it seriously, unable to relate these outbursts to scenes from "I Love Lucy."

This was years before government support of single mothers and you had no choice really but to stay in your marriage and tough it out, because that was the only decent thing you could do, and neither of them would have considered separation. I vowed I would not be caught in this position nor would I "stay together for the children."

At home, being her birthday, I would have been placing her wedding photo on the mantelpiece – Mum standing alone, in a long, very 1930's style dress trimmed with roses and a large picture hat, smiling and attractive, about to embark on a torrid and at times very disappointing and unfulfilling fifty-seven years. So many women of her generation accepted being turned into stunted bonsai trees – never able to cast a shadow of their own.

Mum needed to nurture and to be loved and cherished. My father, an insensitive slave to discipline, needed to be a full-time army man with an unconquerable mountain to climb with a wife at home ironing shirts (five white, two sports.)

I am now writing postcards and a letter and have turned the computer on, hoping Caroline might pop up again, but it seems I can't get on to the Hotmail area at all. I began tidying up and wandered around keeping my eyes on the screen, looking at the clock on the wall from time to time. It was 11 am and she had usually come on by then. The door burst open and I gasped, not expecting anyone.

"Oh sorry. Did I give you a fright? I've come to put some more deodorant on. I've got to ride to my afternoon school and interview some kids."

Rachel smiled and hurried past me in to the dressing room. She glanced at the computer. "Can't you get through? Oh, I can't believe it. I filled the forms out and everything, for it to be disconnected at the end of July and they've done it in June instead. Typical Japanese ways."

Oh no! Now the only line of communication I had with the outside world was gone. That had been my one relief. It was too hot to walk outside according to the natives, I had no Japanese language, no car, no radio, no music, no newspapers or books to read, no English speaking TV, no neighbours or animals to talk to and no way of telephoning someone and having a good old chat or even a whinge to get things off my chest. And now no internet which meant also no Caroline.

The days were very long and the only outlet was my diary as my confidant. I sat twiddling the pen in my fingers. I didn't even have anything to write about.

At forty-one I had been divorced for five years and living in Warrandyte and of course, Ed had remarried. As the America's Cup was going to be held in Perth the following year, 1983, I figured property would rise quickly from where it was then, lower than almost anywhere else in Australia. I just might be able to get ahead with the finances. I was tired of being tripped up by obstacles at every turn but at the last minute I decided that after all, I could not leave Mum. Rachel's teenage reaction to this defeat was a very stormy one. She wanted to get away and go somewhere new. I think she felt as I had earlier, that a move like this would begin a new direction for all of us. What she really needed was a volcano or an earthquake. I feared she was having a late reaction to the family break-up and insecurity I had placed her in. She wept. Both girls had seemed to have sailed through my broken marriage and relationships unscathed. They seemed happy and were doing well at school and I was beginning to grow up beside them and we were good friends. Now at seventeen, it seemed Rachel was showing signs of insecurity. The age I had been when I fell for Nick, and Rachel was still a child!

No wonder Dad had put his foot down.

I was a bit shocked when the old house sold immediately it was put rather tentatively by me on the market and I knew then there was no going back on my decision.

Hurriedly, I went alone by bus to Perth, inspected eight houses and bought a nice little place with a big pool very cheaply within three days. I had always been impulsive. I didn't know what the black spots all along the sides of the pool were but I was sure I could fix them and the girls would be absolutely ecstatic. I had improved their lifestyles already and I no longer had a mortgage. We were going to start over, ten minutes from the Indian Ocean plus a swimming pool!

A week before we moved, Dad shifted my car for me which was parked in his driveway barring his exit. The seat was in a position that suited me but it didn't suit his long rather stiff legs and his foot jammed somehow and we watched him career across the front garden where a very large maple tree stopped his journey. He was unharmed but stricken with remorse and humiliation, which was heightened when Brad arrived (who knew very intimately what went on under my bonnet) to oversee the damage and declared the old yellow Morris that had re-connected us so many times with its breakdowns, was indeed this time "a write-off."

I made the mammoth move with the girls, two dogs, a cat, a houseful of furniture including the old player piano and an eight-foot long spear from Thursday Island, (the last inherited remnant from Dad's overland trip to Darwin.)

I didn't want to go, especially now, going into a totally new world without any wheels.

"I want to change my top" Rosy spluttered pulling it off over her head as she walked in from school all excited about the trip to the ice-cream parlor with her Mum. I closed my diary, suddenly remembering that I was in Japan and in the 21st Century.

"Well, why don't you put that pretty dress on that you wore to Tokyo." It was only 2.30 and she had to wait at least until 4 pm for her mother to come home.

I had been watching TV shows on and off while doing a bit of writing. Most entertainment on TV entailed eating and the experiencing of new food concoctions – like Megumi with the *natto* she made me try. It seemed *tasting* shows were really the thing in Japan like sport in Australia. This was before the onslaught of cooking fever which was yet to get Australia in its grip, and I was beginning to find them tedious.

Rachel and Rosy returned contentedly from their icecream parlor experience around 5 pm and we began a dinner of noodles and raw vegetables. As we were halfway through our meal, the doorbell rang and in leapt Megumi and Miko and Megumi's youngest boy Jun. They stood over us all, chatting, and Megumi produced a little bowl of pickled plums.

"For Mummy to try." I pushed my bowl aside and took a small bite in to what was like a ball of wet salt and my face puckered up.

"Ugh!"

She laughed but looked a little embarrassed. I spat it out in to the bin. "Sorry Megumi. Very sorry. Natto much better."She shrieked. I imagined how my stomach would have welcomed a bowl of those.

She patted me on the back. "Good with rice. "

"Lots and lots of rice" I said spreading my arms wide.

Miko wanted to know what would be the best time for them to take us to their favourite old town that contained some fascinating shops.

"They don't need to constantly entertain me Rachel."

It had been already arranged that we would be going with them to a "big noodle place" on Saturday.

Megumi ran off and then returned again full of concern.

"Soup, soup." She truly believed I needed feeding. Two small bowls of mushroom soup - the odd-looking Japanese ones, small and skinny with a button top. I grabbed some spoons from the drawer. Rachel motioned to me with cupped hands as she chatted to Megumi. I drank from the bowl. It was very good. There were some squares of tofu in the bottom of the bowl.

Eventually the little crowd left.

Rachel said "See what I mean… you wouldn't walk in on people while they're eating in Australia like that and disrupt the meal."

"Well, it's a completely different culture isn't it" I added thinking of Megumi's very good and kind intentions.

I was desperate for something to read. I didn't bring a book with me and searched Rachel's small collection on the shelf. I didn't think Sherlock Holmes was my style and decided on a book that after three chapters was obviously one of Paul's and which I found quite gross.

I had been lying awake for hours that night, going over my life and feeling a haunting old depression trying to claw at my insides, re-opening old wounds and regrets and a desire to self-destruct. I could hear Sandy cleaning her apartment above us and Megumi's boys were crashing about next door, with her tinkling laughter in the background. As usual all of them were up until after midnight.

A man across the street began calling out in conversation to someone and his voice was the last sound I heard.

No-one could understand why I had chosen to move as far away as Perth. Well, apart from the chance of ridding myself of a mortgage I couldn't afford, I needed to get away. I didn't like the example I was giving my daughters. I should have known it was a sign of things to come. Meeting someone in a phone-box.

Superman? Maybe he was. He certainly lived a double life.

The heady sweet aroma of cigars. Tender kisses on a crowded city street corner and our song, Bertie Higgins' "Key Largo."

I was also interrupting my Uni studies by moving to Perth. I had finished the first year of a Fine Arts Degree and was trying to catch up at long last with my life's ambitions. I had done two years of night-school to get the subjects I needed to apply to Uni. I had waitressed and house-cleaned and worked with a landscape gardener doing pick and shovel work. I baby-sat for a teacher and I studied for my own exams sitting outside in my car while the girls attended piano lessons or I read my set books in the gymnasium while Caroline swung from the bars and did her floor routines. The girls had lots of interests and we even managed to lease a horse for a time. They seemed happy.

I had to be a survivor. It was sink or swim. I needed more that this man was in a position to give. But, he was always there for me when I needed support or approval and he'd rescue me each time my old yellow Morris broke down, which was once a week. I was vulnerable with few defences. He had his life just how he wanted it. I had been addicted to romance and my needs went further than just being "the other woman" who literally *at the end of the day* was alone with her conscience tapping her on the shoulder. I had to end it.

Now if I'd become a nun and gone to Nepal none of this would ever have happened. I might have been meant to be a missionary like many in Dad's family, some even disappearing down the Amazon River never to be heard of again, suspected of being eaten by cannibals. I'd been forced to ignore this calling. Why did I let "You just want to be a hero" influence my direction in life? Too late now. At least if I put the Nullabor Plain between us I might be able to continue my artistic ambitions and cleanse my conscience.

On hearing of my intentions to move interstate, and knowing of my connection with Brad, my sister-in-law Liz surprised me greatly with "Don't you think you're cutting off your nose to spite your face?"

We travelled the three-day journey by train, having originally planned to have our car on board as well, but of course, now we didn't have a car. I didn't know then that when we arrived at our new house, having sat up for two nights in a rowdy uncomfortable train with hard seats, longing for our beds, that the furniture van would fail to show up for several days, having lost the page with our Perth address. This meant no refrigerator, no beds or furniture including eating and cooking utensils and no clothing. It was a weekend of heatwave weather in

Perth. And why hadn't the dogs and cat arrived as planned? Having no phone connection, we went in search of food and a phone box to hunt the animals down and they arrived the following day a little jet-lagged having been sent to another city. We all sat on the floor together in the heat, with a tiny store of perishable food that would have to be consumed quite quickly and pondered the fate of our furniture van. I tried not to consider this a gloomy omen to our move but there was still more to come.

####

Its 4 am in Japan and a murder of crows have woken me and I wonder what they are attacking, or whose garbage they are marauding. A feeling of gloom hangs over me and I feel the three weeks ahead are going to be quite a task, especially without contact through the internet now. I am doing too much self-analysis and soul-searching for my own good.

Rosy refused to rise from her bed and I got an angry retort from her mother for describing her condition as "Dead to the world." I tried to reassure Rachel that Rosy was not seriously ill with a brain tumour, but was obviously just run down for want of sleep and Australian food.

"It's not easy to gauge just what nourishment she's getting when you've got little bits and pieces of weird stuff in bowls and she's serving herself, and Anthony is eating everything in sight."

It was hard to say anything with impact in that small confined area. I couldn't stride off to my room because I didn't have one, nor was I able to seek solace anywhere and so I leant on the kitchen window over the sink and looked out from my cell at the *taiyo* glaring brightly at me. It was decided to let Rosy have the day at home and she slept soundly.

"I don't know what I'm going to do about my farewell dinner next week" Rachel said, opening the front door to leave. I remembered being told earlier that there was an invitation for both of us.

"If we *both* go and Megumi looks after the kids, she'll let them stay up all night and it's a Thursday and they'll have school the next day."

"I'll stay home and you go. I don't mind really."

"Well I don't want to go at all but I *have* to."

That's OK. I'll stay with the kids. That's what I'm here for" I said resignedly.

Rosy and I spent a pleasant day, painting, photographing a dragonfly (*tombo*) and eating snacks. I read three or four chapters of a rather classical story about a mouse called Despereux that her Mum was reading to her at night. She became embarrassed at her tears at the sad bits and I hugged her. When she'd had enough of Despereux she suggested we fold the corner of the page down where her Mum had left off, so that she would read it again to her when she came home. She adored Rachel, following her around, telling her she looked like a princess and waiting eagerly for her return each afternoon.

Megumi called in to say "If Rosy is not well we'll skip the big noodles tomorrow." I didn't mind at all.

The snoring had vastly improved since the window in the tatami room was opened and jammed with two taiko drumsticks which had been my solution. It was quiet at last, but for the odd outbreak of distorted breathing and the cry of the new baby down the road that broadcast its need for a feed all day and night and a crow or two on the overhead wires. I lay and listened to the baby in the dark silence or was it a cat? And I thought back.

We'd been in Perth for a month in 1986. Perth was new and shiny with a green Indian ocean, a blue Swan River and elaborate mansions were rising from the still waters crowded with snowy white sails of boats like clusters of seabirds. It was a provincial beach city, a desert city, a city about to rear up from its sandy streets and revel in the wealth of mining and tourism and soaring real estate. In Fremantle the light was dazzling, the bars noisy and the air heavy with international voices, the nouveau riche, fish and chips and sunshine. It was an exciting place to be.

"I'm sorry" said the voice from the university on the phone. "We've been doing renovations and extensions and seem to have mislaid half a dozen or so folios. We have no record of your application. I would suggest you re-apply for next year. The sculpture classes are full now."

Despair! I needed to find work. I had no money.

At the same time as this revelation, I had a very unexpected phone call from Brad somewhere out on the Nullabor and then he landed on the doorstep admitting that "this is bigger than both of us" and after a week of turmoil, guilt and desperation he was gone again. I found myself in an emotional spin. Things were going awry.

Dad made an arduous three-day journey to Perth by train, determined to come and buy me another car, dangerously encumbered by my mother's rapidly declining health which he thought would have been more difficult to handle on a plane. He was wrong of course and I don't know how they both survived the agonizing three-day train journey.

Alzheimer's – it wasn't fair. It was she who had sparked the children's faith and nurtured it through my agnostic years. They'd sung hymns with her around the piano that she played with a fervent ardour. I can hear it now *"I am so glad that my father in heaven tells of his love in the book he has written...............Jesus loves even me."* And this was the thanks she got.

These days I find a quick reminder of a guide to life in the Prayer of St Francis of Assisi. Mum found a lot of help in her Bible, going by the heavy underlining here and there, particularly in Psalms. I opened her much used Bible only recently looking for some answers and found several scraps of paper that had been there for years among the verses used as book-marks; one that read *'Turn the mountain into a gold-mine with God's help,"* and one note that she had scribbled hurriedly to Dad when Rachel and Caroline were little and had then used as a book-mark among the verses in Psalms. Now I open it at that place, to the greatest words of comfort for me in her familiar hand-writing:

"Fred, kettle has had it. You'll have to use a saucepan to boil water. Also use milk on left at bottom of fridge. Carton on right is for the children."

I trained on the job typing letters at a major hospital and found that the medical area was very interesting and paid somewhat more than "pick and shovel" work or baby-sitting for five dollars an hour. It kept my mind almost totally occupied and we three and the dogs and cat eating regularly.

I was at a club in Northbridge with a crowd of medical people one night after work, farewelling a colleague. As we chatted I noticed a lone man sitting in the centre of the room in a red leather jacket, illuminated by the light above him. I handed my drink to a radiologist I'd been talking to and said "Excuse me just a minute – but that's someone I know."

The expressions on the faces of my group were ones of surprise and some trepidation as I pulled out a chair and sat down beside him. We talked quietly about his being in Perth for the role he had in the Jack Davis play "No Sugar" but he couldn't seem to remember the day he posed for us to paint him at Smoky Dawson's and I felt he didn't remember me at all. It had after all been about sixteen years. He'd been in a hundred movie roles he said, including the film that starred Mel Gibson – "Gallipoli."

I returned to my drink and the radiologist and was asked "Do you do that sort of thing often?"

A couple of days later he tracked me down somehow to the Medical Centre, having walked miles around the city. He had some tickets for the play for me. He walked into Reception wearing long robes and beads surrounded with his usual air of charisma and charm after smiling and greeting everyone including the crowd of seated patients. I proudly introduced him to my colleagues and as we walked off to the cafeteria for a coffee and chat he said quietly to me "You know, I had no idea who you were the other night, and then later on I remembered – and to think I was a bit sweet on you back in them days."

As the radiologist walked past later, he plonked the x-rays he was holding on my desk and said "Do you think some time you could give me some lessons on inter-racial communication?"

I answered him "I thought I already had."

Rachel began her Asian Studies majoring in Japanese. Then she met Paul at the gym, an instant attraction for both of them. They married in Perth the following year and moved north to the Pilbara for Paul's work. The Pilbara is one of the remotest areas of Australia, about as far away from Perth as London is from Athens. A red earth country, rich in iron-ore and short on people, where *"chic"* didn't exist, only in Chad Morgan's hillbilly song "The *Sheik* from Scrubby Creek." Rachel would have to do with K-mart for her clothes as that was the town's only fashion boutique.

After two years of being the slave of a swimming pool in suburbia, Carrie and I moved to a cottage in the hills which was similar to what we had left behind in Warrandyte but without the Yarra River. That was home for the next seven years, and I travelled daily to the hospital in Perth to keep our livelihood going.

2013 – Le Cardinal, my refuge.

I wake in a sweat. Is it 4 am in Paris? No, I realize it is only twenty minutes after midnight! The cold has moved to my chest and it hurts to cough. People are still awake in next room but they chat quietly. I take a touch more sleep-inducer and finish my glass of water. My pjs are very damp. I cough painfully. Now there is an argument in the next room, probably what woke me. Her voice is raised in protest and he answers defensively.

6.30 I have slept six more hours.

8.30 After a late breakfast I return to my room, which is stuffy and I open the long windows to the instant waft of cold air and traffic noise, the roar of motor bikes and buses.

My Moroccan fruiterer is loading his stall with oranges, *pampelmousse* (grapefruit), tomatoes and big green apples fresh from the markets.

8.45 A church bell chimes. I am in jeans. They actually dried hanging on the open window handle. My long aqua top over aqua singlet, bright scarf in mauve, aqua and hot pink, and red high heeled sandals. Will take it easy today and just hang around St Cloud.

The effect that the smart business woman attains here (there was one at breakfast), is chiselled hair in short chic style, shoes that look expensive and have never been worn before and clothes that look like they've just left the store and an expensive one at that, together with perfectly manicured and painted nails. She doesn't speak and remains in her own impenetrable world.

I look across from my room to the apartments above the fruit shop. Their almost floor-length windows are open for airing. Their little balconies are stacked with pot plants, one also has a kid's bike and a watering can. There are seven floors with attic rooms in the roof. One window is covered in ivy to screen out the activity and perhaps filter the fumes from below. The Moroccan boy has finished his display and Isabella Coiffure next door to him is not yet open for business although the lights have been switched on. Through the huge leafy trees I see a bus pull out on its way to Hotel de Ville.

"Amour Gloire et Beaute" and here I am again, watching year-old episodes of the B&B that I've seen before but dubbed in French. Why the heck am I doing this in Paris?

It is quite cool here in "The Cardinal." I can't get it right. Everyone is rugged up in jackets and boots and here I am in summer clothes and sandals.

A beautiful African woman struts past with legs even skinnier than mine – all in black – her ankle boots tipped in gold.

The waitress says *"Oui"* to my order of cappuccino... *"et croissant Madame?"*

"Non, non croissant."

Two Jack Russells have a go at each other in the street, their owners dragging them away.

The woman at the next table with blonde smart coiffure wears blue jeans, black ankle boots, black jacket and very nice cobalt blue scarf. (Cobalt blue seems to be the fashion colour here.) Her boyfriend looks younger and is wearing a blue shirt, sleeves rolled up and beige slacks. My coffee arrives – tall glass and two inches of froth, 4.80 euros. I stir and lick the froth from the sides of the long spoon. This time it is really hot. Perfect. Nectar of the gods.

Water is streaming down the gutters washing away the *chien merde*. Shoppers are out, the iconic bread sticks alert in their bags. I am the only one who wanders here, but Paris is for wandering. Everyone else is in such a hurry in St Cloud. I guess this area being more residential, they are all just going about their business. The buses, the garbage trucks, the motor bikes, the taxis, all spin around this suburban roundabout. I spoon out the last of the froth reluctantly. I don't want to leave yet.

I deposit a five euro note on the table. A Chihuahua and a tiny weeny terrier go past on leads. I have seen them before but today the woman is carrying an additional dog in her arms. I feel I could catch a taxi on the run from here when I leave on Tuesday. There has been a constant supply since 10 am.

A black worker sweeps the gutters now with a green broom and now the footpath around the autumn-tinted trees to cleanse it of the cigarette butts and *chien merde*. The gutters continue to flush. He's earning his money. I wonder where he goes to at night and to whom. Does he say fondly as he sweeps—

"I am in Paris!"

Yes, I could live here in Porte de St Cloud – if I needed a suburb that was convenient to the city, where there weren't millions of tourists, souvenir-laden Africans and devious gypsy beggars tripping me up. This is a place you come to escape all that.

The bell chimes 10.45 and the street cleaner sweeps up a pile of crisp golden leaves and tips them into his bin.

Yes, I am feeling much more at home here. There are a lot of very conservative Parisians in St Cloud, including older ones - established suburbanites, well-dressed fashionable Africans and quite ordinary mothers with kids. At lunchtime the place is alive with smartly attired businessmen. I have seen no derelicts or beggars at all.

I thought they predicted 27 degrees today. I am a bit too cool for someone with a cold.

A middle-aged woman in red, white and blue sneakers enters. She could be a tourist. An obvious Parisian man walks in, light beige suit, a two-toned charcoal grey scarf knotted loosely around his neck, black shirt and black shoulder bag. He stands in the doorway and makes a call on his phone. He wears a wedding-ring. His suit is somewhat crumpled, linen I suspect. The clock chimes and it's only 11 am – a reason to sit a little longer. I sip my water.

The buildings running out from the roundabout are my favourite, Haussmann in style, but most buildings that surround this centre are a mix of modern constructions with verandah railings and probably built in the 1960s. This is the block the McDonald's inhabits.

The waitress who comes in to do lunches arrives and we nod to each other. I down my water and go. I hope to find that little boutique open, the only one that I could find which was closed yesterday. The sign said *Vendredi* 12.30, so I'll call back later.

Apart from a bridal salon that never seems to have any customers, there doesn't seem to be any fashion on sale here anywhere in sight. Stroll along street and photograph a *boulangerie*, restaurants and *patisserie*. One restaurant looks a bit grubby and another one is dearer than Le Cardinal, so it will be Le Cardinal for lunch again. It seems to have adopted me for coffees and lunches. It's very clean and smart and the prices are reasonable. Look in real estate window. Quite expensive apartments. There are a few around 300,000 Euros for 35 square metres in St Cloud. Collect *"Le Parisien"* at the news-stand and buy couple of novelty things for my two grandsons. There go the bells for 12 noon.

I'm now back in my room til lunchtime sitting on bed. The African housemaid lets herself in. "Sorry, sorry, sorry!" She cannot be persuaded to come and clean while I am here.

The waitress from this morning makes a great fuss of me when I return once more to Le Cardinal's door, rescuing me from the hands of the *maitre d'*. I am ushered to the same table as the day before yesterday and I order a *vin rouge* with a note of urgency.

"*L'eau – gaseuse?*"

"*Non gaseuse s'il vous plait.*"

I am given bottled water. That will cost extra. The bread and olives arrive. The superb bread and butter and olives would be a meal in itself for me with the wine – after all, that's all I ask in life. I roll the brittle crust around, mixing it with the *vin rouge*, carefully avoiding my front tooth. Hope they don't hurry me through the bread and wine ceremony and whisk the olives away like they did the other day. I cut another slab of excellent butter and repeat the process.

Three men are debating, lounging back in their chairs. This is a most civilized first class restaurant. I could have *escargot,* but not for me – yuk! Le Cardinal buzzes with conversation. There is another woman dining alone in leopard-skin, about my age. Short-cropped hair, glasses. She gives me a glance and turns away. Perhaps she thinks I stare at her leopard-skin and am envious because I don't fit the elegance bill.

I settle for roasted figs.

Two men meet, kissing each other on the cheek. They sit down near me and discuss intensely over a laptop.

It's 1.15 and the place is filling fast and so am I, having almost demolished 30 grams of "*Beurre E'chire* product of France" and the best bread I've ever tasted anywhere in my life.

The sun is out and the sky is blue.

The men with the laptop get up and noisily leave, having drunk nothing and totally disregarded their basket of bread.

I check that the loose top button on my jeans is secure. This is not the place I want to get up to leave and have my jeans around my ankles – especially as I only have grey cotton knickers on.

Have they gone to Barcelona for my figs?

I approach another piece of fluffy bread and more beurre and my figs arrive, looking almost red and meaty, on a bed of rocket with dried tomatoes, shaved parmesan and a drizzle of soy sauce. Delightful. The olives are whisked away. Who would risk eating anywhere else when Le Cardinal is here. Absolutely delicious! I pop my diary into my bag to make room on the table.

After my meal, a woman came and sat next to me while waiting for her husband to arrive. She turned to me and spoke in friendly sounding but rapid French. I hesitated, then my usual *"Je n'comprehend Francaise tres bien Madame."*

"Oh you speak Anglaise?"

"Oui – Australien."

She said her daughter had honeymooned in Australia, loved it and wanted to return. She asked me where I learned to speak French!

"Dans la maison – mon maison ...and when I get back to Australia all will be gone." I knew what I meant. Berlitz Basic French in my living-room at home after lunch, lying on the sofa, Aubrey Beardsley on my chest. *Bonjour Madame, merci beaucoup Monsieur, un chocolate chaud et huit croissants tout de suite!* And as Madeleine drummed into me last year at the Chateau "Julie, Julie, Julie - Not *tray be yen – trrrraaah bien!* Trrraah trrraah

trrraah," as she made like she was kick-starting a motor-bike.

From then on we continued conversing in a language we both understood with my occasional drift into the French phrases that only *I* understood. She was charming, born and bred in France but now living in Switzerland. I made comment on the swiftness of Parisian life, people and traffic and the fact that in Australia everything was much slower.

"And what are you doing in Paris?"

I showed her photos I had taken in my room at my Hotel in Rue des Ecoles, (Stravinsky Fountain and Luxembourg Gardens – my rained-on affects.) I also showed her the recent paintings I'd done at home, one of my little grand-daughter at ballet. She commented "Ah Degas." She seemed quite impressed with the photos of my house and garden full of roses and the mountains in the background behind Healesville. I didn't mention my addiction to writing on this trip, which would now include our chance meeting, my diary my silent witness. (Surprising that I hadn't as yet ordered a coffee for it.)

She said that they were visiting Paris to see her first grandchild Leopold who had arrived five weeks early.

I recommended the roast figs as she scanned the menu and she decided to order the same. Her husband arrived, an older, short, very French man and she introduced us. I ordered a second glass of wine.

"And why are you a vegetarian."

"J'adore animaux."

She had been a vegetarian for ten years "… but with a husband who eats meat it is difficult." I understood.

A lovely little interlude and "*Enchanté*" we both said and off they went to the Metro and Leopold. "Bye bye."

It's now 2.30. Damn. I should have taken their photo! I drag out my diary for an update.

"*L'addition s'il vous plait.*"

20 euro 80! That was my most expensive *dejeuner*, but it was my most memorable.

Walk back to my Moroccan fruiterer. He stands at the door smiling, watching me as I gaze thoughtfully over the fruit.

I am reminded as I sort through the stack of ripe bananas. Funny how it took me until my mid-thirties to rid myself of the compulsion to wash my hands after handling bananas. I see myself as a tiny girl in the greengrocer's store, clutching my mother's skirts after her quick reprimand at my fingering of the curious fruit. My hand would spring back as if I'd touched a hot stove each time she said to me:

"Don't touch the bananas! Chinamen sit on those to ripen them."

I think this superstitious and racist remark had been bred on the gold-fields along with my grandmother and my great aunts and uncles. They worked alongside many nationalities, all chasing the same dream. The poor and the professionals, their credentials aside and their sleeves rolled up showed great respect however, for the skills and medical advice of the Chinese herbalists when there was no doctor to treat their rheumatic ills and broken bones.

"Bonjour, bonjour .....Un banan and un poir s'il vous plait."

Wiping his hands down his apron, he smiled and took my hand and then with a questioning sound in his voice *"Madame?"* he kissed my right and then my left cheek and then dropped onto one knee, took my hand in his and kissed it. I blinked at him. He rose and said something rapidly but musically in French.

I stumbled *"N'comprehend..."*

"In Morocco – this is how we do it." He dropped on to one knee again and kissed my hand once more. "Where you from again?"

"Australia."

"Do they do this in *Australie?*"

"Non c'est difference!" and I stepped back and we shook hands.

"Ah – la difference!"

I wander across the street with my *banan* and *poir* and the boutique is open.

"*Made en France?*" I question as I choose two scarves, one to suit Caroline and one in autumn shades for my littlest grand-daughter in "Smarties" colours and spots.

"*Oui, Francaise. Vous Anglais?*"

"*Non – Australien.*"

"*Ahhh – Australien!*" she smiles.

"*Merci Madame – pour ma fille et ma grand-fille.*"

She nods "*Merci Madame*" as I hand her 20 euros.

"*Au revoir.*"

"*Au revoir.*" And back to the hotel.

I photograph the dining-room where we have *petite dejeuner*. My room is tidy but no towels at all.

3.10 pm and after two glasses of wine all I want to do is sleep. My towels arrive. She apologizes. I open the window and enjoy the sunny day and gaze at the view of the fruiterer's stall and the cars.

The clock chimes four. A fashion show on TV. School is out and what I think is a dog-fight is some dark-skinned kids screaming abuse at each other down in the street. This is the first sound like this that I've heard here.

I just realize – I'm really lonely! I so miss Bonnie and Mat and Ralph and Steve the fifty-three year-old pretending to be forty-seven, and the robust laughter at the volunteering of usually secret intimate memories we shared, probably never discussed with anyone else before but then with total strangers, punctuated with sympathetic reassurances and advice that we stirred in to our cafe crèmes, cafe noir and red wines, nose to nose in cafes all over Paris.

I know I'm lonely at home too, but I realize what is missing on this trip and in my life generally is purpose. My attempts to change the cruelty of the world through letter-writing, protest marching and painting have been too easily defeated. I have to change things when I get home.

I watch CNN News from my bed as usual and must have dozed off. I can hear someone trying my door. I fumble for the light but it will not turn on. Then I feel someone firmly holding my hand! I hear the beginnings of a scream fill my throat. Who had me in their grasp?! Some huge man – I can see a looming shape.

My scream wakens me and I find the light after much grappling. I find I actually am alone. I was dreaming. I should get up and try the door though, just in case and it isn't locked! I *think* I was only dreaming. I lock it severely and rattle it to make sure this time. I sit on the side of the bed and over my shoulder I feel figures looming at me. Of course – my curtains have French Revolution scenes on them, larger than life. The figures are at arm's length from my bed, so that explains it. A soldier in a bear-skin hat and two women in low-cut empire dresses. I breathe a little easier. My imagination does go a little awry in the wee hours.

Such activity outside. Buses and cars and it's only 11 pm. Traffic with car-lights beaming. The street looks very lit up and the fruiterer's stall is still open for business. There is so much activity in the hotel too, coughing, climbing of stairs, scraping of chairs, flushing toilets and lots of footsteps above me. It is Friday night after all.

I wake at 4.15 am after dreaming Caroline had a unicorn horn growing out of her forehead! It eventually fell out leaving a gaping hole which worried me and I wake relieved it was only another one of my crazy dreams. There had been on the French news a plastic surgery breakthrough, where a man suffering loss of his nose in a car accident had had a nose successfully grown on his forehead! Made in China of course, and it would be transplanted to his nasal area once it was established.

I hear someone on the floor above returning from a very late night in Paris. I just can't bring myself to wander the city at night alone. I wouldn't do that in Melbourne for a million dollars. Upstairs they struggle for a long time with their key. Did they have the right room? Finally. Then the sound of peeing for a long time. They'd obviously consumed quite an amount of *vin rouge* tonight and then the final flush of the toilet and now silence but for the bus pulling out for Hotel St Ville. I switch the light on – 4.30 am Saturday.

7.45 It is almost light. The streets have been washed and I'm going down for breakfast. Have been trying clothes on and off and decided as it's Saturday – jeans and my striped top that I wore so many times in Paris painting last year.

Breakfast is a busy affair and crowded as one by one and two by two, German tourists arrive. One very pretty young woman comes in, indicating she cannot speak for her sore throat. I silently sympathize.

I return to my room. No sign of people out on the street, just the swishing sound of the street cleaner's broom as he cleans the gutters and a quieter but constant buzz of early drivers.

My Moroccan Woody Allen sets up at 9 o'clock and I wait for a weather report on the TV. I feel I can't take much more of this French language on TV. I feel excluded. Cliff Richard's song "Theme for a Dream" plays and although I haven't been a Cliff Richard fan since my teens, it's now music to my ears as a panel of morning presenters laugh and discuss it at last in *English,* on an English show.

Can't believe it! Fourth try at the Metro machine and I can do it without assistance. *Liberte Equalite* …! I have renewed *"joie de vivre.*

2004 – The Mountain Trip

"Sunday and it's a beautiful day. 8 am and we're ready to go and the two cars have pulled up outside.

"Here, take a towel Mum."

"No thanks, I don't need one."

It amused me that everyone carried a face-washer or a small towel as if it were a fashion accessory. They mopped the sweat from their faces and the backs of their necks, blotting their gleaming chests and fanning themselves with it.

"You'll need it to dry your hands on if you go to the toilet."

"No thanks. I'll wipe my hands on my clothes" I replied defiantly.

There was Naoto, a short middle-aged man, Kaito and his wife Hiromi, both short and middle-aged and beaming, bowing.

"I very excited for today. It is a lovely day and very nice to meet you" said Hiromi, bowing.

These were people Paul and Rachel had met at a function somewhere and Paul had agreed to teach them English as a group in Hiromi and Kaito's home. Along with them was a young, tall attractive girl called Natsumi whom Rachel said had a crush on Paul. She had quite openly admitted to Rachel "He is medicine for my eyes."

She greeted me very politely and smiling. I was to travel in car number one with Kaito, Naoto and Natsumi. Hiromi pointed to my rather ornate mauve fabric scuffs and showed her disapproval, shaking her head, eyeing them thoughtfully. She was wearing an ankle-length, floating sheer floral tunic over a long Bali inspired printed outfit, together with a pair of clumpy white sneakers.

"Are we going to be hiking, mountain climbing or wading through swamps Rachel?"

"We could be. Put something more *knock-around* on."

"Give me the key." I went in and dragged out my most "knock-around" shoes which were woven leather scuffs that would probably satisfy everyone's wishes but weren't particularly comfortable. I returned to the smiling little gathering. "Is this better?"

Hiromi took a deep breath and began her formal greeting again, bowing in a well-rehearsed second take of our meeting:

"I very excited for today. It is a lovely day and very nice to meet you" and after smiling and shaking hands with everyone, which the men did very proudly instead of bowing, we piled in to the cars.

Rachel said the children should go with her in car number two and I did not protest. I was hoping to sit in the front as Rachel asked "You don't get car-sick do you? The drive up the mountain is a series of hair-pin bends—you've no idea. And I must take something for Rosy's ears because they give her trouble going up there and she doesn't know how to unstop them. She won't do as I ask and she just screams." I could imagine. Poor Rosy, but I was glad not to be travelling in her car. I was put in the back seat with Natsumi whom I found to be a very sweet girl. She had a good command of English.

We drove out through the winding streets of our town and Natsumi asked me where I lived in Australia. I tried to describe my town to her and the view I had of the distant city of Melbourne, the bush and the river. She was quite in awe.

As she and I chatted Naoto turned to me and said "Your Engrish very crear...easy to unnerstan. Austrarians hard for me to unnerstan...Sun*day*, Mon*day* ...they say *Sundee, Mundee*."

"Where did you learn to speak such good English?" I asked him.

"In Engrish grass, with Racher's husband."

Kaito asked over his shoulder "Do you want armrest?"

"Are you cold?" questioned Naoto. They were obviously all pleased to be able to practise their English on me.

"I'm very comfortable thank you," followed by many attempts by Naoto to pronounce *comfortable*.

I saw a green highway sign saying "Om."

"What is Om?"

"Om"... they looked at each other. Natsumi looked thoughtful.

"Om? is it a place?"

"Don't know Om." she said, obviously also puzzled.

The two men in the front chattered in Japanese and we pulled in at a shopping centre. We had been travelling forty minutes and we "had to have a rest" a toilet stop. This was the place we'd come to with Megumi and her family.

"Do you want the toilet Mum?" Rachel asked coming around to the car door.

"Is it going to be a hole in the ground?"

"Probably not."

"OK then." I opened three or four doors to cubicles. "They're all holes in the ground...ugh!" Now I knew why they all took their shoes off before entering the house. There was no water in these. I pressed a button but this time at least it flushed. They're not just holes in the ground. They're shallow earthenware gutters with a sort of raised "catcher" at one end. I couldn't work out which way one was supposed to face.

"See" Rachel said poking her head around the corner as I washed my hands. "You should have brought a towel."

I made a point of wiping my hands down my white cotton slacks. They were dry before I got back into the car.

Naoto handed me a bottle of "Aquarius" mineral water. "Here Jurie…I get this for you."

"Oh thank you, I mean Arigato Arigato. Aquarius is my star sign."

"Oh you Aquarius? I am Ribra" and Natsumi said that she was Sagittarius.

We got through a series of toll gates and I offered to pay.

"No, no, no" Natsumi said. "We will add up all expenses at the end of the day and divide cost."

I was amused at the English on the bottle which described the drink. Everything else was in Kanji and Katakana. *"To ease the parched body and spirit."*

Natsumi said "I wish they would check with native English speaker before they translate into English. It is sometimes embarrassing" and I agreed, laughing, thinking of the T-shirts.

The jagged mountains drew closer, scribbling endlessly along the horizon and larger ones loomed behind these, through the haze and up into the clouds. Workers in the fields wearing baggy clothes and coolie hats were bent at their labours.

In about fifty minutes we arrived at a town that I would have liked to explore had I been on my own. There were old bric-a-brac shops that obviously held lots of mysterious antique treasures. I wished Rachel had been placed in a town like this. We left the car to look at a shrine with a big incense burner like the one in Tokyo. I remembered how rotten I'd felt last week despite the so-called "cleansing" that I'd given myself at that one, but I still put my hands into the smoke as the others did to please them.

We all took photos of each other. Hiromi hobbled over to me on her walking stick.

"Jurie, how old are you?"

"Fifty-nine."

"Oh, so young. I am sixty-four. Oh you so young."

We got back in the car and on we climbed, eventually arriving at the world of the Nikko Toshogu Shrine. Nikko's history went back to the 8th Century. It was a centre for Buddhist monks and later was chosen as the site for the tomb of the first shogun. He was interred there in 1617 and work on the shrines began in 1634 with 15,000 artisans mostly from Kyoto coming to work on them. The temples were so ornate and decorated with gold leaf, red lacquer work and relief carvings, designs within designs, paintings, mythical beasts and birds, forming a bizarre madness. The Three Wise Monkeys emblems of Nikko, The Sleeping Cat, the Sacred Horse. There actually was a white horse, a real one, its head in a feed bin munching away. It was given to Japan by the New Zealand Government as a goodwill gesture and it seemed a little out of place. All I needed was the prince, but here he'd have to be a samurai warrior. My man on the plane belonged to the 21st century but I cast him for the moment in that role.

We entered several temples, removing our shoes and joining fifty others who knelt and listened to a young woman lecturing in Japanese. I understood not a word but we all bowed low while on our knees two or three times and then clapped our hands twice and I wondered why we were doing this on a hot Sunday morning in Japan. I was being carried along by a crowd of strangers with no idea of what I was performing. I might normally be on my knees now in the Anglican Church at home freezing to death in the winter cold, reminding myself of my place in the universe and my value to its creator, despite my personal failures.

The temple had a rather heavy smell to it. I felt it was the tatami straw flooring and all the feet that had trodden it over time, which combined to give it a peculiar odour. I found it a little oppressive. We moved on to other temples and went through similar procedures and I noted Rosy a couple of rows in front of me. When it came to bowing, she bowed so seriously and reverently, her little forehead touched the floor.

We climbed cold copper stairs and hundreds of stone steps finally coming to the high point of the tomb of the "very *fast* shogun" as Naoto referred to him.

On the way down again Kaito said "You Rachel…you look like your mother. He turned around and faced us. "Same face, same style."

"You same backsides!" was Naoto's comment coming along behind us. There was much laughter and repeating of the word "backsides."

Rosy at this point kept running off with Hiromi's walking stick forcing her to hobble along bent over on the rough ground and when Rosy wasn't doing that she was wrestling with Anthony all the way along the paths. They darted in and out of the crowds of tourists trying to slap each other. I would have liked to slap both of them. As we were about to leave the area, an enormous gong sounded which meant it was noon. We watched a young man, a heavy timber pole suspended and resting on his bare shoulder, running at the huge metal gong, hurling it with great force. It sounded to me like someone was due to be decapitated somewhere.

I looked back at the temples up the hill behind us now surrounded by cedar and beech trees. I felt it amazing that the area had managed to come through the war unscathed and Rachel said that the US purposely avoided bombing it.

Anthony was *starving*.

We found a formal Japanese garden. I don't think any of the others had been there before and I indicated that I would really like to see it. Paths meandered through it with low timber posts and ropes and sometimes bamboo railing, stone steps in gravel, stone lanterns, maple trees, shady and cool. A very large pond stocked with koi fish looking very clean and healthy. They came to the surface watching us and Rachel knelt down to look closer and said how they were like puppies coming to greet us. There were moss covered areas, undulating gently with azaleas, some still with the odd pink and white flowers and rhododendrons. A tiny teahouse sat out over the water. We posed for photos on the low stone bridge, then returning to the cars, drove down into the town, stopping at a food store.

I found a Western-style toilet, thank goodness. Rachel was in the store putting a lunch together for me of salad and sushi. Hiromi stood at the door and as I reached her she smiled looking me up and down. "You very good shape."

We piled into the cars and were off again. We crossed a bridge and catching a glimpse of a blue river below, rounded another bend and parked the car. We followed our guides along a narrow track through the trees, cherry blossoms green with summer foliage and more maples. We walked happily along swinging our lunch bags and I overheard Natsumi saying to Rachel in melodious tones "…..and he is really very nice and is at present living in Melbourne."

The countryside was split by a roaring thundering river. It frothed and churned, dropping, turning and twisting like a liquid dragon, snaking its way between gigantic boulders. With a powerful force it headed off on its steep downward journey through the beech trees, now so brilliantly green. I wondered what opalescent effects the maples would have on the water when they turned red and gold. The water was truly blue before it exploded into trillions of milky bubbles. I was used to the quiet brown Yarra River that "flowed upside down" and Rachel and I both gaped at the surging water.

Kaito led us down to a gazebo set on a rocky ledge, stopping to issue slightly frantic warnings to the skylarking children about the danger of the area. A tatami mat was set down and we lay out our lunches unable to take our eyes off the breathtaking spectacle of the river below us. "Beautiful. Just beautiful" was all I could find to say.

Motionless dragonflies sunned themselves beside us as we ate with chopsticks and shared our lunches with each other. We took photos and then picking up the remains of our picnic wandered up-stream along the river.

The stone figures along the track were weather worn from the years of the flooding river and looked as if they'd been there since the beginning of time. They had more appeal for me than the ornate and garish statues at the shrine. This was really beautiful. The heads were missing from some figures and I stopped and posed with my head where the stone head once was on one of them, to the delight of Naoto who captured me on camera.

Hiromi caught up hobbling on her stick and said "Now you are Buddha." I hadn't realized they were Buddhas because they were so worn away. I hoped I had not done anything to offend them. She wrote on her translator "Floods….right up here." She indicated with her hand above the stone figures where the river rose. "River wash away lot of Buddhas."

The children began posing in the same way to the amusement and laughter of Kaito who continued to photograph them. Then Rosy took her yellow sun-hat off and jammed it down on the head of one.

"I think that's going a bit far. This will offend the Buddhists amongst us. Rosy stop doing that! Rachel that's showing disrespect for their culture. Imagine if that was a statue of J.C."

I looked back at the river for the last time with the thought that I would probably never see it again in my lifetime but it would be roaring and tumbling down its pathway, blue and bubbling while I was back in Australia sleeping in my bed, just like that spiritless lion would be pacing up and down in his cage.

Rachel stopped and encouraged a dragonfly (tombo) onto her finger. She examined it for a long while. We had a lesson in pronunciation with Hiromi, Naoto and Kaito who had considerable trouble saying "Dragon*fly*." We all laughed and stumbled together along the track in the heat.

I saw what Rachel meant by "hair-pin bends" on the trip up the mountain to Kegon Falls. We stopped a thousand metres above sea-level and Rachel sent another photo to Paul in Perth. Naoto said as we drove on up "It will be *crowded*. It will be very very *crowdy*."

"Oh well, it's the weekend. I guess most places will be crowded" I added.

Natsumi put her hand over her mouth and giggled. "He's giving you a weather report Jurie. He means it will be *cloudy*."

"Are these trees beech trees or cedar?"

"Both" said Natsumi.

"Not *beach* where you swim..but *beech* B .E. E C. H."

"Yes" said Naoto "Beech. Like *frower* and *frour*."

"Yes, *flour* to cook with."

"Yes, I make cakes." He smiled proudly. "I will make something for you Jurie."

We were arriving at Lake Chuzenji and I was trying not to look out at the scenery flashing by as Naoto spoke to me and we twisted and turned up the steep mountain road. If I was going to get car-sick it would surely be on this bit of road. But I was OK. Once at the top we were all crammed into a lift with twenty-nine others and I looked around. I was not as tall as Bill Murray was in the movie but I smiled at the thought of the scene where he was looking down on everyone in the elevator. Rachel had shown me a funny photo of Paul in a similar situation. Paul being a cheeky person, managed to wander in to the middle of a gathering of complete strangers on the street at a Japanese wedding and Rachel took a photo of him in the crowd as they posed for the wedding photographer. There he was, six foot five inches of him, an easy head and shoulders above the tallest in the crowd, an amused droll expression on his face.

We climbed down steps where water dripped from the ceiling and stepped out onto a landing where the air was full of fine spray and the magnificent spectacle of Kegon Falls dropping one hundred metres with terrific force from Lake Chuzenji into the blue river below.

"Now we go to farm" said Kaito as we slipped seat belts on again once in the car.

The countryside was so different to anywhere else. The closeness of the trees, the thin trunks, the deep green of it all and the dwarf bamboos covering the ground. Natsumi pointed out a deer. I had noticed a sign back further, warning of some kind of furry animals crossing. Natsumi said they were raccoons.

"I can't find the toilet" yelled Anthony as he emerged from the main building, "and I'm absolutely busting."

Naoto began singing "Oh give me a home where the *buffaro* roam and the deer and the *anterope pray – pilay – pilay*", he struggled. "Where *seddom* is heard…" and then I joined in with "a discouraging word and the skies are not *crowdy* or grey. How do you know that Naoto?"

"It's his hobby…singing songs in English" laughed Natsumi.

Back in the car again after ice-creams, a product of the farm, Naoto turned around. "Jurie…you give me your name and address prease." He handed me a scrap of paper with his name and address on it. "In case of emergency Jurie."

Kaito roared laughing. "Naoto say to me again and again "Rachel's mother very beautifor. He keep saying." He roared again.

On the way home we had to make one more stop. This was at a stately hotel, one that I'd seen from the road not far from our lunch-time picnic spot, and high on the hill above the Yu-Gawa River. The Nikko Kanaya Hotel had a gracious history going back to 1872 and was referred to as Nikko's oldest and classiest hotel. Rachel, Paul and the children had stayed there in the autumn and Rachel fell in love with it.

She beckoned us to follow her through the rotating door which was attended by an attractive young man in uniform who bowed low to us. "They said I can show you through." So we all tracked after her.

Anthony and Rosy disappeared into a powder-room. The rest of our party stood looking at the collection of old sepia-coloured photos and memorabilia from the last two centuries. There was a framed complimentary letter in very tall sloping writing from a lady and gentleman from Melbourne Australia who had stayed there in the 1890s.

Kaito decided we should have some refreshments.

"Cheese-cake and coffee?" he asked full of enthusiasm.

I looked at my watch. "It's getting late." But we were led back up to the dining room where everyone ordered iced coffee and cheese cake while we sipped on iced water. I looked at the menu and I wasn't sure of the prices at all. The iced coffees arrived and they were black. We took up two tables in the lounge and I heard

Kaito telling Rachel as his camera flashed at us across the aisle "Naoto has been saying all day Rachel's mother is *so beautifor*." I looked away, wishing he would not annoy Rachel with more of this nonsense. After all I was used to being invisible in the company of Rachel or Caroline. After forty-five that's how it is, especially when one has two beautiful daughters.

The cake was not cheese-cake as I knew it at all but something very synthetic-tasting. We got on to the subject of natto.

"You have tried natto?" Hiromi asked, wide-eyed and surprised and I gave her my impression. Natsumi laughed and said how she hated Vegemite at first and now she liked it. Their limited English and my nonexistent Japanese kept the late afternoon tea tete-a-tete very simple. I poured my coffee out of a small blue and white china pot into a matching cup and saucer. I was aware of those moments that are fleeting in life, like sunshine on a winter's day that I refer to as happiness. I felt a warmth from these sunny people, a caring and a sharing of special moments in time. It was comfortable being with them. I felt approved of and welcome. I slipped down to the desk and paid the bill.

"That was a very nice thing to do Mum" said Rachel as we left the hotel. "Well, they've all made such an effort to give me such a wonderful day. It's the least I could do. I've been thinking all day how I was going to repay them and then when they suggested coffee and cake I suddenly thought that could be my treat.

"How much did it cost you?"

"Ten thousand five hundred yen."

Her eyes widened. "Gosh!" She went off to extricate Rosy and Anthony from the toilets upstairs.

We drove off towards the town that held the next official toilet and refreshment stop.

Natsumi had at last decided on the meaning of the "Om" sign I had asked about earlier.

"It means zero makes to travel behind car." I accepted this explanation without further question.

"Today was just lovely" I said sincerely to everyone.

"Ruvvery, ruvvery, ruvvery, ruvvery" sang Naoto. We laughed and he continued on with his rendition of Eliza Doolittle's song and then stopped, unsure of the last line which I sang for him "Wouldn't it be ruvvery."

I offered Kaito money for the toll fees and he waved his hands around with an emphatic "No!"

We put the kids to bed without showers and Rachel said "They'll never wake up in time for school tomorrow. I really missed Paul today. We have such happy memories of that place. I really was wishing he was with me."

"I suppose you were."

I lay on my bed on the floor feeling happy about the day and how much I'd seen and enjoyed. It had ended up costing me nearly half a week's wages, but so what. I had been well entertained.

Off To The World of Super Chic.

I get on the No. 9 train and an African man stares at me for some time. I am wearing dark glasses so he can't meet my gaze. A woman gets on with a Jack Russell on lead. He stands very patiently. He's used to this. I lean forward and tickle him under the chin (not the African man) and he calmly ignores my advances. He stretches and lies down. He is so well behaved. The train stops and he looks up at her with a questioning gaze. She reassures him with a fondling of his ear. I see she has a container in her bag in the shape of a pink bone and a plastic bag peeps out – a "poo bag." She is about to get off the train. He shakes himself, prepared and on the ready to meet whatever Paris streets have to offer this morning in the way of dogs.

A grey-haired French woman who has been smiling at me over the top of her newspaper, comes and sits down beside me and continues reading her *"Le Parisien."* She has been aware of my prehistoric recording of information onto paper with a ballpoint pen and she is reading the news from an old-fashioned tabloid. Neither of us is plugged into computers or iPads. We share a special connection to the stone-age.

Four Americans get on board. I smile and get no response from them. The younger woman hanging on to the pole makes the comment with a New York accent to the older couple "You can have lessons doing this you know, with the right music." They laugh.

The grey-haired woman beside me packs up her paper and stands, waiting for the train to stop. Turning back to me she beams "And have a very nice day." This is said with a very friendly emphasis. All I can manage is "*Merci*" and the warmest smile I can muster in appreciation.

I arrive at the most expensive upmarket centre of Paris and set off to the Printemps store. On the way I am accosted several times by women waving boards with requests for "signature please!"

"Go away – go away." Gosh they are persistent not taking "No!" for an answer. One traveller is cornered and stands blinking at the wretched woman forcing her intimidating persuasion upon the unsuspecting man.

"But why? But why?" he shrugs, trying to lean out of her way.

I circle him "Don't do it. Don't do it!"

It's raining a little. Lucky I brought my umbrella.

I escape into Printemps and the world of Prada, Dior, Miu Miu and every fashion name you can think of. Why did I come in jeans? I catch a glimpse of myself in a long mirror, the tourist contrasting with the immaculate outfits on show that the immaculate Parisienne woman dresses in. There are rich Japanese women cruising around, fingering the clothes. Caroline comes to mind. Can I buy her something? Apart from minding my dogs for me – she loves Paris like I do. Scarves – 345 euros! Dresses, simple little dresses 1,500 euros and upwards. Shoes 750 euros! Don't think I'll be buying anything here. The fashion seems to contain very bizarre patterns in bright colours with tops covered in sparkles and borders in gold geometric patterns.

I explore the goods from floor to floor. This is where Angela and Brad shop and the business women of Paris. Probably Diana shopped here too.

I am now at "Triadon Haussmann" café on Boulevard Haussmann and ask the waitress to show me on the map where the café is situated as I am completely lost. This is yet another Paris and quite foreign to me. The coffee is 4 euros 60. Was expecting it to be 10 euros. I can see a sign pointing to Gare St Lazare. I think I go in opposite direction. Here goes!

I reach the Arc de Triomphe – my triumph for the day. This was one place I was determined to see again as I didn't have time last year. I am satisfied that I have accomplished what I set out to do today. I have no intention of climbing up all those steps though. Twice in my life was enough.

When I was here in 2002 I remember spending the day photographing all the fashion houses and climbing the stairs of the Arc and marvelling at the view. I think it is a better view than from the Eiffel Tower because you can see the Eiffel Tower as well as looking down on all the streets radiating outwards which is amazing and the best place to view the theatre of traffic and the madness of the Parisian drivers. I had been photographing, photographing and then stopped to lunch in the Tuilleries Gardens. Along with my usual banana, I found the roll of film in my handbag instead of in the camera and with steam coming out of my ears re-traced my journey, climbing the Arc's 140 steps and whizzing around the fashion houses once more. Photographing, photographing, this time with the film in the camera, but it just was not the same. I didn't feel quite so bad when I returned to my tiny hotel in the Latin Quarter however, as the young man on the desk said he used to be a professional wedding photographer until the disastrous day when he photographed a whole wedding only to find out the next day that there had been no film in the camera!

"And that is why I am now on this desk Madame."

I feel a few rain drops. Where's my umbrella? Oh no. I left my umbrella at the café. Damn and blast!

I can almost hear it screaming out at me, "Come back!" This one was born and bred in France – well no, probably in China but it has been abandoned in Paris. And I was emotionally attached to it. I have gone too far from the café to return for it. Maybe it just escaped, wanting to remain in Paris. It doesn't fancy life in Australia.

I wander along Champs Elysees feeling very wrongly dressed. I should be in Montmartre wearing this outfit. My outfit of navy clingy dress and cape jacket would have been perfect. I feel like a jerk and such a tourist, map in hand, stopping to take photos every thirty seconds.

I have to find something for Caroline on the Champs Elysees.

This area is definitely the centre of the Universe. There are Americans everywhere. I've never seen so many people packed into a square metre since Camden Markets in London twenty years ago. Determined to find something now for Caroline (I should have got something at Printemps – miser!) I go into umpteen fashion stores looking, looking. I actually try on a black and white top to check the size for her and am so devastated by my appearance half naked, that I leap out of the top and slide my skinny body under the door and scoot out of the store. Maybe it was the lighting.

I look at labels. Some say bluntly "Made in China" and I leave those behind me. I didn't come all this way to buy "Made in China." Nearly decided on a blue and white jumper at 35 euros but think it would have collapsed after one wash.

I find some interesting clothing in another boutique – quite complicated and the prices out of this world. A St Bernard dog follows its owner inside the store.

At about 2 pm I enter Naff Naff and finally after combing the place, find an off-white top with embossed sleeves, rather different, simple and I think Caroline's taste. 25 euros. SOLD!

I walk on and am facing the Tuilleries having just had the worst coffee *ever!* Cappuccino – an egg-cup-full with foam four inches high. (Lunch money was spent on Caroline's top).

I do my best for my friend the umbrella. I retrace my steps and find my way back to "Triadon Haussmann."

"Excuse moi Monsier" to the middle-aged maitre d'. "*Le matin – mon* umbrella - *sur la table?*" I stumble on atrociously, pointing outside to where I'd had my coffee earlier this morning. He looks at me a little stunned, straightening the snowy tea-towel on his arm and loosening his shirt collar with a be-ringed finger, and then a little sympathetically at my absurd attempt at French, he turns from me and calls a young waiter over. They chatter in beautiful *Francaise* and the young man smiles sympathetically and says in beautiful melodic *Anglaise*: "Ah Madame, I remember you from this morning – you ordered a café *crème.*" I show my flattered surprise awkwardly at his remembering me from this morning. (He didn't serve me this morning!)

"But I am sorry to say there was no umbrella there Madame." He turns on his heel and answers a request elsewhere, disappearing from me – "*...M'sieur?*"

I sigh "*Ah – merci beaucoup Monsieur,*" and dismiss myself. I walk in circles like a lost pigeon around Haussmann Boulevard and Boulevard Malesherbes, my map flapping in the breeze like a sail. I know I look like the most "*stupide touriste.*" No wonder the waiter remembered me from this morning, in my navy and white striped top and jeans and my tangle of coloured scarves.

I somehow find my way to St Augustin Metro and get out the Metro map. Yes, I am nearly home and hosed.

The train is full, humid and stuffy, made worse by a couple of lovers, who go unnoticed by everyone but me, squeezed against the door, eating each other's faces, her eyes watery and her face crimson with blatant desire. Only fourteen more stations to go.

As I am about to alight I notice a poem on the wall —a bit of framed Metro folk-art, and in English. I scribble it down on my Metro map. The story of me in Paris, on the planet actually. Maybe a message from Mum.

"Time is running out, A ghost's keeping me alive
I get what it means – You have to survive!!"

I arrive at Port de St Cloud and *Sorte* takes me a different way out. There are five gendarmes on the steps. I follow them out but I am lost but then "Le Cardinal" beckons ahead, my saviour many times here. There are police everywhere and the traffic is held up. If laid-back Melbourne had this kind of a Police force we mightn't have a murder or a stabbing every day as we do. They are always around in Paris – on the ready.

When Caroline and I moved from the house with the pool in Perth to a cottage in the hills, we found we were part of a little community, with an Irish couple living in the house behind us, and my next-door neighbour, an ex-school-master from Melbourne.

Our neighbours from Ireland introduced themselves as I worked in the garden one afternoon. They were old enough to be my parents. I had discovered a new source of support and companionship. At weekends we wined and dined together, enjoying the mild velvety evenings, sometimes entertaining their overseas friends to dinner on their verandah or in the gazebo in my garden surrounded by huge groaning gum-trees and monolithic boulders like sentinels on the green lawns.

We went on long walks daily with our dogs and sometimes I'd stop for coffee with them while they breakfasted together. I often came home with a recipe, a jar of marmalade made from the abundance of oranges on Kathleen's tree, a great book and always the smell of her cigarettes on me. She had suffered with emphysema for years but still continued to chain-smoke. She was a tweedy sort of woman who had bred horses in Ireland and now that her life had slowed down, the West Australian wildflowers had replaced the horses.

My other neighbour Jim, was an 80 year-old classical musician and retired school-master from Melbourne whom I accompanied to the local Rep Group's Shakespearean production of King Lear and to the movie "The Piano." He could not hide his embarrassment at having me witness Harvey Keitel's nudity instead of a piano recital he thought we were attending.

On Saturdays as I pushed the hand-mower around the half acre of lawns I could hear the piano being caressed by Jim, the strains mingling with the smell of freshly cut grass around me. We would all get together for drinks of an evening, the four of us usually, and listen to the couple's adventures of their ten years sailing the Caribbean together. I didn't realize it then but I would look back years later on this interval in my life as one of the happiest.

Jack and Kathleen had run away from their marriages and their families because they were in love. Why hadn't Brad and I run away? I knew very well why. Jack and Brad already had wives.

I now felt torn as to what to do for the best for my scattered family. I didn't want to be too far away from

Rachel in the Pilbara. She was now as far away from me in Perth as Mum in Melbourne and I really felt I should be with my mother. I felt pulled in all directions with Caroline still living at home whilst at Uni. I was allowing myself to be guided by everyone's advice.

Alzheimer's didn't get the exposure in the media that it gets today and we didn't know much about it. My brother Bruce was relaying stories of Mum's state of mind over the phone to me. We had to laugh at some of the incidents. It had to be treated in a kind but light-hearted way or it became an insufferable agony for everyone involved. My heart ached for her when he told me in a despairing voice how he had stayed the night there because Dad was going to an Anzac reunion and Mum couldn't be left alone. He had just purchased an expensive new golf club, a wood, in an immaculate fluffy white sheepskin cover. He'd left it in the kitchen. Around midnight he was woken with a lot of banging coming from the kitchen and it was Mum, bucket of soapy water at her feet, mopping the floor!

Bruce and his wife Liz supported Dad in the finding of a nursing-home for Mum, after a long struggle with him trying to manage her at home. My sister-in-law reassured me continually that I wasn't needed in Melbourne and to "stay in Perth for your daughters' sakes!"

"A nursing-home with a parent with Alzheimer's was no place to be spending your time" came from my concerned friends. But how could I accept that?

My twice-yearly holidays were spent travelling the three-day journey across the Nullabor Plain and back again in a Greyhound bus. I would sit with Mum in the nursing home for the hour that Dad allowed each day. His day was ordered and planned and he kept to it as he would one of his military exercises, keeping an eye on his watch. I observed her on one of these mornings locked in the prison that Alzheimer's had forced her into. She was still there in body but she was gone from me as if she had died. I had already lost her.

"She doesn't know who you are. She won't speak to me at all" Dad insisted, but I didn't believe him because, although he refused to admit it, he had lost his hearing so their communication was non-existent. One morning I fell on to my knees beside her and took the hand that had cared for me and held it to my face. I wished I had supported her more. I had been trying to sort out my own mess. I should never have left Melbourne. What had possessed me? "I'm just so sorry Mum." My tears spilled down, too late to be of any value or comfort to her and I choked on the words "I'm so sorry I have been such an awful daughter."

She looked up at me with recognition, took my hand in hers and patted it, whispering "Don't say that dear. Don't say that—there's no need."

She was more peaceful in the home than I had ever seen her. She had staff around her who made a fuss of her, even Max the cleaner. I always found him leaning on his mop chatting and laughing with her whenever I walked in the door. He was wonderful and she seemed appreciative of the respectful care and interest shown her by both he and all the staff there. She was enjoying more respect and attention than she had ever known I think.

I would climb back on the bus to Perth again and once home, would walk my dogs through the hills, find that shady place hidden by boulders and cry in despair on the flattened cool green grass, for the loss of my mother.

####

Monday morning, and the kids have gone off to school surprisingly well apart from the usual mucking around that goes on. I had done the house-work and the washing-up by 11 am and had written three postcards and eventually walked off to the post office. My calf muscles felt stiff from the climbing of all those stone steps yesterday. It was incredibly hot and had been airless and quite suffocating all night in the apartment. I wasn't wearing my hat.

There was the tree trimmer at the big corner house, trimming the shaped trees, branches of bamboo acting as supports. His head was wrapped in a cloth and he wore a loose white and indigo patterned tunic-type shirt. He wore very full indigo-coloured trousers that bloused right out and then were drawn in tightly at the ankles. He didn't see me although I passed almost right under his ladder.

There were sunflowers in rows further on, their faces turned to the sun and lines of ripening corn. An old lady, tiny and wrinkled, hidden from sight almost by the tall sunflowers stood staring at me, a handkerchief covering her head. She watched me grumpily from her garden beds. The sky was a steely grey. Would it rain?

I crossed the main road that led to the shrine and walked down the narrow road to the Post Office carefully dodging the bikes and stepping back from the cars. I handled my money more competently at the Post Office, at last realizing it cost 70 yen to send a post-card to Australia. I sent three.

I went onto the supermarket and searched for sugar. The salt looked like sugar and I did not want to make that mistake. There was nothing in English on the packets to indicate to me whether it was salt or sugar. I shook it and squeezed it through the plastic. I found sugar cubes in the next aisle and decided that was the safest thing. I also bought some broccoli, eggs and bananas. The bread was dearer than the other day so I gave that a miss.

I seemed to be feeling more at home in Japan. I looked at my watch. It was still morning and I even managed "*Ohiyou gazaimous*" to the check-out lady and then an "*Arigato*" as I left. It was a shame to leave the shop which was really cool and outside I felt the unforgiving blast of hot air.

That night I watched a British show on problem animals in the UK dubbed in Japanese of course. As I watched a big rabbit chasing and attacking the family dog, I could hear Rachel giving Anthony a really serious talking to in the bedroom. He kept answering her back with denials and protests but she would not be beaten. She was the teacher and mother in one, calm but determined. The dog on the TV had been dripping blood from the attack from the rabbit but now some time later, stood grinning at the rabbit that had had retributive counselling at the vets and his aggression was no longer a problem.

I'd had a reply to my first email to my friends at work, saying they were all amused by the image of me on a bike. Everyone had had the flu and on one day there was only one girl working out of the five. I felt a guilty pang. Judy's father had died and Maria had had another baby girl and it was freezing cold in Melbourne. I imagined how behind work would probably be at the hospital and how I'd have to get cracking when I got back and make up for lost time. I felt guilty for taking the two weeks over my annual leave, but I had offered to resign if they weren't happy. They could have got a temp in surely.

Rachel had been my first concern. She could not have continued on with Paul not being there for Rosy and Anthony. I had two and a half weeks to go yet. Keeping my diary made the day fly past.

####

This morning is another hot one following a stinking night. It was impossible to get to sleep.

Rachel came home extremely irritable. She'd had two days of working in a small classroom with a hundred and eight children with no air-conditioning. She said kids there were not allowed any form of cooling as it would "make them weak" and when she was teaching she had to cope without any sort of fan, and must not even fan herself with a book in front of the pupils. Staff rooms were usually cooled but not at the school she had been to that week. Anthony and Rosy had come home hot and sweaty too, but in happier more cooperative frames of mind than I'd seen for many days.

Sandy came down from upstairs in need of someone to grumble with over the day's conditions they had shared together at the same school. She stayed on til 9.30 and I thought she'd never leave, the kids refusing to go to bed while she was there and showing off and being quite revolting. Sandy said she heard all the drama and the yelling that went on before bed and at breakfast time.

She finally took the hint and went back to her quarters when I changed into my pyjamas. I suggested to Rachel that we had better start whispering from now on seeing as she could hear everything from upstairs, but we were all back to loud hostile tones once more next morning with the usual prodding and urging to get the kids off their beds, eat and get dressed. Rachel had relaxed a little about Rosy's health as she had been weighed at school on Monday and she'd begun putting some weight on and was now 20.2 kg.

Today had been "burnable rubbish" morning again and I helped Rachel carry the bags around to the park where they were placed with everyone else's under the big nets where the crows couldn't get to them.

I waved goodbye to her as she pedaled off to school and put some washing on, then refilled the shampoo and conditioner dispensers from the refill packets. All this packaging amazed me. The packaging industry must be worth an absolute fortune. The refill packets had spouts inserted and dotted lines and were quite intricate. The biscuits were all individually wrapped within the cellophane packet, the eggs in containers wrapped in cellophane, with a sealing strip that had to be pulled before the cellophane came away. All the packaging was things within things.

####

Sixteen more sleeps. Last night after dinner we went on a short excursion down to Rosy and Rachel's ice-cream parlour and then on down to the shrine. Rosy made me carry her sticky empty containers and insisted on washing her ice-creamy fingers in the traditional "cleansing water" at the shrine. Rachel told her that it really wasn't for that purpose but for "cleansing one's mouth and hands before entering the temple." Still she washed her hands in it and I looked over my shoulder hoping it wasn't being witnessed by anyone, particularly Buddha. My own hands were now thoroughly sticky and would remain so.

We walked back slowly along the dirty river. Many dogs on leads passed us looking listless, all needing a good brushing, their coats very matted. The weather was heavily oppressive and humid although only in the low thirties, quite different to Perth's dry climate or even Melbourne at its most humid. It is a bit milder out in the evenings but seems to warm up again by bedtime when we shut the place up again and put the air-conditioner on.

The days are getting longer for me and we are not doing much that is of interest for me to write about and since the internet is out of action, I can't contact anyone. It is too hot to go out and hang around during the summer days. Nobody goes out in the heat of the day and there are often comments about "The danger Mummy is putting herself in by wandering around in the sun."

I wait for the sumo wrestlers each afternoon until I am heartily sick of them. I am just longing to go home now.

The evening walks reminded me of the traditional ones in the Christmas holidays we took as children and the balmy evenings when it was light until 9.30 but this was the dirty Argebori dyke in Eastern Japan, not the darkening sea on the Mornington Peninsular back home, where phosphorescence washed in on the tide and where the sun sank in to the sea like a big stewed peach. We'd go home and check our peeling skin after roasting ourselves all day and my brother Bruce was always able to peel off the biggest piece from his shoulders. I wondered if maybe I should go and live by the sea again. The air-conditioner was turned off before we slept and the fan roared all night aimed at the stuffy tatami room.

I threw my bedclothes off and sat staring at the clock. I had slept later than usual. I headed forlornly towards the kettle on the stove. Strange, but I had never dreamed of Brad before. I turned the tap on and the water ran, along with the cold realization of the fact that I had been wakened from a dream and that I was actually in Japan and the year was 2004.

It was 1983 and the English teacher said "Now, I want you all to define love." I had looked around the class-room at the other high-school drop-outs and hopefuls. In response to a couple of inhibited written attempts of mine, my teacher later wrote at the end of my paper "Too stiff and formal. You have arrived at a dictionary/encyclopaedia entry rather than a detailed explanation."

I proceeded to satisfy his request beginning with Elizabeth Barrett's poem "How do I love thee – Let me count the ways…" I had clung to that rapturous poem and memorized it when I was a tragic eighteen year-old, until I found myself stumbling into it automatically beside my mother, when she and the rest of the congregation at the Methodist Church began The Lord's Prayer. It was a prayer. It was certainly a form of worship. I believed this poem to be the epitome of passionate love, an expression of my unfulfilled longings, my life's agony – Nick. But that had been much earlier days. There was now another unattainable man in my life.

"Love is the prayer for my children's safety after they've both left for school and I find myself standing alone in their room, fondling the ear of one of their oldest and most cherished toys; the emotion I felt for my small daughter, lost in a forest of legs at her first Sunday school anniversary years ago, when she stood in a tear-soaked dress, twisting the hem and my heart into knots, each sob, audible between musical rests, urging me to rescue her."

I sighed, thought and then continued, "Love is collecting his cigar butts when he is gone, and keeping them just because the aroma brings him close again. Love is laughing about it together when he finds them in the glove-box of my car."

My English teacher was satisfied.

My History teacher's last words to me before the exams were: *"If you mention Chinese men and bananas in your exam paper – I will have you failed on the spot!"*

"*Bonjour Monsieur*" I say to my Moroccan boy as I gently feel his avocados. Our eyes meet and he gives me a subtle "No squeezy my fruit please" look. I choose one and a tomato.

Dejeuner....." I say. "*Avez vous fromage?*"

He points inside the shop. It is actually a tiny supermarket. Paris is full of these little supermarkets fronted with shelves of fruit and vegetables. I spend ages examining his *fromage* and don't fancy the selection.

"*Mineral eau?*" He offers me the choice of two brands of bottled water.

It takes ages to cross the street. Cars are banked up and police stalk the street. I get my key and go up to my tidy room and kick off my boots.

I'm feeling separation anxiety for my umbrella that used to sit on my luggage in the corner of the room, the first thing to greet me when I walked in. I hope somebody gives it a good home.

I don't have a knife of course and begin to peel the avocado with my thumb nail. "What's this? Mould? Yuk – rotten! This won't do."

I get back into my hot boots, zip down in the lift and plonk the key in front of the man on the front desk. I notice he's kicked his shoes off too.

"*Cinq minutes Monsier, cinq minutes.*"

My fruiterer looks stricken.

"Ahhh sorry Madame, so sorry, so sorry" as he greets me over a huge box of pamplemousse. He tosses the avocado into a bin out in the street.

"It's Ok, OK" I pacify him.

"No, no more avocado – just *banan,* grapes and *poir.*"

"Ah so sorry Madame. Have a good day. *Bon soir, au revoir – so sorry*"

Back in my room I kick off my boots once more and towels arrive. It's 4.45 and I'm starving!

The church bells hurl out their abuse at 6 o'clock as I map out my trip to Abbesses tomorrow. A police siren interrupts with a deafening challenge. Something's been happening in Port de St Cloud today and there's only soccer on the TV.

I get out Dad's French/English dictionary. "*Parapluie*" (umbrella). The front page has his name in his slanting writing on it and "Damascus 1941." Little did he know while he was in the Middle East during the war that his daughter, not even a gleam in his eye at that stage, would be making use of this in Paris 72 years later – *mon Dieu!* Thanks Dad.

All sign of my cold has gone. It's Saturday night and some of the apartments across the road are lit up. Some people have closed their shades and gone out. The fruit shop is still open and a woman walks a little white dog past. It's raining. The streets are wet and shining and there is a throb of music managing to emerge through the noise of the traffic.

This is the third Saturday night in Paris that I am alone in my room again. I don't go out Saturday nights at home and I don't when I'm in Paris. The Eiffel Tower will be putting on a light show I can only imagine. Being married to show business for fourteen years has conditioned me to spending a lot of Saturday nights alone. And I was a very young woman then. Now I am an "older woman" and I feel it is inappropriate for me, but not everyone mind you - to sit at a bar or a restaurant and dine alone at night. I can't do it.

My daughter Rachel and my 15 year-old granddaughter Rosy are presently in Japan on a school trip with the elite ladies college Rachel teaches at. This weekend they will catch up with her old neighbours and friends she spent twelve months with a decade ago. I experienced my six week Japanese adventure too at that time and I hope she remembers to send them all my best wishes and tell them that I think of them often. During that time I also kept a daily journal. Again, it was my friend and life-saver in what was a very foreign, sometimes unhappy but poignant and amusing time in my life. At this stage I don't know what to do with it. I'll probably delete those spontaneous scribbles and musings, but as yet I can't bring myself to destroy the work I put into it, along with memories I brought back to life, that helped to fill in my time and the pages. Now it would seem like putting an old faithful dog down.

Looking back now, I find it hard to believe that Rachel and I had had such a tense time together. Instead of taking Caroline's advice of "a little bit of counselling" I began writing. I guess it had the same effect as gradually, with wisdom gained in time, most of the animosity faded from my manuscript as it faded from our relationship.

Cucumbers and Cockroaches

I tidied up and threw out some of Rosy's papers and scribbles, did some washing and turned the fan on full blast. I watched the geisha soapy that was on every day from 10.30 until 11.30 and wrote a postcard to Caroline. We'd had no contact for over a week now and I realized she hadn't had one post-card from me yet. The only appropriate one I could find was from Ginza in Tokyo, the shopping mall area and I told her about our trip to the mountains and the hotel.

Then I braved the heat, hat on my head, down to the Post Office. I crossed the road and went by Rosy's old Buddhist kinder. The kids were all in their swimsuits about to get into a big pool and were going through some sort of drill. It was very noisy with their laughter and shrieking as they splashed about. I was about to take a photo of them and decided it might be "inappropriate," so walked on to the Buddhist temple. It was deserted and I sauntered along the straight path, taking in the stone figures—all very angry with fierce eyes and gestures. I looked at the worn timbers and stone of the archway as I walked through. I usually have the desire to touch really old structures, feeling I have contact with the blood, sweat and tears of ages ago, but I had no desire to have contact now, in fact I avoided it. Did I feel too much alien spirituality oozing from it? I don't know. I sat on a large flat rock in the sun feeling I was frying myself like an egg, so I moved across to a spot in the shade, near the graves, where a cool waft of air reached me. I sat there maybe fifteen minutes with the sounds of the children and thought about the sea. Was it because I was so hot?

I closed my eyes and imagined the gentle flick of shallow waves on the shore, far away, the fragments of shell and stone and worn smooth glass that I collected by the handful, glinting amber and green in the early morning sun and the quiet whisper along the shoreline as tiny waves etched shadows on the damp sand.

The sea made me very melancholy and introspective and I could still remember a poem I wrote as a young teenager during one of these moods alone on a stormy beach.

I stand and watch with frightened stare God's symphony among

The waves that curl and fling themselves like giant dragons' tongues

To lash the silent shore.

I stand and watch with silent gaze, the swirling mass of violet haze

Heaping foam of green and gold on rocks and sand and stone and me

Until we cling together then, and beg forgiveness for some deed we must have done.

I remembered the enchanting mornings I had spent, totally alone on that same shoreline, clambering around the rock pools, peering into the blue-green and inky depths at the life there, with just my two dogs at the time for company. I was there for three weeks in my parents' holiday house. It was late winter and completely deserted. The sunny early mornings were magic. Being totally alone but for the dogs, one of which was a very protective German Shepherd, didn't bother me.

The two girls had gone to Queensland with their father to visit their grandmother. I had hoped Brad might surprise me with a visit but he didn't.

These memories had not haunted me for a long time and now here in Japan twenty-odd years later these scenes were coming back to me along with Liz's remark.

"Aren't you cutting off your nose to spite your face?"

I walked slowly back to the apartment, not wanting to return but not having anything else I could really do. I stopped and looked at some lipstick pink roses careering over a front fence and reaching up, I was able to gently pull one down to my face and smell its lovely perfume.

I arrived home and made a toasted banana sandwich.

Half-way through eating it the phone rang.

"Hullo, Hullo!" came an anxious voice.

"Who is that?"

"Oh, Obachan. I speak English then. Maddie-Rose needs full change of clothes. Clothes wet. She need all clothing for full change. You come! Come right now!"

"Yes. Yes. I will come right now."

"You come to Classroom 1-1. You know her classroom?"

"Yes. I come now – right now. OK?"

"Very good. Bye-bye."

I gulped the rest of my sandwich down and grabbed a set of clothes and was off again not bothering to grab my hat.

"Nanny I'm in here," loud and with a note of urgency. Rosy burst out of the sick-room area followed by the school nurse.

"*Obachan*... Maddie-Rose. Good. Maddie-Rose put clothes on!"

"What happened?" I asked as I helped her step out of her wet undies.

"I got water all over me."

"Well it's a very good day for getting water all over you isn't it?"

The sick-room was freezing cold and I was hurried out again by the nurse nodding, smiling and bowing.

If she'd left her in her hot class-room she'd have been dry in less than ten minutes but instead she made her stand sopping wet in the freezing cold air-conditioned sick-room until I arrived with her dry clothes!

##

Fifteen more sleeps.

I've been awake since 3.30 am. It's now 7.00. The fan is roaring, aimed at the tatami room and I woke tied up in knots with my sheets as damp as I am.

Anthony emerged as I threw myself out of my uncomfortable bed. I got not so much as a grunt from him as he drifted past to the toilet and back to the sink and began cooking toast. I folded my sheets which would go into the wash again and folded my bedding out of the way.

What could have got off to a good start went completely the other way, when Rachel who was particularly silent and grumpy at breakfast, retired to the toilet. She locked the door and for some absurd reason Anthony decided to unlock it with a bread and butter knife, exposing Rachel to me in the kitchen. This caused a tirade of anger and hysterics from her which went on for some time.

Rosy refused to stir from her bed and became a limp rag-doll, refusing to eat or get dressed until finally Rachel forced her into her clothes and she eventually ran off after her "line" that trudged daily to the saltmines. They had left her behind for the third day in a row.

I was amused by the commercials on TV for the most amazing "beauty aids." There was a harness that you stepped into and pulled up and it supported the buttock cheeks so that they looked more rounded in one's clothes – sort of a bra for the bum!

They also demonstrated strapless, backless bras that stuck to the breast skin and then clipped together at the front giving one "great cleavage."

Then there was the hair-piece that was worn on one's crown to cover the balding spot that *all we women* must inevitably produce at a certain age according to the Japanese.

I went into the bathroom and checked my hair from all angles with Rachel's hand mirror, to my satisfaction. I wondered what a let-down these women would be to their men once they actually got to the love-making and discarded all their props.

I searched the cupboards for something for lunch. It was time we started taking stock of what was left before we started buying more stuff, now the countdown had begun. Rachel and the kids were to leave on the 26th but I'd go on the 24th.

I found lots of cucumbers in the fridge, gifts from Anthony's teacher. This seemed to be the number one vegetable here apart from the daicon (white radish). I found black sesame seeds and some seaweed. I chopped it all up and dotted it with some mayonnaise and soy sauce. It was bitter. It was the cucumbers that were bitter, but I ate it anyway. I made some more coffee which was awful. The soy milk was going off in the heat and I tipped the remainder down the sink.

I thought of how the night before Rachel came face to face with the most enormous cockroach in the sink. She was about to grab it with a bunch of tissues and flush it down the toilet but it began to drink from a little pool of water around the edge of the plug-hole and she wailed, the tissues on the ready, "I can't kill it now. Look, it's thirsty! It's drinking water. I can't kill it." Instead she waited until it had finished its drink, bundled it up in the tissues and disappeared out the front door. She took it to the neighbour's vegetable garden across the road and released it there. She could have mercy on a cockroach. I was touched – I loved her. If a cockroach could appear cute and pathetic maybe I should try drinking out of the sink.

That evening Sandy called in and sat talking and then Megumi arrived with Jun. We hadn't had a visit from her for a week which was strange, and there was a call from Kaito to say he had the photos from last Sunday. Could he come over? When he arrived it was a full house, the kids on the play station and making a terrific row. He said we could order some copies which he'd bring over the next day. I was thrilled as I thought I had probably lost most of my photos at the weekend, having opened the camera with the film not completely rolled off. He told everyone about Naoto's "love at first sight" nodding at me. I could see this had annoyed Rachel and it was embarrassing to me.

There was an email via Paul in Perth for me from a colleague wanting me to keep them informed of my doings, but with the internet disconnection I couldn't keep in touch. I wondered if Sandy would let me email on hers upstairs.

2013 – Wet Sunday in Paris

I thought I'd have a sleep-in but I'm ready and dressed for breakfast at 7.30. Stomach rumbling loudly. Haven't decided what to do yet today. Am wearing new "discreetly-Paris" T shirt, long olive-green cardigan, jeans and sneakers. It's cold when I open the window. There's not that much traffic this morning.

I'm the first in to breakfast as usual. I breakfast to ABBA. Then Roy Orbison's "Pretty Woman and "The House of The Rising Sun." Ed used to sing that. The radio station sounds similar to one of Melbourne's.

There is more of an array of food on offer this morning and I decide to "steal" a hard-boiled egg. I thought my "Continental breakfast only" was what I'd paid for and that anything beyond the traditional croissant or baguette would be off-limits. The egg goes down well.

A mother and daughter arrive. Then an obvious runner in yellow T-shirt, green shorts and running shoes – middle aged. I wonder if he only eats the yoghurt but he consumes the same as me. Then two young girls arrive both friendly. And then four more runners dressed in the same outfits as the first man. They must be a team. They greet each other in German and one of the women is a very bulbous shape and zips up her fly continually as her body attempts to escape. They all gather at the table next to mine. I would like to stay longer but the half-hour it takes me to slowly consume my Continental breakfast goes quickly. I can't fit in a third cup of tea so I leave.

What to do today? I don't know. Sunday at Luxembourg Gardens or attempt three trains to Abbesses?

Back in my room "Marley and Me – The Puppy Years" is on the TV. A delightful movie about talking Labrador pups. The dog next door at home is called Marley.

The bathroom basin has been leaking all week and the maid looks at the water on the bathroom floor and rolls her eyes at me. When another maid joins her, equipped with my fresh towels, they attempt to retreat out the door again when they see me sitting there.

"*Excuse moi!*" I show her the wet floor and say "sink leaking."

"*Non non*" she tries to reassure me, suggesting with an accusing glance that I am the culprit, flooding the bathroom just for entertainment. She bends down to inspect the floor and the fittings.

"*Non, non*" she shakes her head. "No leaking."

"Well it's not me. Every time I turn on the tap – water on floor." I am getting angry. She doesn't understand a word I say of course. She eventually finds the leak at the back of the basin, where I knew it was all the time.

"Ah!" She runs off and returns with a big plunger and proceeds to "solve" the problem. She lays a huge towel on the floor and begins her operation.

"Is that a clean towel?" I question, hoping it isn't a dirty one from next door where they may well be suffering from gastro or quite possibly "*sepsis of unknown aetiogy.*"

"*Oui – oui.*" She assures me the matter will be addressed tomorrow.

"Tomorrow" (pointing to her eye – 'I' – meaning herself) "tomorrow." (We speak a similar lame language. It also reminds me of Miko in Japan. When she said 'I', she pointed to her nose.)

"OK." I get up to get out of her way and she says "No matter" withdrawing her accusations.

I tell her to leave a towel on the wet section of the carpet. "Not good for carpet."

"No – thank you, thank you" in a pleading tone and beaming at me.

I am writing this while she is here and occasionally she glances my way. I think she suspects I am drafting a letter of complaint to management.

8.45 The church bells ring out. It is Sunday. Just as I am about to head for the Metro, down comes the rain – pouring *"chats et chiens"* and no *"parapluie."* I sit and watch at the window as it saturates the slate roof across the way. Well, I'm going nowhere until this stops. I am in light clothes and coughing again. Everyone is in coats. I put my cord jacket on and the blue scarf I've never worn yet. Maybe I'll get coffee at Le Cardinal nd wait for the weather to clear up. A whole week has passed since I met Penny and Mark at the apartment in the Marais. I wonder where they are now.

I choose to sit behind the glass screen with the smokers. There's a dog in here too, a German shorthaired pointer. It's pouring and Le Cardinal is cosy if not a trifle smoky. A dark-skinned well-dressed young man at the next table turns to me with a smile and a *"Bonjour."*

The young man on the desk at the hotel always says "Hello" to me and I say *"Bonjour"* to him – and he says "Thank you" when I hand him my key and I say *"Merci."* - Silly isn't it.

The young man next to me writes away on his smart phone and I from the "stone-age" write with a pen in this cumbersome book. It's left over writing material from my two year stint as a volunteer in the reading program with 13 year-olds at the Aboriginal school back home. That was the year that the bush-fires took 173 lives and totally consumed the town of Marysville not far away from me. Only a wind-change diverted that and another fire at Kinglake from reaching Healesville and Warrandyte where Caroline lived.

Funny how people react in emergencies. I left the house during the first evacuation with dogs, cat, two dining-room chairs that belonged to my grandparents, (hadn't yet taken possession of the armchairs,) a few of my own favourite paintings and some ancient family photos. A friend of mine put her dogs in the car and ran back to the house to shave her legs.

The teenage boy assigned to me at the school wasn't up for participating in anything to do with reading. His only ambition was to be a top footballer and that was the reason he'd come to Melbourne. I eventually gave up my attempts to interest him with books at his six year-old's reading level. I could not compete with his vocal interruptions and joyous re-enactments of wading through the pristine waters of One Arm Point in the Kimberley, spearing fish and turtle. I listened transfixed as he nurtured repeatedly, the experiences that his young and independent heart took him back to and that he longed for. As I came away from one of my first sessions, the Head called out "Learnt any language yet?"

"No, but I learnt how to skin a kangaroo today."

A cappuccino is the best coffee Le Cardinal does. Again, in a tall glass and very hot. I shouldn't have chosen to sit in this area. I am passively smoking Rothman's and Marlboro. Two men sit smoking as they enjoy their *petite dejeuner*.

Church bells chime. Two churches this time in a raucous duet.

Baguettes by the armful are carried through the rain. People carry bunches of flowers, probably off to lunch at family or friends' homes.

I really need my *parapluie*! I'll be hopping from café to café to dodge this rain all day. Better to be here in the smoky atmosphere than in my empty hotel room and there's not much point going to Luxembourg Gardens in this rain.

Fourteen sleeps to go – and the heat is on.

Kaito rang to say he'd arrive with the rest of the party at 1 pm, so Rachel went off to the supermarket on her bike, telling me to stay with the kids.

I had felt I needed to get out of the house as I could feel myself sinking into a gloom and doom mood that morning. Was there a storm brewing? Should I be gathering tiny white pebbles like the ants do, to build a shelter from an impending bushfire? Rachel had gone silently around house-cleaning and frowning while I tried to do my bit, but I felt an atmosphere of resentment growing around us.

When Rachel had gone I sat down opposite Anthony who was poring over a book of Australian birds. I attempted to make conversation with him.

"Do you know Anthony, I would have been very lost without my diary to talk to." My words seemed to fall on deaf ears but after a long pause he eventually looked up vacantly.

"Why?"

"Because I'm here all day when you're at school, with no-one to talk to, nowhere to go and nothing to do. My diary is my one friend I can to talk to."

I waited for a sympathetic reaction, even maybe a little light repartee from my grandson. Following another long silence he looked up from his book slowly and very steadily fixing my gaze with his huge blue eyes said very dreamily....

"Do you know – the willy-wagtail, little penguin, black swan, pelican, sulphur-crested cockatoo, sparrow and Australian magpie... are on my 'Seen in my lifetime' list?" Then he added, our pupils locked together and with a pronunciation as crudely as he could manage with his continuing blank expression, "Do you know that *mai-**asa*** means every morning and *mai-**bum*** means every night?"

Rachel slumped inside with bags of shopping, hot and angry.

"You're really going to have to help me with the shopping in future!"

"But I asked you did you want me to come and you said that meant the kids would have to be on their own."

"I did not."

"Rachel you did. I would have come. You told me to stay with the kids."

"Why can't you just be an ordinary grandmother?"

Then together with the shopping, a lifetime of resentments poured forth and lay around me like scattered broken toys – that I'd broken. No man can hurt you like your child can.

"I'm very sorry I can't undo the past Rachel."

I reached for the door but hesitated. I couldn't disappear and hurt the feelings of her friends who were about to arrive.

"... and why must you be so charming to my friends' husbands *anyway*?"

"Well, I certainly won't be here when your friends arrive," and I grabbed my diary and followed my shadow down the road to the rumble of thunder and the echo of her last words.

I walked to the temple attached to the kindergarten and slowly followed the path with the stone figures. A woman with bleached reddened hair tied in a handkerchief ahead of me, a garden worker, bowed and said "Konitchiwa." I said "Konitchiwa" back to her and nodded, trying to swallow the rising lump in my throat. Then she pointed to the sky and mumbled something else and I nodded and she hurried off. I sat on the rock that had been my shady seat the other day.

Yes, in hindsight I could not deny that I had made some very foolish choices in life that might have seemed the answer at the time. One could look back in hindsight, with the wisdom that only comes with age and retrace a smoother track to follow, but the journey is a one-way trip without a rehearsal.

Maybe I'd go slowly to the shrine now. The apartment would be full and they would all be there until about five o'clock when Rachel went to her taiko lesson. I had to stall for time.

It began to rain softly. Walking into the road I found a shop that sold happy shoes. I would have to remember that, as my niece had asked for some happy shoes. There were some very drab dress shops and even drabber food shops. The air was alive with the whine of insects. The thunder still rolled as I reached the shrine. There were people worshipping inside and in the area outside under red and white awnings. It looked like a baby was being blessed.

I walked to one of the little pagodas and sat on the mossy steps. I began writing in my diary again and the peacocks began calling. The crows in the tree above me squawked and squabbled with hoarse sounding cries to each other and those in the woodlands behind and around me joined in. The rattling sound of a train every few minutes broke through the atmosphere which had become very sullen. The drums in the temple sounded slowly and ominously and then quickened. The railway crossing sounded its signal for a long time and the drums stopped like an animal on the alert. In another two minutes a train signal sounded again raucously and the crickets set up a chorus beside me once more and the drums resumed. It was a cacophony of badly choreographed sound.

Another train went past, causing the steps I sat on to shake. I hadn't experienced an earthquake yet. I had been told it was almost a daily occurrence, but after four weeks I was still waiting. That's what I needed right now.

An enormous black butterfly flitted through the tall canopy of trees. The doves set up a repetitious monotone that I had at first thought was the recording of a man's voice speaking Japanese over the loud speakers. They said "Dear dear ho ho." They had basser voices than Melbourne doves. I watched some land in a group just ahead of me and proceed to toddle like Charlie Chaplin impersonators, chasing each other along the path, just like they did in Paris. Someone was playing the flute very badly.

As I walked past the enclosure with the unhealthy looking rooster and the peacocks, I saw the priest again, dressed in aqua robes with a long lilac-coloured coat and he looked like he was blessing a car. It was a silver station wagon and appeared brand new. He walked around it waving white paper streamers on a stick. He then disappeared into the temple once more and the car was driven away.

"Dear dear ho ho, dear dear ho ho."

I turned off the main shrine road and passed a tiny nursery and found myself at the train station where we'd caught the train to Tokyo. Then I walked back along the filthy river that moved stealthily as a khaki serpent through the green banks silent and purulent, whispering Ed's words - *"You're gonna end up a very lonely old woman – you know that."*

Some of the homes here were quite ordered with gardens and colourful pot-plants. The road separated these houses from the river and somehow bits of the gardens had wandered across the road to the banks and there was a tumbling of exotic flowers down to the water's edge. There were small cemeteries dotted around the town and at the two shrines, and the stink of the drains came up through the pavement. At this point of the walk my foot was being eaten into across the instep by my scuffs and I began limping. I passed the ice-cream parlour that we'd been to the other night and a different, much older woman was there and she bowed as I passed the window.

Where was my Mum when I needed her? I found 500 yen in my wallet and decided it was time for comfort food. I chose a very nice ice-cream and chocolate sandwich wafer from the cabinet outside and went in and paid for it.

I walked back down the road to Rosy's temple and sat on a rock outside, feeling it might be disrespectful to take food into the temple grounds.

My foot looked raw and it was 4.30. Maybe I could walk back very slowly. What would I do though if they were still there? I really wanted to arrive just before 5. I certainly didn't want to hear how *"beautifor"* I was ever again. I decided to sit for ten minutes on the sheltered rock where I'd begun my retreat that afternoon.

When I reached the apartment Anthony was outside on his scooter. I watched him leap off, tossing it aside and race in calling out "She's here!"

"Have your visitors gone?" I asked him as he returned and looked at me with a screwed up face, shielding his eyes from the sun.

"They're just leaving." The tiny twin friends of Rosy's shot past me like two sparks out of a fire.

"Not them."

"Oh, two car-loads have just left. Mum told them you thought it would be too crowded so you went out. They've left presents for you."

I groaned in despair at Rachel's weak excuse for me and went in, meeting Rachel in the doorway as I kicked my shoes off.

"Can you mind Rosy while we go to taiko?"

I stared at her. "No. Last time you left her with me to go to taiko she cried all over Megumi's husband. Take her with you!"

She grumbled something and with drumsticks in hand said "C'mon then Rosy. Just remember, you can't play the taiko tonight."

I had two hours of peace ahead of me and I sat in the darkening room with a glass of water staring at a cooking show. I watched some kind of sandworms, very long with hundreds of legs writhing in a spicy red sauce. A smiling woman sliced through them a couple of times and then attacked them with her chopsticks, gobbling them up alive. I jumped up and turned the TV off. I could not watch such macabre eating delights.

They arrived back later than usual at 7.30.

"Don't make me anything thank you. I'm not hungry," as I sipped my water and sulked.

"You've got to eat and I've bought this sushi especially for you and I'm not going to waste it."

I sat on the floor and disinterestedly began dishing up some food and Rachel said "I'm sorry we had that upset this morning but...."

"I'm not discussing it with you while I'm eating."

Sitting uncomfortably on my knees, I put some corn and beans into my bowl.

The moments of glum silence were interrupted by the increasing sound of a very heavy truck rumbling down the road towards the apartment. The room was going back and forth and suddenly the lights began swinging madly.

The children and Rachel screamed in unison – "EARTHQUAKE!"

I put a piece of broccoli into my bowl, carefully checking to see if there were any grubs in it as always was the case in Bali, turning it over twice for close examination and then lifting it to my mouth. The three of them leapt up to the window.

I chased some corn around my dish with my chopsticks. It was a bit tricky trying to pick corn up with chopsticks. I was aware then of Rosy's plate smashing on the floor.

Rachel and the children now stood by the window peering out into the darkness. There was stillness once more but for the kitchen light still swinging. I watched the pendulum effect as if mesmerized.

I couldn't have cared less if the roof had caved in.

Later in my bed, I despaired. Then I heard my mother's distant voice from years ago saying "You don't trust me. That's what really hurts. You take your father's side and you don't trust me."

"I'm so sorry" I whispered tearfully into my pillow.

####

Thirteen more sleeps.

I made myself invisible, sitting on the back doorstep sipping my tea.

As Rachel tidied up she handed me a kimono that Hiromi had brought for me, with a bright egg-yellow obi to go around my waist.

"I was really looking forward to yesterday you know" I said as I took it from her.

The group we'd been with that Sunday had arrived with a kimono lady, especially to dress Rachel up in a kimono that was to be a gift and Kaito had taken photos. I was evidently expected to dress up for photos too.

"I had told them when we parted on Sunday how I was looking forward to it and then – to just not be there – how rude. They would think it was very odd."

"Yes, well it was *your* decision. You didn't have to go out. I told them you'd probably got lost going for a walk. They waited and waited."

When we sat down at the table at lunchtime we were a silent little group. Then Rachel began reading aloud a text message from a colleague who had left Japan earlier for Europe. She had a new baby and made a practice of texting everyone she'd had contact with in Japan with the greatest trivia about her baby's daily progress, with details of what went in one end and what came out the other.

I sat morose and silent until Rachel read out "and we look forward to games of hide and seek." I looked at Anthony and leant towards him and whispered "in the middle of Tokyo." He laughed and Rachel went on. "We will soon be moving to double breastfeeds."

"She's grown two more…" I whispered again to Anthony and at this point his eyes lit up and he spat the milk he had in his mouth across the table. Then Rachel began laughing and we were all laughing.

As I went to the sink with the dishes, she came across and putting her arms around me, said in a warm and almost sympathetic tone "Give me a hug." We held on to each other for some time. This was my child, who at thirty-six had been addressing a gathering of officials at the Japanese Embassy in Perth. At the same age I had been telling my English teacher at night-school how I measured love in stale cigar butts!

"You're not pulling your weight. You're here to support me." Was that my Mum's voice? I had let my mother down. Mum had let me down too in many ways that she wasn't aware of, but she had done her very best. Now I had let my daughter down it seemed, again and again. My only enemy really was loneliness and a lack of confidence which led to a continuing need for approval while I'd been with them. Rachel's enemy was stress and having to dog-paddle in the deep-end while keeping the children's heads above water, seeing me as just another added weight in her battle to achieve one of her life's ambitions. Where had our empathy gone?

Anthony switched on his play-station at my request. His mother went on wrapping blue and white china in bubble-wrap, asking my opinion on how to pack and what to pack. I sat on the floor and learnt how to make little people co-operate with me on the screen. Life certainly was not like this game. Wouldn't this generation be disappointed when they found out that life was not all about pushing buttons to get people to do what you wanted, unless of course technology overcame that problem too in the future. He eventually tired of our game and went next door, returning soon after complaining that the boys had sent him home. Later Megumi came in complaining that Anthony had been in there teaching the boys English swear words and that she was sick of it. After he had had another good talking to from Rachel she sat down and worked on her speeches for her farewells the next day.

When she went off to bed she hugged me again.
I said "Rachel, I couldn't have loved you any more than I have. I've always been so proud of you and what you've achieved. I boast about you to everyone."

2013 – A goose in St Cloud on a Sunday.

Well, I didn't get far. Left "Le Cardinal" with every intention of spending the day at Abbesses. I was about to descend the stairs to the Metro.

Ahead of me, down the street as far as the eye could see, markets have opened up. Delighted, I wander down, taking photos as I go.

Boulangeries, fromageries, fish, escargot, flower-stalls bursting with blooms for apartment balconies. Jewellery, clothing, shoes, rugs for apartment floors. If only I was buying for an apartment for myself somewhere in Paris.

Dogs on leads. Two beggars. One, an old black African with hand held out begs, seemingly invisible to everybody. I feel horrible passing him by, not once but twice.

Here, huge pink gaping fish, standing up on their tails in beds of ice, heads turned in profile, staring with dead eyes, like that beggar.

I walk up and down gazing at stalls. Crowds of shoppers carrying heavily laden baskets. I decide to buy lunch and dinner for myself. Stop at one of the many fruit and vegetable stalls and buy bananas, tomatoes, spinach leaves, *poirs*. Then go inspecting the *fromage* stall – *Brie*!

"*S'il vous plait Monsieur – un petite brie pour moi – petite.*" I indicate with my fingers. He holds up a slab.

"*Oui – petite brie.*" He cuts a slice. "*Merci beaucoup.*" One euro 70.

Then to the boulangerie for bread.

"*Petite pain pour moi s'il vous plait Madame.*" She points to baguettes.

"*Non* – too hard!" (I have no idea what hard is in French). She understands and squeezes one to show me they are *not* hard.

"*OK Merci Madame.*" I take *le deux baguettes* and hand her a 20 euro note. I hope she gives me the right change.

I come away knowing I have food for the rest of the day and now cannot pass the black beggar without putting what I have left in loose change, amounting to a measly one euro 20 into his crinkly hand. That was lousy but everyone else was ignoring him totally and he could get a baguette or a sample of brie with that.

Merci Madame – Merci" he bows with thanks, and nods with eyes that stare vacantly over my head.

Porte de St Cloud with its market is a great place after all.

I return to the hotel. The same young man is at the desk. I don't know why I speak to him in broken English with a sort of French accent as he speaks perfect

English back to me. But then I am a real goose. I say *"Le Marche est tres bien."*

"Yes" he says.

"Raining" I comment, lost for the French word for rain and too busy trying desperately to think of the word for umbrella.

But he says "Yes and where *is* your umbrella?"

"Ah Oui" I sigh – "I left it in café on Boulevard Haussmann yesterday and when I go back – gone!"

He looks at me as though I am indeed a goose who can't even speak English properly.

"You won't let it rain tomorrow will you" I add taking my key from him. He laughs and I waddle off up to my room as a goose does.

The cheese is really gooey and I scoop it up with my baguette. It's the kind of ripe brie that almost makes your eyes water – like Caroline and I were used to buying twenty years ago when we roamed Paris together from market to market on the cheap. Poor girl, she often reminisces "Remember that time in Paris when we didn't have enough money as usual and we shared a lettuce for lunch (or was it dinner) and you said 'Well we're in Paris aren't we?'"

Each time we laughingly recall that incident in 1993, I apologize to her once more, and she now comes back with "But you've always taught me *resilience* and I'm grateful for that Mum."

I wash the spinach and eat a few mouthfuls with some cherry tomatoes. All that's missing is the wine, but I decided to keep my meal as cheap as possible for the day.

I should have given that African man a decent amount in notes. But he doesn't understand I have a car thousands of miles away waiting to be repaired and I've broken my front tooth which means a couple of thousand for a crown and I'm trying to be as frugal as I can because I'm on a holiday I can't afford. "That's not good enough" an irritating little voice inside whispers! "He's probably got no idea where his next meal is coming from." (At this point I'm not going to make comparisons about myself being married to a country music singer for fourteen years!) I should have bought food for him and put it in his hand. I'm the one on the "glamorous sounding holiday" and as for teeth – he may not have any at all!

When I get home I am going to have to change my lifestyle. After all, I do live in a tourist area. I hardly ever go to the markets and rarely go to cafes. My dull life confined to a studio with a cat is going to change. Could I volunteer at the animal shelter again without adopting three more dogs? I don't think I could. If I can afford to, when I get back after the dentist and the mechanic have taken whatever money I have left, it will be coffee at the "Mocha and Lime" in Healesville every other day.

I finish off with a huge beautiful golden *poir* for dessert. I have eaten well. I feel much better for some food – strange that.

It's 1 pm, about 10 pm in Sydney and Melbourne I think. I've got to get out of this room.

At the market they are beginning to pack up their produce. I slowly stroll the full length of the stalls, still fascinated by the variety of foods I've not seen before. Large birds hang upside down, yellow and naked. They look as if they've been smoked – quite ghastly – with long necks and heads and bills still attached, the wings still covered with feathers.

"Goose or duck?"

He answers *"canard."* I'll have to check Dad's dictionary later.

I clutch my last handful of change, having scraped together a lousy 80 cents which is gladly received again by the same African man.

The fish stalls still hold the big gaping faces and I hope they've not died in vain. The fishmongers are obviously well tuned mentally with all the brain food they go home with.

A bus goes past and I wonder how Diana would feel about Naomi Watts playing her, with the image of her on the back-side of every Paris bus, and that face, one of a pretty imposter!

I come to the end of my inspection of juicy olives and earthy mushrooms of every kind and goat's cheeses covered in ashy mould. I stand for a reprieve for a few seconds at one of the flower stalls, a hint of pure fragrance instead of the fish and meat. There are many azaleas and cyclamen and tortured stunted olive trees.

I pass by the Metro and wonder if I should hop on a train but I'm really not in the mood now to set off on a journey, even a small one, and I wander around the central point of town and past the D'Eglise-St Jeannede-Chantal Church that has the over-worked bell-ringer.

There is a film crew with a bunch of young people gathered near "Le Cardinal." A black van is parked at the roundabout in the centre of the road with a large sign saying "The Much Much" printed in large white letters, (something lost in translation here?). There are cameras and loud clothes. The girls are dressed like glamorous young things in extreme outfits, perhaps young prostitutes. A movie in the making? No it turns out to be a fashion collection being shown off by young "just graduated" design students, so I learn later from Mr Google. I walk past my hotel and up the street again, checking the window of the Patisserie and feel I'm beginning to look like a street-walker myself.

I return to "Le Cardinal" and take a seat outside. At the next table are two loud young Americans drunk with their own awareness of "doing a stint in Paris." They both have professional looking cameras. They must be with the film crew. They talk about where they "shot her" and compare shots. There is a lot of the F...word and blasphemy. They sound like they love the sound of their own voices. They are nauseating. One so patronizing o the other with over enthusiastic ravings of his "work."

"Fuck man – I mean – your work is mind-blowing!"

I am glad when they get up to leave, loudly blaspheming because where they have to go "is a fucking 45 minutes away you know - dude!" (Excuse my French.)

I order a cappuccino and watch the hands on my watch almost going backwards. I should have gone somewhere on the train today, but it's not inviting, the thought of going into central Paris at this time of day with the migrating wildebeest. I'll go tomorrow, Monday.

It's 3.15 as I sit and watch the crowd. An old couple in their seventies come by beautifully dressed. The man is a real gentleman in his tailored clothes, the woman obviously once a great beauty. I think that when this generation, somewhere between mine and my parents' have died out there might be a different population of people here – I hope not. The French are too protective of their culture to allow that to happen.

2004 – Lunching with the girls

12 more sleeps. I walked around to the supermarket near the kid's school. Kaito caught up with me on his bike. I apologized for not being there Saturday. I thanked him for the photos and endeavoured to explain in a combination of sign language and pidgin English that Rachel and I had had a "little disagreement" and that's why I had not been there for their visit. I don't believe he understood a word. I thought he understood English, which puzzled me and off he rode. Maybe he didn't wish to speak to me after my atrocious behavior of disappearing before they arrived on Saturday. I watched as he pedaled off down the street. I don't think obachans in Japan get a lack of respect from *their* children let alone their grandchildren and he wouldn't know what to make of any of us.

At the supermarket I bought quite a few things including what I believed to be tomato juice.

I went upstairs when Sandy got home and was about to send off my reply to my work colleagues, but as Rachel had the nurse from the High School arriving in a few minutes with flowers and presents for both of us I decided against it. She wanted me to be there for this "special presentation," from the nurse with the white arm, the one that directed my eyes to the invisible Mt. Fuji in the distance and who giggled about the Hugh Grant look-alike. Her present for me was a very large framed photo – glass and all, of Mt Fuji with a train zooming across the plains. Not a photo I would really want on my walls at home and how was I going to get it in to my luggage and get it home without the glass breaking? It was huge. Still, how nice of her to give a present to me, someone she had met only once, and I had nothing to give in return. The Japanese were such generous gift-givers.

Megumi and Miko arrived shortly after and I was informed that my tomato juice was a cherry drink.

Miko said she had our weekend planned for us and together with Rachel, went off to a big shopping centre at 8 pm to help choose farewell presents for a number of people.

I had the job of getting the kids organized for bed.

####

11 more sleeps.

I stayed in all day just watching the TV news in Japanese and Angela rang from Australia at 5 pm and we talked happily for three quarters of an hour while the sumo wrestlers staggered around on the television. Her estranged husband had moved in with her. Was that OK? "Yes." Why not? The more the merrier, as long as the dogs and cat were OK. I could hear Coco barking in the background. She was still alive and well by the sounds.

Rachel arrived home tonight with another lot of flowers and more goodbye letters from students and photos of her goodbye ceremony with a big banner which read "THANKS RACHEL."
Megumi and Miko called in.

####

Ten more sleeps and Bastille Day in France, July 14th - but I am in Japan.

I attempted to find my way to the library just to read some Melbourne newspapers but didn't take the map with me. I took a wrong turn, went around in a circle and eventually arrived back at home base. I always did this in Paris but this was different. There was nothing to see while being lost. I couldn't face the entire day in the apartment, but this only occupied half an hour of it anyway.
I watched TV all day ending with an hour of sumo wrestling. It was a worry to have to resort to sumo wrestling for entertainment but this kept me occupied for the hour. Huge stag beetles locked in battle,

throwing their opponents to the ground, slapping their whalemeat thighs, lifting their legs out sideways like elephants locking tusks together.

Rosy arrived home and was in a pleasant mood, although she claimed she had been sick today at school. She changed into a dress to go to her old kindergarten for a visit as arranged.

We met the kindergarten staff. The building was two storied and overlooked the temple and garden. It was all very formal, with Rachel and Rosy passive and sweet, their lilting voices chatting in Japanese as I tiptoed along behind them in courteous silence.

Megumi came in when we returned and asked if tomorrow, being her day off, would I like to go to lunch just with her and Miko.

"I'd *love* to."

####

Nine more sleeps...

I went with Megumi and Miko to lunch. It was a fiercely hot day, but I had a pleasant time spent with just the two of them, laughing and trying to communicate together with our phrase books in hand.

They took me to a Bean Restaurant and we had a walk around a small Japanese garden there. Inside there were displays of art and craft and a painting of a beautiful woman with long dark hair wearing a red kimono, with a black cat stretching on her knee. It reminded me of Rachel and I wondered if I could paint her in a similar pose. I did get around to attempting a painting later but Paul refused to hang it, saying he didn't want such a formidable image of Rachel looking down on him.

We had a tasting of hot soy milk and then soy milk with soy sauce, which was like a bean soup with tofu in it. It was a different consistency to what I had tried before, more like a paste with slices of spring onion. Then we had lunch. This was the most Japanese style meal I had had. Too much of it though. I had soy noodles in a milky liquid with thin slices of squid or some kind of rubbery fish, green seaweed and some little dry flaky balls. Quite nice, but I couldn't finish it all. Then we went to a green-grocery store-come nursery. There were flowers there that I didn't recognize.

That night Rachel had her break-up party to go to. We had had a really severe thunder storm earlier. Rachel was sent home early to avoid it and Anthony was kept at school until it was over. This was followed by torrential rain.

####

Eight more sleeps…

The kids finished classes at lunchtime and the house soon became a complete mess of papers and junk.

Rachel walked in around 1 pm to deposit more gifts that she'd been presented with. She'd had a morning of "cleaning" tasks in the school grounds, assuring me that no, she hadn't been on her hands and knees scrubbing floors but I would not have been surprised at all. Then the staff had taken her out to lunch. She seemed very sad to be leaving Japan behind her.

The girl Anthony sat next to at school arrived and the TV was taken over again and there was more mess everywhere.

Rachel came home after her farewell from the Yakuba with more flowers. "I'll really have to take you to meet them."

"Why do you want *me* to meet them?"

"Because they'd think it strange if I didn't. Sandy took her brother when he was here from America."

I had no intention of being taken down to the Yakuba so they could look me over just to save face for Rachel.

She was horrified at the mess in the house and began going through it with Rosy. None of the mess could be attributed to my doing and I didn't know where to go to get out of her way. There was nowhere to go.

I went into the tatami room and opened the screen door and leant over the railing. I saw a man on a bicycle coming up the road. As he reached me I realized it was Kaito. He seemed unsure of whether he should recognize me or not and I called out to him and he smilingly turned his bike around and came over to the window. "I've got the photos" he grinned. "I bring them around tomorrow." I indicated to him to come around to the front door.

"Rachel's here. Just five minutes" and opened the door to him.

Rachel greeted him at the door and he was all smiles. He asked her questions in Japanese and she told him we had plans to go out the next day and Sunday too. I heard him mention Naoto and he pointed to me and laughed. I left the two of them talking and went back to the tatami room and stood, enjoying the cool air pouring in. The kids across the road were laughing and playing with buckets of water, making very muddy deep puddles and jumping in them.

After Kaito left, Rachel sat crying quietly on the couch.

"I'm just so sad to be leaving" she sobbed. When her tears subsided she said "Sandy upstairs wrote me a lovely letter. I'll show you. Do you want to read it?"

We'd said goodbye to Sandy that morning. She had left at 8 am for her four-week summer vacation back home in the States. She'd brought around the cereal and soy milk she had left. Rachel had gone upstairs to say goodbye to her and was gone for quite a while. I briefly said goodbye to her at the door and wished her well.

The letter went on to say what an inspiration Rachel was, what a wonderful teacher she was, how she would always be inspired by Rachel and her determination to follow her dreams. How wonderful it had been for the children and how she had watched them blossom over the year. *"One day your children will thank you for the wonderful experience you have given them and they will benefit in life because of it."*

I wondered if Maddie-Rose would thank her when she was all grown up.

"You must feel very happy with your achievements. This has been a truly rewarding experience for you. You must feel very happy. It's wonderful to have so many lovely things said about you, isn't it?"

The thunder began rumbling again and the doorbell rang. It was Megumi and Miko.

####

Saturday morning and it is incredibly hot and muggy. At 9 am we are waiting out the front for Megumi.

We all marched off to the station, Rachel was light-heartedly chatting in Japanese. In the train it was lovely and cool and I noticed for the first time that the green fabric on the seats was the exact shade of green that the endless rice fields outside were.

We passed through Miko's home town where she had been born. Her grandmother lived there still and her sister was building a house in the next town.

Rosy was busy further up the carriage entertaining the men by turning her sandals almost inside out and flopping about in them while pulling absurd faces.

It took about an hour to get to Ashikaga. We were heading into mountains, and we crossed a river before we came to the city. This area was a pleasant surprise. There didn't seem to be the maze of telegraph poles as in the area around the apartment and the roads were wider. The whole feel of the place seemed more culturally refined and the people didn't look like they were farming a quarter-acre block, particularly those coming and going from the art gallery.

I stood in the cool entrance, taking in the large oil painting there that I was rather intrigued with. It was a Michelin man with all kinds of images superimposed over him. Miko had only brought us to the art gallery so we could use the toilets. I could hear the usual noise that accompanied my daughter's family wherever they went, particularly in wash-rooms.

I was sorry to leave the gallery and would have liked to look around, but we were led out by Miko to a long narrow street with its shops, restaurants, old houses and boutiques and curio shops. We found one that specialized in indigo dyed fabric, clothing, wall hangings, table cloths and norens. Miko bought a beautiful noren in indigo and white with an intricate design and asked me if I was going to buy one. She pointed to a beautiful indigo and white wall-hanging. "You like?"

"Yes it's beautiful."

"Then I buy for you – present" she said, pointing to her nose. Whenever Miko referred to herself she pointed to her nose.

"No Miko. No. I couldn't. Really, you must not."

"Yes, I buy for you." And she had the old woman in a kimono get down a boxed one for me. I felt embarrassed in front of Rachel who would wonder what I had done to deserve a present.

Rachel came over to me. "I think I'll buy one of these. I love them."

Miko looked up from the noren that was being wrapped for me. "You want for you Rachel? Let me. Let *meee*." She pointed to her nose again. "Present for you."

"No, no no," said Rachel waving her away and there was a bit of a verbal struggle as to who would pay.

Miko had been eyeing off another wall hanging twice the size which was tacked to the wall nearly to the high ceiling. We looked at each other.

"Let's buy Miko that" I suggested. It was a little more than what she had spent on ours together.

"Last one. Last one" said the kimono lady in Japanese.

"I wonder if she'd let us have the one on the wall."

The old woman called out to a man in the back room, whom I imagined to be her son and he arrived with a very long extension ladder, rolled his eyes at her and proceeded to climb up to the tall ceiling.

"He says it's a bit dusty. We can have it for 1000 yen instead of 3200 yen."

"OK. OK."

Miko was delighted with it and I'd bought a tablecloth for Caroline as well. Altogether between us we'd spent quite a lot of yen and there was much gracious bowing and well-wishing and sayonaring as we left.

The shops were full of beautiful handcrafts and fashionable clothes and we zigzagged back and forth along the street, browsing through them, having Miko translate the menus in the restaurant windows.

We chose to have lunch in a little restaurant where an old man sat on a high stool at the counter cutting up long beans with scissors. The eating area was a raised platform of tatami matting with low tables and colourful cushions. We removed our shoes. There was a lot of laughter and talk between Rachel, Miko and the people behind the counter.

I ordered a vegetarian meal of fried noodles and vegetables and drank barley tea, which only went down well with savoury food.

We continued to meander around the town.

"This is the kind of place I had imagined I would come to" said Rachel. "I said I wanted mountains. Seventy five percent of Japan is mountainous but I got sent to the twenty-five percent flat country."

"Yes, If only you'd been sent here Rachel, but still, you wouldn't know Miko and Megumi."

"No and I've loved the schools I've been teaching at and the kids have been just wonderful, but I said to Paul that Mum would wonder what on earth we saw in Japan. Our area is so uninteresting. But at least now you've seen some of the places I think of as the *real* Japan."

Miko's kids bought what looked like long bread sticks but which tasted like fairy floss and had been made with brown sugar.

We found the school, the oldest academic institution in Japan built in the 9th Century. There was a gingko tree in the grounds, 550 years old, with a trunk like stone and an enormous girth. And a graveyard where many smooth grey boulders sat on end interested us. This was a mass grave of samurai warriors according to Miko. We wanted to photograph it but Miko was horrified.

"No no no!" she cried waving her hands to stop us.

"Photograph shrine and *accidentally* get graves in picture but not graves only!"

She had stopped us taking photographs a little earlier when I found some ancient stone figures of children and I had called all the kids over to sit amongst them for a photo.

"No, no, no…….graves! No photo!"

A lot of the buildings were built in the sixteenth century. There were some very pleasant two-storied houses lining the streets and I thought Ashikaga could be a very agreeable place to live.

The main building had been erected in the 18th century after lightning had struck the original thatched roof of the 9th century one. This looked like it was made of cedar and the roof was also thatched. There were lots of sliding doors with the milky paper panes opening on to verandahs that peeped through leafy bamboo to formal gardens and ponds. Tatami flooring was laid throughout and the whole building smelled strongly of fresh straw. It was beautiful.

We had quite a long walk back to the station but it had been a wonderful day. We'd been on our feet for six hours and Rachel had her taiko lesson at 5 pm.

It was 4 pm by the time we hopped on the train. Rosy sat next to Miko, opposite Rachel, leaning like an abandoned rag-doll against the woman on the other side of her, who also slept with her mouth wide open. She omitted the occasional whine and moan that I heard coming from the tatami room at night. Rosy was exhausted and so was I and we still had that long walk from the train to the apartment. We got her legs in motion once off the train and she gradually managed to keep up with us, irritably refusing to take the hand I offered.

Rachel walked straight in and then out again to her taiko lesson, not changing the rhythm in her step, drum sticks in hand. I wondered how on earth she kept going at that pace.

I was left to find something for all of us to eat. When I looked in the fridge there was nothing, only bits and pieces of left-overs but I managed to make up enough to keep them happy. Saturday was the big food buying day and we hadn't got around to it—in fact it had been forgotten.

All I wanted to do was curl up on the floor and sleep.

I decided to put some rice on in the rice-cooker which I'd never used before. I had never used one at home either. I didn't know where the on-off buttons were. I only knew Rachel washed the rice first and used a measuring cup. I put two cups in and too much water because I was scared it might dry up and burn the precious rice cooker which she'd bought herself, and which now belonged to the apartment, therefore the property of the Yakuba. All the buttons had Kana or Katakana writing or whatever, so there was no indication or directions for me to follow. I knew Rachel cooked Japanese rice for 45 minutes which seemed to me to be 36 minutes too long. I kept opening it and checking what was happening and moved Rosy's seat further away in case it exploded on to her. I knew I would probably get into trouble when Rachel got home – but if I prepared nothing I might be in trouble too.

"Why did you put rice on? I thought we'd had a big enough lunch not to need dinner. I'm not hungry" as she walked in the door. "Yuk. It's like porridge. What did you do to it? You have to go exactly by the directions and you don't interrupt the cycle. It just turns off when it's cooked."

"Well it's all in Kanji and Katakana. How can I go by the directions? I can't read it and I don't even know what buttons I pushed."

We were pushing each other's buttons again.

"Oh for heaven's sake!"

The kids were still fighting sleep and each other, but I went out like a light.

I was aware during the night, of a struggle going on in the tatami room and a child being dragged off to sleep alone in the dressing room and angry sounds coming from Rachel. Then a heavy-footed return to the tatami room followed by more arguing. I was disassociated from it and I drifted in and out of sleep, lying heavily on my futon, while the characters in this drama stormed about.

****

Eighteen days in Paris alone has been too many.

Fourteen would have been plenty. Have I fallen out of love – again?

It is still Sunday and there are several elderly couples out walking together this afternoon, the men in their cream trousers and linen jackets. I suppose this is the Sunday tradition which I continue to sit and observe over my now empty cup.

A shiny light-grey car pulls up amongst the taxis, a private car. There is repeated tooting of the horn. The elderly driver eventually gets out, angrily slamming the door. Someone inside "Le Cardinal" is not responding. He waves apologies as he weaves in and out of the taxis and half runs with a bit of a limp, to the entrance of the café in an extremely agitated state. He calls a name repeatedly but *"Googie"* makes no response. He gets back into the car and then jumps out again five minutes later and runs into the café once more, only to re-emerge with a little white fluffy dog on a lead. Is this "Googie?"

He puts her into the back seat and climbs in behind the wheel again. I wait for him to drive away. Another five minutes pass and he has remained stationary. Then out totters the real "Googie," an elderly faded woman in shades of faded blue. She stumbles along to the car and climbs awkwardly into the back seat. Either too much wine at lunch with friends or a little of the Ol'timers. After backing up and bumping the car behind them, they roar off.

Another old man with a dog like an Australian Shepherd with a walleye sits at the table next but one to me. The dog is old too and overweight, sitting, panting. He takes the lead off him and while I sit, the dog rolls his eyes towards me and wanders over for a pat. I stroke his head as he pants and stares at me (this is the dog I'm talking about.) His eyes say "You needed that – I could tell." My eyes well up. I talk to him of how he would love Coco and wonder if he understands English. I ponder over what a comfort a dog is the way it gives and receives affection and empathy so readily. When I stop stroking his head he slowly totters to the group of teenagers at the next table who are smoking and blustering their shallow flirtations at one another. I wonder how long I can put up with their overlapping smoky hormones. They show no interest in the dog and he realizes he's out of his depth too and wends his way back to his master, then remembering me, does an about turn to my welcoming touch once more. I feel teary in our silent communication and thank him quietly as he wanders back to the man.

I have a nice dinner to look forward to tonight! Produce from *le marche*.

It's 4 pm – midnight at home.

8 pm It's bucketing down outside. I should have bought another *parapluie* for 5 euros at the market today when I had the chance.

It's 9.30 pm in Paris and I find on TV a French version of the British show "Grand Designs" (one of my few favourites.) An ultra-modern house in French countryside. Horrible. Weird. "These houses" he says "blend in with nature and the ancient farms." I think they look like a meeting of polished steel covered-wagons and African huts. Stone walls lined with woven reeds or rag. Very strange.

10 pm. There's a lot of tooting of a car horn outside. Maybe "Googie" and her dog have escaped back to "Le Cardinal."

Japan's 'Welcome to summer' 2004 celebrations.

Sunday – I woke at 8 am to the sound of a snoring household. I dished up half of the cold porridgey rice, stirred in some strawberry jam and with soy milk it was *delicious*. There was nothing else and when Rachel staggered out sleepily to the kitchen she had the other half with the last of the kiwi fruit, cherries and grapes.

The children slept on until nearly lunchtime and this gave us enough time to get on with quite a bit of packing of suitcases and culling of the kids' clothes, as we saw fit without them wailing and interfering in protest. It also gave Rachel time to tear down to the supermarket on her bike to replenish the stores.

Megumi and her family were taking us to Kawagoe for the afternoon. Rachel had arranged to take us all to dinner and Megumi wanted to see a fireworks show after that. This was the "Welcoming of Summer" celebrations which was an annual event.

While Rachel was at the supermarket I had been instructed to get Rosy into her clothes. She chose a pink blouse that was amongst the washing I'd only just hung out. She went and tugged it off the clothes line and came to me with it on and buttoned up crookedly.

"I'll have to iron it." I said. "It's wet and it's crushed."

"But it's got stains on it Nanny."

"It has too. They look like rust marks. You can't wear it. Take it off."

I turned the iron on. The game Anthony and I sometimes played was face-down on the eighteen inch long ironing board and the counters went all over the floor when I turned it over. I bent down and began picking them up.

"I'll wear this" said Rosy, dragging another blouse out of the drawers.

"OK. Please yourself."

At 12.30 we drove off with a full day ahead. It wasn't til we were twenty minutes into our trip and pointing out Tokyo disappearing into the far distant haze behind us, that Rosy complained that Anthony had wiped something on her shirt and it suddenly hit me..... *Did I turn the iron off?* I was becoming like my mother.

I replayed to myself mentally exactly what I had done and I could not bring to mind the act of actually switching it off. All the family's clothes were now packed up in that room where I had used the iron. All Rachel's precious blue and white china and gifts were there and if a fire should spread to the living room hundreds of irreplaceable photos and the computer, not to mention all the furniture the new fridge and TV would be destroyed. I felt sick and my pulse was throbbing in my throat. It would then spread to Megumi's apartment next door and then up to Sandy's. And Sandy was in America.

Megumi and her family were taking us further and further away from the apartment, good-naturedly showing us Japan and of course my plane ticket, passport and money were right next to the iron. But that didn't really matter if those things went up in smoke – I wouldn't be going anywhere. Rachel would kill me.

I fell silent. I couldn't say anything.

Then I thought of Miko. She lived in the narrow street behind the apartment. If fire trucks arrived she'd ring Megumi on her mobile. But she sometimes worked on Sunday. She might be away too. It wouldn't catch fire unless the iron fell over. How would it fall over on its own? I didn't leave it down flat – I wouldn't do that – would I? I said a prayer that the iron was off.

We arrived at Kawagoe. We found ourselves on a crowded busy street. Exotic shops, so old, tiny and packed in tightly. Women with sunhats, umbrellas, kimonos and jeans. We clambered out of our people mover, the dashboard TV now showing a movie that Megumi's husband's eyes were glued to.

It was so hot. The sweat streamed down my neck and dripped down my back. A rickshaw flashed past with the rickshaw boy panting loudly like a dog.

We wandered the length of the main shops. There were also side streets packed with shops but I'd need several days there to explore them all.

"There would have been plenty to do here if you'd been placed in this town Rachel."

"I like Ashikaga best" she said "…but yes, anywhere else would have been better."

I could have busied myself here every day exploring the shops. Rachel said there was a junk shop I would like not far away.

Another rickshaw flashed past.

We went into Rachel's favourite shop that sold metal handcrafts and I bought a little bell for my boss back at the hospital, for her garden. Rachel bought Megumi an ashtray she'd said she liked and a small metal horse for herself. I bought a small bell in the shape of a fat little bird to hang on my door at home. We would do the junk shop later.

Some of the Summer Festival crowd was gathering in an open area that surrounded a stage. There were three children sitting slowly beating taiko drums in a very boring monotone. Rachel said they were asking people to come up and play taiko.
"Well go on. You'll be better than they are. Play the usual thing you play at your lesson!"

"You've got to play what they tell you."

"So, go and play! Live dangerously! Just break out on your own. Do your own thing!"

She put her name down on the paper that a tall attractive man in an indigo and white kimono held out to her. I took a photo of him when he turned away. He was rather impressive.

The children joined in with a little crowd of kids who were lined up with bamboo water pistols in a contest to see who could hit a young man who stood laughing and dodging them all and then they began turning them on each other and were all soaking wet which was great fun in the heat.

We thought we'd only be waiting a short time before Rachel's turn came around, but it was an hour of trying to fend off the sun before they were ready to begin. They were first given a lesson on rhythm using rubber tyres as drums. It looked like Rachel wasn't going to be able to do her thing after all.

I had noticed the cooking of shish-kebabs over a fire at a stall. The flames had caught my eye and I quickly turned away and watched the stage. I said another prayer that the iron was off.

Megumi's phone rang and I turned my ear towards her. She chatted away to her husband telling him where we were. Obviously his TV show had ended and he was sitting in the car somewhere, alone and bored. He was really so easy going and good natured.

Rachel impressed the tall man in the kimono with her taiko skills, as well as her looks, and I watched him eyeing her as we walked away. I was a bit disappointed though that we had waited a whole hour and Rachel had not done her special drum solo.

We continued browsing and eventually came to the junk shop Rachel had promised to show me and she got to do her drum solo after all. There was a huge old taiko drum amongst the antiques and the proprietor came out and gave a little solo demo himself.

I pointed to Rachel and grinned proudly and he offered her the sticks and she was away. "SO-RE!!" To the amusement of the proprietor and the passersby who stopped and stared. She couldn't get too carried away though as there was a collection of antique vases standing right behind her that jumped a little at each thump. Anyway I was now satisfied. I could see she had a lot of the entertainer in her from her father. I was watching Rachel the performer.

We walked back and forth across the street. I wanted to find a fan for a supervisor at work, as an introduction to the heat she was going to feel as she would be coming to Japan in August. They were all quite expensive and I hadn't seen one that was pretty enough.

It was about 5 pm and Megumi beckoned us over. Her husband had the car running at the kerb. "Let's go."

We piled in and I thought Miko would be home now if she had been working and would have phoned if there was anything wrong. There hadn't been any shock phone calls so far. I said another prayer. We wouldn't be going home for a while yet.

We stopped for a meal at the Saesana Restaurant which is one of a chain of family restaurants. The children could misbehave and we could relax. We looked at the menu and I chose a prawn and cheese fondue. There was wine and beer available.

Megumi was going to have a beer but her husband could only have water, as he was our driver. Grudgingly but smiling, he went off and got water for the kids and himself. His hands already full, he returned with none for us. Rachel was going to have a glass of wine with me so I said "I'll get us some water to drink first. Do I just go and ask at the counter?"

"No. You serve yourself."

"OK." I always felt a bit shy doing things like this where I can be watched and observed by a crowd. Caroline calls it 'performance phobia'. I walked the fairly long hike to the counter, feeling extremely foreign and alien and took down two glasses. There was a peculiar tap and some ice in a small tray beneath it and rather tired looking lemon slices amongst the rather tired ice cubes. I managed to pick up a few bits of ice and ragged lemon which I placed in each glass with tongs.

At this point a wrinkled old woman stepped up and nudged me. She chuckled, shaking her head from side to side and pointing to a cabinet. I slid back the lid as she indicated and there were larger ice-cubes and certainly fresher looking slices of lemon in there. I nodded thanks to her awkwardly and tipped out the contents of the glasses and started again, wondering why the first ice cubes I put in the glasses were off limits. I couldn't work the tap. Megumi's husband came to my rescue and we re-filled the glasses and returned to our table.

The meal was a very substantial serve for a Japanese meal and hot and spicy. Anthony and Rosy's dinners came out last and they were instructed to hurry up and eat so we could get to the fireworks. I hoped there weren't fireworks going on in our apartment right then.

Megumi's second son who was about Anthony's age and on the way to being obese, the one they were planning on being a sumo wrestler, had two dinners placed in front of him and Rachel said that that was their usual procedure. They had to build him up so he was always served two dinners!

We finished our meal but not before Rosy danced down the aisle between the diners, uninhibitedly kicking up her heels and smiling and grinning toothlessly at a group of young men who burst out laughing at her antics, making me realize that the performer was definitely coming through in this generation too.

It was twilight and uncomfortably humid as we drove through miles of rice fields. Crowds began filling the road. Rachel said this was part of the Summer Festival and the men and women were dressed in their summer kimonos. How hot they would be with the wide obi tied around their middles. Elegance is a necessity to show the kimono off to its full advantage and the women in Tokyo looked very elegant in theirs, but these were mostly teenage girls who did not walk properly with the grace of the older generation and the kimono said little.

All the paths through the rice-fields were filled with people pushing bikes towards the fireworks display.

On the narrow road it was almost impossible to make any progress as drivers had parked their cars in no official manner, just leaving them parked wherever they decided to stop. If a car came from the other direction, it meant one almost went into the rice paddy water to avoid them. There were no signs or indications of where to park, so there was a lot of backing up by some drivers and racing forward by others and general chaos.

The boys opened the sun-roof and Jun disappeared up through it to see if there was any sign of fireworks yet.

Rachel suggested we stay in the car as we would be eaten alive by the huge mosquitoes outside. Rosy burst into tears.

"I don't want to stay in the car. I want to get out!" So everyone scrambled out except for Megumi's husband, always just the chauffeur. There was another movie running and he was content just to sit and watch I suppose. I wished we could just go home.

It darkened quickly and suddenly I had a gripping pain in my stomach. What had I eaten? I felt a bit like I had felt after the day in Tokyo. The first of the fireworks exploded across the night sky and I felt the internal workings of my stomach doing the same thing in unison.

We walked along the narrow dirt road between the rice-fields and looked up at the sky at the rockets that exploded raining down on the crowd ahead.

Girls in kimonos walked past us, hand in hand with boyfriends also in kimonos. Old ladies in the same attire passed us on bikes and cars kept rolling along from behind us and we had to get on to the grassy edge of the road, inches from the water and the rice, the fireworks offering the only lighting in the dark.

My stomach pain seemed to dissolve. I caught up to Rachel who was waving the persistent mosquitoes away.

"I've got an agonizing pain in my stomach. I think I'm getting sick," she groaned to me.

"Oh really. Not you too! What did we eat? It could be the coffee jelly. Maybe it was MSG do you think?"

"No, I think it was probably the wine. It tasted a bit funny. Maybe it was off."

"Do you think so?"

"Well that's all it could be – the wine. We didn't both eat the same meal."

"I think my stomach ache has settled, so yours will too in a minute I'm sure."

Back in the car, Megumi's husband asked Rachel proudly "So what do you think of Japanese fireworks?"

I was glad when it was over. I always worried about all the terrified dogs and would have been very happy to see fireworks die out of fashion in all countries.

Rachel still complained of her stomach but it was settling a little she said.

We had an hours' trip ahead of us and there was a dreadful movie playing - a very gruesome murder with a horrible knifing scene and Rachel was ordering the wide-eyed Rosy not to look at it.

"Don't look! Don't look! Wouldn't you think that they'd turn this off when there are little kids watching, not to mention *his smoking*. They just don't think."

Megumi didn't understand a word Rachel was muttering and just looked back at us smiling happily and nodding at both of us.

Anthony and the boys were discussing graphically and with delight, the torturous things that stag beetles and rhinoceros beetles did to each other when you put them in a confined space. I empathized with these creatures' plight with great sympathy and suggested Rachel not stand for the torment of bugs.

She pointed out a tall Hotel we were passing, a "room-by-the-hour for straying Japanese husbands" she drawled. It was lit up a little way off the road with a greenish light.

I wondered if it was the ice! It had been ice that had upset me in Bali.

Suddenly it dawned on me what the ice and lemon was for at the bar. Of course – what a fool! It was to cleanse sticky fingers before and after eating and I put it in our glasses! Oh no! Now, did I remove it all? Why didn't I get fresh glasses? Because I didn't know everyone had been dipping their grotty fingers in it and squeezing the slices of lemon. I'd contaminated the glasses and the drinks! Who knows, they may have just left *that* Hotel that Rachel had pointed out to me with *very* suspect fingers.

Well, I couldn't share this with Rachel. She was an anxiety freak like me. She'd have all the symptoms before we got home! Home may have burnt down.

Which of my misdemeanors would upset her most - hepatitis or the Great Fire?!

We arrived home at long last. I sighed back into the seat, my body heavy with the relief. All was quiet on the Eastern front and the block of flats stood tall and solid – well, as solid as anything else in that country. Japan was either rocking back and forth with earthquakes or awash with floods so I didn't feel anything could be terribly solid. However the shrines had been standing for hundreds of years and it obviously wasn't yet time for the apartment to go – not in a fire anyway.

I was dying to get in and check the iron. Rachel was dying to get in to use the toilet, but naturally Anthony beat her to it and locked the door from inside. A lot of pleading went on and a lot of emotional blackmail and eventually Rachel and I were able to relieve ourselves, she in the toilet and me seeing the iron that was switched off, unplugged, smug and innocently erect.

I lay on my bed trying to retrace my movements at the bar and whether or not I had removed *all* the ice from Rachel's glass.

The children stayed up til 11 o'clock. They just refused to take any notice of threats to call Paul in Perth.

I also began trying to retrace my movements for the past decade and a half while the others slept.

I thought of my brother Bruce. Mum chose that name for her son because she thought it "very strong and manly" – and he was! He'd always been a bit of an actor. Dad often referred to him as *Walter Mitty*. He tricked me into seeing the famous western movie "Shane" twice after he had already seen it five times himself. He'd swagger through the door Saturday nights smelling of his horse, hat down over his eyes, and proceed to gun me down. A horse of his own had been the motivation for him to come in at third place in his third year at high school when he was fourteen. A saddle hadn't been part of the deal unfortunately, and the bony little chestnut filly that had been broken in just three weeks earlier had the indignity of being saddled up with a pillow strapped to her for some time before the Alan Ladd effect could be realized.

He progressed from horses to motor bikes at eighteen and when "The Wild One" and "Streetcar Named Desire" were playing at the movies, we would get impressions of Marlon Brando's "STELLA!!" all over the house for weeks.

He seemed almost a generation ahead of me, being eight years older, so he was grown up when I was still a kid. On Saturday nights he and his best mate Mike went to the "Berg" which was the local dance. Bruce would get in to his white sports coat with a pink carnation and while he spent half an hour getting the right frontal flick with his comb and the hair oil in the bathroom, Mike and I would fox-trot around the lounge-room to Marty Robbins or Frankie Lane with me standing on top of Mike's blue suede shoes.

He went on to building cars and boats and racing them. He was a keen sportsman and artist in one and a workaholic. He was amazing. He had married the right girl who was also clever and creative, with all the social graces and a love of the absurd – so she fitted in well and he and Elizabeth and their two grown-up kids were very happy and settled – so why Bruce?

Caroline was in London and it was 1992. I'd paid for the plane ticket to London as her 21st birthday present, as she had taken a position as a nanny over there. I was really feeling an urgent need to be back near family and especially Mum, whose life I was sure was drawing to an end. I made a sudden decision to leave Perth, my job and the house and run back to Melbourne. I told my neighbours to watch out for the young man that the real estate agent had found to rent my cottage. I knew they would make him welcome and I wasn't sure when I'd ever be back.

A week after I arrived in Melbourne, I took a typing position in a Melbourne hospital. At the same time the phone call came from Liz in Asia. They had moved there for a work project of Bruce's the previous year and before he had seen out his contract he had become critically ill. They were on their way home. The prognosis was not good. "Can you warn your Dad?"

That big ripe peach that sank into the sea had a rotten side to it after all – melanoma secondaries.

Three months later I walked out of Dad's kitchen to face what looked like a cocktail party in a 1960's movie. Everyone stood nose to nose with a glass in their hand. I squeezed between them with a platter of smoked chicken. Dad's entire bowling club and dozens of relatives overflowed from the house. Not having been able to eat anything for three days, and being unable to cope with the thought that Mum was actually gone, I felt decidedly fragile. It was quite a new and terrible experience to lose one's mother. After everyone had gone home, I tried to reassure my disapproving brother (who was desperately fighting any outward signs of fragility himself) "…really Bruce, Mum would have *loved* a party."

"Thank God" was all Mum had said to me when I'd given her the news just six weeks earlier that he and Liz were on their way home from overseas. But that was all she was to learn and had it all happened during her earlier years it would have killed her. At least she had no idea what was going on. Alzheimer's had spared her that agony and her beloved Brucey was coming home.

After Mum's funeral, the next six weeks was like waiting for a damn to burst and engulf us. The final words my brother said to me were "Will you be staying in Melbourne, or do you think you'll go back to Perth?"

I had hesitated before I answered. "I have to go back to Perth eventually – for Rachel."

"I thought as much" was all he said quietly.

Rachel had thought the world of her Uncle Bruce and flew over from Perth to join the hundreds of mourners and we clung together during the service, weeping openly in each other's arms.

I turned the light on as I walked into the bathroom at Dad's house afterwards and peered into the mirror at my tear-stained face. The light suddenly went off. I switched it back on and a few seconds later it went off once more. I said without a second thought "Stop that Bruce!" I went to join Liz and the family in the living room and as I entered, the lights went out there also. I shrugged and said to Liz "I think its Bruce. The lights were going on and off in the bathroom too."

She smiled through her tears and said "If anyone could work out how to contact us from the other side it would be Bruce." I knew it and we both began making the teas and coffees for everyone.

He had stressed emphatically "No cocktail parties for me when you see me off, thank you very much!"

2013 – Back to the Latin Quarter!

7 am Monday morning. I had an upsetting dream. My two daughters came to see me off on a train to Luxembourg Gardens. Rachel had come all the way from Perth to visit me and I was telling her I had to catch a train to the airport instead and I wouldn't be living in Paris after all. Now I had missed the last train and lost my wallet. Woke in a sweat – and where am I? – Paris of course.

8 am Dressed in new navy clingy dress I haven't worn before, blue/black scarf, black stockings and my old faithful black high heels – will have to take extra pair in case these ones finally fall apart – I still haven't had the heart to throw them away and they are tired from the miles of cobble stones I've forced them to endure.

Breakfast with ABBA singing in the background – Anna's "The Winner Takes It All." That song always makes me melancholy. She really lives that song and it makes my eyes sting. I relate to the lyrics but I haven't worked out who the "winner" is yet.

All Germans again at breakfast. The only tourists I've seen here have been Germans. Funny that they say their room numbers in English to the waitress, yet they smile and say *"Bonjour"* to me. I had three cups of tea along with my second stolen hard-boiled egg, my baguette and croissant.

On TV there is a promotion of Hugh Jackman's latest movie. They dub his very Aussie accent as he is interviewed. He makes no attempt at any French. "Prisoners" is the movie. The French presenter is just commenting on how "genial" he is. His only attempt at French during the interview is *Merci beaucoup* at the end.

9 am Woody Allen is stacking the shelves with fruit and because it's Monday here comes "Days of Our Lives." It is even more painful in French than English.

Three bananas left, so that's lunch today. I repaint my nails. I open the window. It's cold, and lean on the wrought iron railing, mainly to dry my nails. A curtain is flung aside at an apartment across the way and a black cleaning woman stops and gazes at me. Does she think I'm going to jump?

A bus revs up and pulls out for Hotel de Ville. I slip on my long green cardigan. 14 degrees this morning but it is expected to reach 21 later on.

On the train a young woman quite well dressed munches on a croissant in a paper bag. I wonder if she has a toothbrush with her.

At Sevres Babylone an old man gets on. He's probably younger than me but looks poorly – (no comment.) He stands like I have seen a few of his kind doing on trains here – talking in French very loudly to all the passengers in general and no-one in particular. I don't see an earpiece attached to a phone. Is he preaching, protesting on the state of France, or just talking to himself? I'd better be careful. I could quite easily become like that. Someone needs to give him a journal to write his thoughts in – like I do, instead of spouting them out to the world. He alights at Mabillon.

At Odeon a middle-aged hard-worn Frenchman gets on – dirty or sun-tanned. I can't ascertain which. He is supported by a piano accordion and strikes up tentatively at first with an old Parisian tune. This is my Paris.

Cluny La Sorbonne – and I get out. I am not thinking and walk up at the left side of the stairs and have to move to the right for a young couple who walk down. Drive on right side, walk on footpath on right side, ascend and descend stairs on right side.

10.30. Well here I am at Café Rostand. Home.

Damn! I notice looking down at my stockings there is the odd, eternally embedded white hair from Aubrey Beardsley protruding from them here and there.

It is fifteen minutes before my order is taken at Le Rostand but I am in no hurry at all and happy to sit and watch the joggers coming back from Luxembourg Gardens carrying their bottled water. Port de St Cloud has slightly soured my taste of Paris – I need my sugar! This area is my pace. The Left Bank. *This* is my Paris.

The waiter is carrying my *cafe crème* and another couple's *petite dejeuner* with orange juices and the lot on two trays held on high. He catches one tray with breakfast on it in the folliage of the potted olive tree as he walks out into the street and juggling both, nearly loses it. I think he's new. No *sucre*! *"Exuse moi Monsieur –sucre?"* He takes my sugar and my glass of water that he's forgotten from his tray.

Best coffee deal so far in Paris – *café crème* at Le Rostand with *l'eau*.

I should have stayed the full three weeks at my hotel just a walk away. I loved it. But then I have had a good taste of the reality of living in Paris and Porte de St Cloud. I would not want to live at St Cloud. It would never have the familiar feel for me that Cluny/La Sorbonne/Luxembourg has. A croaky voiced little Jack Russell barks at four tiny terriers that threaten him. If

I'd stayed close to this area for three weeks I would have found it very hard to leave Paris.

The Metro News says only 19 degrees for today.

I have been up and down Boulevard St Michel, searching for the little shop where I got Caroline's earrings, to find a scarf or something for Helen my neighbour (the one who came to my aid with her husband, when my car failed me). That shop has just disappeared! I went into all the shops there, checking out scarves and everything is made in China or India. After two hours of searching I found a nice scarf "Designed in Italy." That will have to do. I nearly bought another top for Caroline "Designed in Italy – Made in Italy" but the quality was not good so I decided against it. Rachel was in France and Italy last year with the family and she prefers Rome to Paris, so I haven't bothered to buy her any more things. I bought some scarves for her last year anyway.

1 pm. Back at Le Rostand. I need the toilet after three cups of tea this morning and thought I'd get a *verre rose* (not that cheap red) *just* so I can use their facilities.

A charming elderly Frenchman is beside me in the corner (not in the toilet let me add), sipping a *savon blanc* – a white ponytail and little white ziff and moustache, dark sweater and slacks and stars and stripes sneakers.

Looks "arty" yet "academic." He just asked my permission in French, if he could smoke. How nice.

I said "*Je n'comprehend Francais tres bien* – but yes."

"*Merci beaucoup*" he nods.

A gentleman. It would be different if he'd just lit up and exhaled smoke at me but he was so polite with his "You don't mind. You don't mind?" which is what I *think* he was saying in French. I wasn't going to say that I minded was I? He reads a book. This is the only type of "old man" I could cope with. (He's probably in his fifties.) I sip my rose. He speaks now on his phone in French, probably to his 30 year-old mistress or wife. "She" will probably join him shortly. He takes off his glasses and at the thought of her arrival any moment I shift a little independently to the far side of my seat. He looks at his watch and takes a sip of wine. I wonder if his ears are burning. He makes another call and I half turn my back to him. I cover my journal with the Metro News. I wonder what she will be like. I open the Metro News and am faced with a big picture of Naomi Watts as Diana!

He takes out a large book and pen, clears his throat – is he going to write? No, it's a book that he is studying. Maybe he's a philosophy professor from the Sorbonne – that's it I bet. It looks like the woman on the other side of me is making notes in a diary too.

The buzz of the traffic and the buzz from the rosé blend together nicely only disturbed but not unpleasantly, by a musical sound from someone's mobile phone.

What I can make of my star sign *Verseau* (Aquarius) is "beginning to have confidence...." The rest I can't make head nor tail of even with the help of Dad's dictionary.

An elderly couple arrive and sit in front of me. She is quite enormous. Her husband is gracious and affectionate with her. He still loves her with her very sagging chins. I could have had a bit of "work" done with the money I've spent on two trips to Paris, but then sat at home with no money to do anything else. He turns and smiles "*Bonjour*" to me. Yes, the older Parisians are precious symbols of times gone by – piano accordions and Edith Piaf songs – before the tourists arrived. Paris has always been tourists! I'm just a tourist!

They give their order. They are Americans. I can be so very wrong.

My neighbour the philosophy professor has a book on the table titled "*Fables Chinoises.*" See, I get it right sometimes!

It was 1993 and I stayed on with Dad in Melbourne for several months after Bruce's death and I was desperate to see my youngest daughter. I missed her terribly.

The staff at the hospital were very supportive, and suggested I would need a holiday now these events had come to a close, but they would be glad to have me back on my return. But Rachel and Paul had returned to Perth from The Pilbara and I had assured her I would be back in Perth after I visited Caroline.

It was my first trip overseas.

The first thing I noticed after Western Australia's intense blue skies and penetrating sun was the appearance of the light or the lack of it, that suggested someone hadn't paid the electricity bill.

We trudged the wind-swept hills around the rugged Cornish coast, climbing stiles from field to field, huge backpacks weighing us down, gazed at by curious blackfaced sheep.

It was on those faraway hills I heard the resonant sound of a bell with an uneven rhythm, calling from over the serious grey sea to me. We'd heard the sound for most of the day, seeming to follow us, rising and fading against the wind. I felt that my brother was out there somewhere, beyond the cold, grey sea, following us, watching over us and a warm yet melancholy mood enfolded me.

Nine hours later we staggered exhausted into a little tea-room at Polruan. The proprietress greeted us warmly, taking her apron off and throwing it aside, hands on her hips.

"It's whisky not tea you'll both be needing by the looks of you."

Neither of us had tasted whisky before but it went down well and once she had tossed her second glass back we were on our way again, happier for the human warmth and the whisky.

We ended our hike at a little white-washed cottage in Polperro. It seemed to me to be right out of a Daphne du Maurier novel and that we had slipped back in time from 1993, to a safe and cosy pre-war England, far away from all the unhappiness I'd left behind in Australia. I gazed through the diamond-paned casement windows at the bobbing boats, inspected the large blister that bled and seeped from one of my socks and fell in love with the story-book harbour and the crying silvery gulls.

We found our way up to Scotland, my old Pop's ancestral country and stayed on the Isle of Skye with an artist friend whom I'd known in Sydney and we laughed around the dinner table, reminiscing about the days spent painting at Smoky Dawson's Ranch and the "1.57 to Brisbane."

Caroline and I parted tearily in Paris after a few days in Holland and spending ten days in France (my first taste of Paris) and I returned to Melbourne alone.

I wasn't quite sure any longer where "home" was, Dad's house in Melbourne or my cottage in the Perth hills. Rachel and Paul had resumed life once more in Perth, so there was my answer.

I collected my little terrier from Dad's and said my goodbyes to Melbourne again.

Once more at home in the Perth hills my neighbours welcomed me warmly.

I don't know why I bothered, but I rang the young tenant who'd been renting my cottage to complain that the goldfish in the pond were all dead.

He arrived that afternoon ready for a heated argument. He "didn't realize he was supposed to be looking after gold-fish!" I offered him a cup of coffee and we talked for ages. He was nice – half my age – lonely too, having moved from interstate after a long-term relationship that had broken up. He told me all about it. We'd just met yet he was confiding the story of his life to me, a total stranger. As he left he said a bit awkwardly, turning at the door, "I might give you a call later. Would that be OK? Maybe we could even go out to dinner some time." I felt elated.

Dad came across for a couple of visits, delighted to be spending his days gambling at the casino while I was away at work, and then it was back to coffees with Kathleen and Jack at breakfast and sherries with Jim the school-master from next door, on the way home after walking my dogs in the evenings.

I wasn't going to tell Rachel about my new found friend but she and Paul seemed to enjoy joking about the likelihood of my "falling over and breaking a hip" now I'd reached the prime old age of forty-eight, "and Mum still sleeps with her old teddy-bear!" I just couldn't help myself any longer and it came out. I would live to regret my hasty retort for years to come, but I could be pushed so far and it was several weeks before they spoke to me again after I interrupted their insensitive dialogue and mirth. "Actually, the teddy-bear you refer to is about your age Rachel."

I was making breakfast one morning when my neighbour Jack arrived in a desperate state at my door. Kathleen had passed away in her sleep. She had been very unwell with the symptoms of her emphysema and had taken to her bed for several days. We both wept as I brushed her hair softly into place and we waited for the doctor to arrive.

Our little group was disintegrating as six months later old Jim next door went unexpectedly and suddenly, his boiled egg still in the saucepan on the stove. It was a great loss not to be hearing his piano, sipping his sherry and listening to his eighty year-old wisdom. This had been a year of deaths and funerals and tears – except for the occasional company of my new young friend.

Jack was desperately sad and lonely and it wasn't long before I came home from work to notes slipped under my door. "Have enough spaghetti marinara for two – awfully good – do come and share – Jack." And so I did, but then the requests began to become more frequent and insistent. He was suddenly very dependent on me as he was lost without Kathleen and his old mate Jim. He needed them. At about the same time his son's marriage fell apart and he moved in with his Dad, which rather benefitted all of us, but now I had two alienated men appearing separately at my door at any hour. They were on for coffee or something stronger, depending on what time of day it was, to discuss the complaints they had about each other. They had both spent their lives at British boarding schools and proudly waved the old school tie.

Jack Senior would call out through the back door "I say – are you home? Can an old man bother you for a chat? That young upstart is driving me mad!"

A grinning Jack Junior would knock on the window a little later with an awkward "Is the Mother Superior available for a talk? That's what you've become you know, listening to the bloody old man's woes and then mine."

They are all gone now and my life in that cottage surrounded by huge boulders the size of cars, salmon-coloured gum-trees, dappled sunlight, dogs and Jack (thawing frozen chickens on a table out in the hot West Australian sun much to my disapproval and the delight of the flies) all seems like a dream. It's only very occasionally around Christmas, when Jack Junior rings me from his old family home in Ireland where he is now living, and a voice from the past says, "I say, is that the Mother Superior?" that I realize it was after all not one of my dreams.

Caroline returned from France the following year and my young friend and I had already parted amicably as I knew we would. We had shared occasional happy evenings together and a relationship that I had no regrets about.

My heart sank with the realization that Caroline would most probably return to London as she walked into her tiny room that I had hastily tried to renovate. She looked out onto the surrounding bush-land and sighed. Perth wasn't home to her any more. She'd spent three years in London and her last three months in France, looking through her window at the French Alps. She chatted now about life in London with the hint of a British accent. I wondered if she could ever make her home again in Australia – maybe if we returned to the place she'd grown up in. She had no contacts left now in Perth. Should we head back East to Melbourne again?

My fiftieth birthday wasn't far off and I suggested Bali to her for the occasion, somewhere neutral where neither of us had been, so we could decide where we both wanted to be. I chose the hills of Bali – Obud, for my birthday treat.

We waded through rivers and walked to the surrounding villages and enjoyed a totally different culture. After all, Perth people went to Bali like Melbourne people went to Lorne or Sorrento.

Bali Belly gripped me for most of my stay. It did cross my mind as I screamed "George!!" down the toilet, that it may not be the ice-cubes in the pink drink that I was given on arrival in Bali after all. Was it due to one of Jack Senior's farewell dinners?

Caroline went off exploring each day without me, returning with horrendous stories of the cruelty she witnessed to the dogs in the district.

I gazed from my bed across the river at the palm trees waving in the stormy sky. I felt I had to go back home to the Yarra River and the waving gum-trees and to my Dad in Melbourne who was needing things like hip and knee replacements. How could I expect Liz to care for him? She wasn't his daughter. I was, and she had taken a lot of the responsibility, caring for Mum when I should have been there. That time with my mother I had lost and would never be able to retrieve, ever again.

Anthony was just a baby and Rachel was insistent about managing with Paul's help only. I had depended so much on my mother's help and advice when my girls were babies, but Rachel wasn't about to listen to any advice from her wayward mother.

I remembered my mother's despair at me in my twenties exclaiming "Why aren't you the same sweet little girl you were at fifteen?"

This was during my marriage to Ed and I had said some very hurtful things to her during those years.

Where was Rachel at fifteen? We were the best of friends. At that stage she had wanted to do zoology and would come home from Work Experience at the Healesville Wildlife Sanctuary full of stories about the native animals she'd handled. I so enjoyed her company, but then in only a few years and the move to Perth, she had suddenly tumbled into Paul's grown-up world. My relationship with her became very like mine with my mother, with me tiptoeing carefully on thin ice. None of us would ever be fifteen again, but debts were being settled. When the time came for Caroline and me to return to Melbourne, Rachel tearfully begged us not to go. Now she would not forgive me for leaving. I had put an even bigger wedge between us.

The ongoing mother and daughter saga. I think of my great grandmother Louisa, who at 19 left her mother who had just lost all her offspring to an epidemic of scarlet fever that had hit England in the 1850s. She and her young husband Henry headed off to Sydney Australia. He had taken up a position in a legal firm with the promise of "a carriage and pair in no time." After Louisa left, it was said that her mother died six months later of a "broken heart" at losing her last remaining child.

The young couple were affected with the spread of gold fever on the ship with the diggers headed for the fortunes of Warrandyte, home of the first gold discovery in 1851, and the "carriage and pair " dreams were now replaced with new ones and they disembarked at Melbourne, where their lives took a completely new direction.

Wandering into the Luxembourg Gardens it is actually the quietest I've seen it.

The sky is pearly grey.

There is no sun.

There is just the soft murmur of voices.

A jogger crunches the gravel and a rake is dragged over autumn leaves.

Beds of hot pink geraniums and purple salvia in many plantings greet me.

American voices pervade the stillness.

I can actually hear the splashing of the water fountain.

I'm glad I didn't come yesterday. It would have been so noisy and so touristy. Today the Gardens are mine and I have to say goodbye.

A white butterfly dances through the salvia, over the maroon wind flowers and the pink and white border of pink begonias. At the corner of each garden bed there is a blue standard form of plumbago. I haven't yet successfully grown plumbago at home. I don't know why.

A pigeon fossicks nearby, hoping that I have something but I have nothing but banana skins. I'll be swinging from the trees soon on this diet.

More joggers. A distant police siren and the clock strikes the quarter hour. An American sitting not far away yawns loudly, covers his mouth and grins at me. I smile back. He and his wife are obese. A noisy crowd of high-school kids walk by scuffing their feet through the gravel and talking together.

It feels humid. I think there's rain in the air. I walk to where the ponies usually are. No ponies today – only weekends. Hopefully they're enjoying a "well-earned rest."

Yes, having a purpose in life is the answer whether it be in Paris or the Yarra Ranges of South Eastern Australia.

I walk to the statue of Thor and sit on a bench, thinking of last year when I was painting with Claude's group right here and I had set myself up on the grass to paint. I wondered why he laughed and called out in a sing-song voice "You'll be sorry!" The sound of a gendarme's whistle and rapid approach followed by "Off l'herbe Madame!" moved me quite quickly much to Claude's amusement.

Now a tiny child totters on to the grass ignoring the calls from the father who is on a seat, reading his newspaper. The child like a newborn baby gazelle, trips, gets up and slips over again and heads off continually stumbling and dusting his hands off.

"Jess, Jess" the father calls, then gets up, pusher in tow and actually sprints across the grass. He or she toddles off with a coloured ball retrieved from the pusher and tossing it ahead, runs away from the father, stumbling and chuckling, delighting in the dismay of the father who has no choice but to follow. A gendarme finally appears on the scene but has missed the little law-breaker and the father by half a minute.

Au revoir Luxembourg Gardens! I feel a pang of farewell and that "I miss you already" feeling tugs at my heart.

After the trip to Bali, I eventually managed to buy a house in Warrandyte, close to the Yarra River, visited by wombats, echidnas, possums, kangaroos and koalas that provided all kinds of jungle-type sounds at night.

And Princess Diana was killed in Paris. Dad and I had been visiting an old friend of his when the alarming news-flash interrupted the program on the TV screen. Rachel said, that in Perth, people were getting out of their cars at traffic lights to inform the drivers in the cars around them of the unbelievable news.

I began working at a local hospital and watching over Dad's life for the rest of the time while he was becoming more and more demanding, a little more stooped, a little paler and at odd times a little more confused. He had become difficult to care for at home, still having a will of iron under the old frame and a desire to be in control and therefore was a little unmanageable. He eventually accepted the inevitability of going into care at the same place Mum had spent her last year or so, after he'd spent a few months living very awkwardly with me. This was something he had always vowed he'd never do but the time came and mentally and physically he was ready for the surrender and actually content to move on to the place where Mum had been cared for so well. (I plan to drop dead in the garden – but will I be carried off voiceless to the wreckers kicking and screaming?)

There was now a big void in my life. Caroline was in Melbourne but was with James, now the love of her life whom she'd known since high-school days.

With both daughters gone, at the end of the day literally, I was alone again except for my adored cattle dog "Moonshine." I'd rescued her when she had fallen off the back of a truck in Perth.

The only social outing I had apart from work was a daily trip to Dad's nursing home as soon as I finished work each night and at weekends where I sat in the gloom staring vacantly at the Collingwood football game on the television while Dad slept peacefully on top of his bed content with just my presence. I was desperately lonely and unhappy and filled with the dreams of "what might have been." I was creating too much of a relationship with the past while the footballers fought their way around the television screen in Dad's room as he dozed.

September 10th the calendar said. Nick's birthday. Wow, he'd be sixty! He was about twenty-five when we had completely lost touch. I couldn't get him off my mind. Was he still out there somewhere – and what might have been if…?

I picked up the telephone and began playing detective. In desperation I telephoned his old number. His mother's name was still in the phonebook. Quite unexpectedly *he* answered!

After a short stunned silence I gulped "This is Julie. Remember me?" (It was only thirty-five years that had passed.)

He was living a couple of states away and was staying with his mother on one of his rare visits to her. I didn't know what state I was in. My old Ford's number plate said "State of Excitement" and that was where I was residing!

Surprise – but yes, of course he remembered me. He still had that photo I'd given him when I was seventeen – in an album. (I knew the one, total innocence in dark olive green taffeta shot with black! And why did I ever find that colour attractive?) And yes, we could meet. Wasn't I married? He wasn't any more either. "But why would you want to meet up with an old man like me?"

I spent the next few unbelievable days floating around like a hovercraft, some distance off the ground.

I was seventeen again, euphoric with outbursts of hysteria.

I rang Rachel – I could feel her disapproval.

I rang Caroline – she was thrilled for me.

Nick recognized me the instant we met. He said I hadn't changed much. His shoulders were still the same broad shoulders I remembered but the twinkle in his brown eyes had faded and his hair was silver and he'd made a few bad choices in wives. We drank coffee in the same place the crowd from the dance used to go to on Saturday nights thirty-seven years before. Was I dreaming?

I wish now I had left myself with the memories. I behaved like a seventeen year-old girl with more knowledge than was good for her, whereas he had been content to retire as a senior cave-dweller away from the mad women from his past. I had dragged him out and sought to catch up on thirty-five years.

On our first weekend I booked a canoe for a trip down the river. Remembering him as a very adventurous man, I thought this would be a novel and romantic way to relaunch this relationship.

"Why are we putting on life-jackets and helmets?" He asked. "I thought this was to be a quiet afternoon on the water."

As we approached the rapids with the tunnel in sight, he growled "Whose cock-a-maimee idea was this?"

"But you used to jump out of aeroplanes."

"And that was forty years ago!"

The water however, proved to be a lot less bumpy than our relationship.

I had been searching for my 23 year old Russian Prince that Tolstoy had coloured my imagination with and I was determined to find him in there – somewhere. I wanted the Prince to kiss the sleeping beauty awake after being asleep for what seemed like one hundred years. Still I persevered. We watched the Year 2000 come in on the bridge over the Yarra River midst the fireworks, which he was personally adept at providing in certain areas – and even flowers on that first St. Valentine's Day. But we were not in love after all and as the temporary insanity passed, I was satisfied that the only white horses he had anything to do with were the ones he lost money on every other day.

A plane crashed in to The Twin Towers.

Neither of us were to blame for the disenchantment. I tried desperately to get back into 1962 but I became resigned to the fact that I no longer wanted to, because my memory was of someone else entirely. His actual words to me were "You have been in love with someone that did not exist."

I realized it had been a one-sided infatuation on my part. I had made a fool of myself and wasted more years on my dreams. I had hoped for the wild passions of Brad, the possessiveness of Ed, the affections of a young man half my age and the authority of Dad.

When my beloved dog "Moonshine" passed away, I was left to dig her grave alone, and after Nick's parting words of "Let me outa here!" as he jumped into his car and drove away, I dug another couple of holes, one for my 17 year-old self in the olive green taffeta shot with black and one for the remnants of a knight's suit of armour, never worn, and I asked myself "Whose cock-a-maimee idea was this?"

I continued working on my art exhibition for the following year and left for Paris. It was 2002 and my first trip alone.

2004 – Farewells, introductions and one very cool headmaster

Megumi came in early this morning with the suggestion that they drive me to Omiya station on Saturday to catch the bus to Tokyo Airport. I said that would be great. I felt it was too much for Rachel to go all the way to Tokyo with me on Saturday and then back again, just to repeat it on the Monday when she would be leaving. I just hoped Megumi got the booking of the buses right. Rachel told me that she got her organizing all wrong but insisted on doing it, so I didn't feel terribly confident about Saturday's arrangements.

At 10.30 Kaito, Naoto and an overweight middle-aged Japanese friend arrived all smiles, with Rachel's photos of the kimono fitting and an apple pie and a basket of fruit and bean cakes.

"I said I would bring *apper pie*" said Naoto shyly.

"Yes, I thought you'd forgotten" said Rachel.

"I have not been here for a *rong* time" he said slowly. "I cannot come here as I am a *dangerous man*." He worded this very carefully.

Kaito roared laughing and explained to the friend how "Naoto - love at first sight with Rachel's mother. Rachel's mother very beautifor" he said to his friend. "They sisters."

While we were dividing up the *apper pie* and dishing out cream, our backs to the visitors, Kaito piped up with "You would be knowing them by their backsides."

"Do you want a fork or a spoon?" Rachel, asked waving them around in the air in each hand. At this Kaito roared laughing.

"*You want fok or spoon*" he repeated, elbowing the friend with Naoto chuckling and repeating "*You wanna fok?*" He raised both eyebrows up and down with more wicked laughter. This had obviously been part of Paul's English lessons.

We talked about Australia and food and the friend asked if we ate koala. "No" we both said in unison. "Kangaroo is eaten but we don't eat koala."

"I think koala would be good meat" he insisted.

"It would probably taste like eucalyptus" said Rachel. "It would be terrible."

They stayed for an hour and after the goodbyes and "Let us know if you are ever coming to Australia" from Rachel, Kaito shook my hand warmly and we said goodbye and Naoto rather sadly took my hand and said "Goodbye Juree."

"Goodbye Naoto." And I brushed my cheek against his. Then he turned to his motor scooter and buckled his helmet on.

"Give my regards to *your wife* Naoto" Rachel called out and off he buzzed on his motor scooter. "The *Mild One*" I added, laughing as he disappeared down the street.

We spent the rest of the day packing. The kids had the day off, their last day tomorrow, when they would attend for an assembly and a farewell to the school year and officially begin summer vacation.

I made everyone sandwiches for lunch and we gradually settled down, but Rachel who was trying to sort through a box of dozens of cards and bits and pieces of Anthony's, suddenly burst in to tears at the despair she felt trying to do all this sorting and packing.

"I can't do this." She sent Paul a message on her phone saying "You said enjoy my last week in Japan – how can I when you've left me with all this? The Scrabble set you got your mother to send to you. I've given that to Megumi. I don't have room for it!"

What! How come I wasn't told there was a Scrabble set?

After lunch Anthony's girl-friend arrived and linked up the play-station to the TV. Her sister arrived too. Soon the apartment was full of kids again. It was stinking hot. There were boxes still waiting to be sealed up, rubbish in four bags in the kitchen and living area and there was hardly a spot to place one's foot.

"Are they going to the park? How can we continue packing with all this noise and all these hot kids?"

Rachel just waved my comments away.

I couldn't stand it. I said I was going out and I took my diary and headed for Rosy's shrine where the ants attacked me viciously. I watched a small boy with a butterfly net, very smartly catch a stag beetle and put it into a tin where it buzzed and rattled frantically.

I was hot and I sat swigging on a bottle of Aquarius *"to restore the body and spirit"* and found it rather difficult to write, but I wasn't going back to the apartment until they'd all cleared out. But towards 5 pm I returned, writing my thoughts as I went. An old lady on a bike stopped and peered at what I was writing. She was intrigued with the writing form not being in Kana and gave me a questioning look as if I was maybe just visiting from another planet.

I arrived home and the twins and their sister were there also and Anthony's girlfriend was still there but at 5 pm the Yakuba played their music and the apartment emptied. The good ol' Yakuba!

We continued the sorting of papers, papers and more papers and another day was over.

We had gone to the florists earlier and Rachel had chosen four potted plants for the Headmaster and three of the teachers which we would take to school the next day. Plants were about the same price as in Australia and four cost her about $80. We wheeled them home in the bike baskets and then had to find a relatively cool spot for them overnight.

####

This morning is the hottest morning I've felt so far during my time in Japan.

At 10 am we took our armloads of plants down to the school. I felt the heat would probably kill the plants and all of us before we arrived. Rachel took us straight to the Staff Room and the Headmaster came to the door smiling. Finally I got to meet *Gregory Peck*. I was introduced just as *"my mother"* and we followed him down the passageway to his office.

We sat back on comfy leather chairs and sipped Mugicha and ice. He read Anthony's note that had been tortuously written under severe surveillance from Rachel and he said it would be his "jewel." I suggested "treasure" and Rachel agreed and he repeated "treasure, treasure." He wanted to know where I had been in Japan. Rachel repeated his question to me in English.

"Nikko, Tokyo, Ashikaga and Kawagoe" I replied carefully.

"Ah, Nikko, Ashikaga." He said he lived one hour away near Ashikaga. We discussed Ashikaga.

"Have you been to Kyoto? You should go to Kyoto. Kyoto wonderful city. You must see." He said that it was seven hours away by car but four hours by train.

"Next time maybe" I said glancing at Rachel.

"Yes. Next time you must go *Kyoto*." He jumped up and went to his desk and brought back a photo of himself, with his wife and son who was who was very tall, somewhere in Kyoto.

He then took us down the corridor to Anthony's teacher from last year. Anthony had been so fond of her. She had said in her end of year report "I will never in the life forget Anthony." Rachel gave her the pot-plant for the classroom and she handed us a large bag containing a big parcel for Anthony. Rachel's face distorted and she wept. I felt like crying too. I think she would have happily stayed in Japan permanently now.

As I watched Rachel crying, a little girl with a very pretty face hugged Rachel and then came over and beaming at me, said something to me in Japanese. She stood beside me fiddling with my hair and the Headmaster said "This is Obachan, she is very beautifor" and I turned to the little girl who was about Anthony's age, stroked her hair and in return whispered "*You* are very beautiful." She beamed again and whispered in her awkward but well practised one English phrase "How are you?"

We were led off then to Rosy's classroom. Rosy came running out wanting to take the plant from her mother. The teacher came to the door and they said their farewells, exchanging presents.

Back in his office the Headmaster answered a knock at the door and Rachel pointed to a long chrome pole with a blue plastic forked prong at the end of it.

"That's the *dangerous person* weapon" I told you about, that they chase the "dangerous person" with. Then they pin them to the wall with it while they wait for the police.

"You're kidding."

"No, *all* the schools have them. It's all part of the Dangerous Person Drill they do."

The Headmaster returned and amusedly picked up this contraption and jumped into a defensive pose with it.

"*Dangerous Person!*" he snapped beaming, then offered it to me whereupon Rachel photographed me pinning him to the wall at his insistence, with laughter rippling from the three of us.

We returned with decorum to our seats again only to have him retrieve from his desk a book, the very one I'd sent to Rosy months ago "The ABC of Australian Animals." Rachel had given it to the school and he had evidently claimed it. The three of us sat poring over "A is for ant." Were they really six inches in length? No, but from the photograph you would have thought so. And I recalled how Rachel, Caroline and I would feed the ants bread-crumbs along the clay banks of the Yarra River opposite our old house, when they were kids.

We went through the whole alphabet, explaining the animals and as we did I smiled at this exercise with the Headmaster, the figure of authority, so eager to show his respectful interest in our country. He was very intrigued with the way the Aborigines cooked kangaroo and was impressed that Rachel had sat with a group cooking kangaroo in ashes and shared it with them while living in the Pilbara.

We told him how kangaroos were regularly culled and how Aborigines were friendly towards the white people in our early history, assuming they were spirits and would leave again. But when they didn't, hostilities began and there was no treaty as with the American Indians. The white people just took over their land. Their culture was very complex and was based on totally different values and had been decimated. We tried to explain to him that this younger white generation was beginning to recognize the value of the country's ancient culture and aiming to turn attitudes around. There was some interest, respect and a growing success in some areas. A lot of this was due to the game of football, the music scene and attempts at political reforms, but despite this their rate of family violence and incarceration is higher than ever and suicides are about four times the rate of non-Aborigines. They had adapted to a lot of white ways that are the negative ones in white society and things would never be the same again.

I have learned that you can't go back and re-build things exactly as they were in the past, moving them into a totally new era.

Adaptation and sacrifice is not for everyone. But there are always those determined to be survivors and they succeed and that is what Aborigines as a race have always excelled at – survival.

I thought as Rachel relayed some of this to the Headmaster, that if Japan had won the war, Australia would have had a complete change in culture and we'd all be speaking Japanese – blacks and whites.

I remember once, hearing the discussion between two Aborigines about the futility of Aboriginal soldiers' sacrifices in the Second World War and the conclusion they arrived at was *"You reckon our mob had a rough time when the English came here. What the hell do you think it would have been like if the Japs had got in? We had to help stop 'em!"*

Dad had been disappointed by Rachel's desire to learn Japanese. I think he was actually offended as his memories were still very much alive in his head and she could only see this as being a racist attitude. She had no memories of any wars.

The Headmaster had been to Sydney. "Sydney very beautiful. Tokyo not beautiful like Sydney. Sydney Harbour, Opera House, bridge, water, boat on water" and he indicated sitting back drinking "...and beer" he added.

We laughed.

"Not many people in Sydney ride bikes. Do many people ride bikes in Melbourne or Perth like Japan?" Rachel looked across at me and translated.

"Some ride bikes but not like here in Japan." He seemed very interested in the bike helmet law and I think he thought it rather a quaint and amusingly unnecessary idea.

There was another interruption with a knock at the door and he leapt up and went outside.

"We'd better make a move" said Rachel and we rose and walked to the door but he turned around and firmly showed us back to our seats once more. "Stay *please*!"

We got back to the subject of eating kangaroo and goanna and he said he liked to eat deer.

"Sometimes too many deer – like kangaroos" Rachel relayed to me. "He likes to eat deer."

Did we eat raw fish? Rachel said yes she did and I hesitated because I thought straight away of the squirming creatures with a multitude of legs squirming in the dish of red sauce I'd seen on TV. "Maybe tuna" I suggested, thinking this might be a safer suggestion for my tastes if I was correct as to where this questioning was leading and I was right.

"I would like you Rachel, your mother and Anthony and Maddie-Rose to come to my house for dinner."

"That would be lovely" we both said.

"You try raw fish, yes?" he beamed at me.

"Er...yes, I try raw fish."

"Ju-*lee*. Very nice name" he said in Japanese to Rachel.

"Your mother very beautifor. I come and pick you up at five past five Friday."

They had come to a decision of Friday over Thursday after much discussion in Japanese together and he wrote in his diary saying aloud "Rachel and Ju-*lee* five past five."

It was 11.15 and the children arrived looking for us, dragging their bags along.

"Anthony Shogi game genius! You drink beer or wine Rachel? And your mother?"

"Wine" I answered.

Rachel said in Japanese that we would bring wine and I said quietly to her "Don't suggest that. It's probably insulting in Japan. That's an Australian custom."

He waved his hands around "No, no. You come to my house to eat and drink wine and beer."

After a couple of attempts to rise and leave were thwarted he finally accompanied us down the passageway, past Anthony's teacher from last year who came out and spoke to Anthony tearily again. Then she called out to me "Your grandson *very clever* boy. Maddie-Rose - very ...ah ...very *cute!*"

I wondered if they realized that at six years old Rosy could read anything she laid her hands on in English. She was a clever little girl who struggled with the Japanese lessons, although she seemed fluent to me and they had no idea of her abilities in English.

They all followed us to where our shoes were and waited while we climbed into them and then stood and waved until we were out the gate and down the road. When we turned the corner into the main road I looked back and the Headmaster and the two teachers were still waving, standing together in the middle of the road, waving until we were right out of sight. When we got home Anthony unwrapped the box containing the present from his teacher. Rachel was quite taken aback.

"A pair of Nike athletic shoes!"

Rosy's end of school report read:

"Maddie-Rose....It seemed to like dabbling and it seemed to be very pleased and it could play...but it is wonderful not to take a rest and to go to school. It is disappointing to take a rest one day in July and it after goes to the Health Room because

it is said that it is the stomach ache which has a headache every day. It got well though. It was said that they were a headache and a stomach ache when a pool began. It seemed to be happy and it was making merry when it went into the water."

I wondered from whom she had inherited her talent for such an avoidance procedure.

Rachel had a friend of Anthony's and his mum and sister coming to visit at 2 pm and so I disappeared down to the shrine to bring my diary up to date.

I set off in 39 degrees and sat on my usual mossy steps at the little shrine. I sat there for two and a half hours writing, visited by huge black butterflies as well as dragonflies and the doves cooed *"Dear dear Coco"* in the trees overhead.

A young teenage boy on a bike stopped near my steps. He was hunting for stag beetles I think and he stopped quite close to me, his head on one side and leant across to look at what I was writing. He straightened up again and shrugged, looked vacantly at me and pedaled off.

When I got back to the apartment Rachel's friend was just leaving. There were tears as they said their goodbyes. Rachel was then rushing off to drinks and dinner with a group of teachers, so I was left to get the kids organized again.

Today was the hottest day in Japan's recorded history with twenty people being hospitalized in our prefecture with heat-stroke. That night the message broadcast on the TV news was:

"SO YOUR BLOOD DOES NOT CONGEAL, PLEASE DRINK LOTS OF WATER!"

####

Wednesday and Rachel insisted I go and see the Yakuba on a "duty visit." I didn't want to, but I went along in another day of 39 degrees.

Kaito worked there too, in the same office area on the ground floor and we spoke to him for a moment. He seemed totally occupied and only glanced at us briefly, and went on with his bookwork with little more than a grunt of recognition. He obviously did not wish to look as if he was distracted in any way by two visiting *female friends* which was unthinkable and rightly so, and we made ourselves scarce.

Then I was taken to the big office upstairs to where Rachel reported each morning before being sent to different schools. It was all very polite and stiff and we were taken into meet and talk with the "Head of the Yakuba!" He spoke no English at all. I felt rather uncomfortable, and stared at the wall during Rachel's discussion with them. I could see a furious image of my father looking down on us, watching us all as they conversed together, their voices rumbling in deep Japanese.

In the afternoon we began clearing the apartment as the Yakuba people would be doing a full examination there the next day. Miko came and collected Anthony to go to dinner at her house as she had two twelve year old baseball players staying from Melbourne and she needed a young interpreter.

Megumi called in with two bottles of Japanese wine and we shared them happily and laughed about our day.

####

Thursday morning and that meant only two more sleeps. Rachel and I leapt up at 6 am and began cleaning and straightening the place up again. Inspection Day with the Yakuba!

In complete silence they inspected and photographed everything, all the equipment and furniture, stalking around with suspicious glances and peering at everything as if they were forensic scientists and completely ignoring our presence. I was surprised that they were not wearing white gloves.

Rachel said when she arrived a week before Paul and the kids, the toilet door fell off, full of white ants, the bar fridge (the only fridge) didn't work at all and the rice-cooker was full of rust and old mouldy rice and everything else was in a bad state of repair.

I questioned in English in a quietly polite but curious tone if this inspection was carried out before Rachel moved in as everything had been unacceptable when she arrived. They gave no explanation in Japanese or English and continued to ignore my presence. I was "crossing he line of formal politeness" according to Rachel under her breath to me. She was feeling uncomfortable at my sudden interference, but it really angered me that they showed no appreciation for her re-equipping the apartment and supplying a new rice cooker, toaster, kitchen cabinet, vitamizer, vacuum cleaner and set of drawers which they were getting for free, as well as a new bike – no charge to them.

I decided to remove myself from the scene and sat with my head in a book, an interesting novel about the French poet Rimbaud which I regretted not finding weeks ago.

They stayed for an hour and a half examining every inch of the entire tiny apartment and its equipment, as though determined to find some offensive particle of DNA somewhere in the cracks.

Megumi raced in when they had left to see how the inspection had gone and Rachel thanked me for my support when they departed. Megumi kept calling in and sitting down wanting to be with Rachel whom she felt had become "like the sister she'd never had" as the departure time drew closer.

I wanted Rachel to rehearse just how she intended to get on the plane with all her stuff while controlling the kids. After all, they were "moving house" after a whole year. She just hoped that it would all somehow fall into place when the time came. I got her to pack all the bags, the hand luggage, handbag and duty-free bag and it was a hopeless situation. I made her unpack each of the three huge heavy suitcases and cull what she could and repack some of the hand luggage into those, which she did. She was reaching a state of despair and looked tired and drawn. Megumi and also the children across the road were about to receive good clothing which either Rachel or Rosy didn't mind parting with, and we eventually balanced the luggage out. I was still worried about the duty-free allowance but she insisted it would be OK.

To add to Rachel's worries, Megumi and Miko had said that there was the "unfortunate possibility" that the other parents at the school may be "put-out" by our going to the Headmaster's for dinner.

"I wonder if the Yakuba mind" I ventured.

"Thank you. Now I'm really worried about the possibility that I've got him into trouble with them!" She wailed.

I tried to laughingly reassure her that he would probably just be shot and to be more discreet in future with what she said to them and that she didn't have to do that for much longer, only a couple of days anyhow. But she was really worried and agonized over it.

"Oh, give me a hug" I said. She looked beaten by all the strain and responsibility of the move.

Miko the hairdresser had been given the job of taking Anthony off for a haircut.

He returned scowling and angry as it was very short and bristly like the other Japanese boys and it did make his ears stick out somewhat. I said it would grow back in time to look perfect for school in Perth. Rosy said she hated how he looked. She had stopped eating again and there was much yelling and threats from Rachel around dinner time and Rosy was behaving like someone possessed.

Rachel sat on the couch after dinner, staring in to space.

Megumi arrived again with a bottle of white wine and three glasses. It was just what we all needed. We sat and laughed and as they chatted I interrupted to ask about the authenticity of *Maibam* (every evening) and *maiasa* (every morning).

Rachel and Megumi would really miss each other, always being on hand for help or a chat. It was decided

Jun would have a "sleep-over? So he joined Rachel and the kids in the tatami room that night.

####

This morning Rachel hopped on to her bike to go to the supermarket. We've run out of all essentials again and we only have left-over rice, jam and soy milk and a couple of eggs. I am making cheese omelettes for the kids and Anthony is stomping around complaining and I can't blame him, but it isn't easy keeping up a food supply when there is only a bike with a little basket on the front to do all the shopping with.

Rachel came rushing back in, to say the supermarket wasn't open until 10 o'clock and she'd seen the cutest little mole trying to get away from a cat and she'd stopped and helped him escape in to a vegetable garden. An old woman had come out and cried out in Japanese "You can't pick those eggplants!" and Rachel told her there was a little animal burrowing there, but she didn't believe Rachel and waved her away. I wondered if mole and noodles would be on the menu down the road that night.

Rachel and Megumi lounged around outside at the back of the apartment with the boys, playing games until it was time to get ready to go to the Headmaster's house for dinner. I suggested he may come to the door in disguise, so that all the neighbours wouldn't recognize it was the Kocho Sensei coming here to take us out, seeing it had been suggested that this rendezvous might upset some parents.

But the doorbell rang shrilly with the subtlety of a fire alarm and we wondered if this was wise but we greeted him quietly and followed him to the car. As we piled in as discreetly as possible, shooshing Anthony and Rosy's voices to whispers, I couldn't believe that he had somehow leant on the horn clumsily and sounded it seemingly on purpose, not once but three times, maybe to announce his disregard of any local disapproval. I cringed, feeling all the neighbours would be rushing to their windows and gasping with the charge of undiplomatic favouritism with Kocho Sensei and the round eyed foreign family in their best clothes getting into his car.

The drive to his house took one and a quarter hours in heavy traffic. We chatted and laughed all the way with Rachel interpreting in the back seat. He said he thought Elvis Presley was "cool" and he loved the Beatles and he had a Harley Davidson bike and I thought how "cool" Kocho Sensei was.

So here I was, calling him "Headmaster" and he calling me "Grandmother" while Frank Sinatra's "Let's Face the Music and Dance" blared away on the radio above our talk. I laughed to myself at the absurd reality of that moment that I was enjoying immensely, and wondered at the same time, if Rachel's continual addressing me as "Mother" was just her total immersion into Japanese formality, (seeing as the Headmaster called me Grandmother quite comfortably) rather than displeasure towards me. I was always referred to as "Jule" by my mother as a child, but if she referred to me as "Julie" I suspected I was in trouble.

We stopped on the way at Kazo which was a surprisingly smart sort of city for him to buy cakes.

I said to Rachel "See, you offered to bring cake and he said no – and obviously he thought you would anyway and they think we expect cake now and he's stopping to buy it because we didn't bring any after all."

She ignored my comment and snapped instead at Anthony who was complaining about being squashed in between her and Rosy. I was pleased we had flowers and chocolates for them at least.

Everyone was a little shy and self-conscious at first. His wife was very feminine and gentle and there was a grand piano taking up most of the living room. She was accomplished at piano and flute and was a quiet classical type of Japanese woman. Their son explained to us in halting English how he intended to become a surgeon.

I told them to call me Julie and not Grandmother and it was *Juliesan* from then on.

There was a spectacular array of food, salad and ham, fried crumbed pork, fish that his wife ate with the heads on, which I found rather alarming, as the heads, eyes and all disappeared into her delicate little mouth. The Headmaster and Rachel cut the heads off theirs with chopsticks. There was sashimi (raw tuna, squid and prawns) sitting on shredded daicon, rice wrapped in seaweed and fried potatoes. There was beer and soft drink and I drank juice and Mugicha, barley tea. We had coffee with the assortment of very delicious decorative cakes that he'd taken twenty minutes to choose in the shop on the way there and then we were given hot Japanese green tea which I liked very much.

I asked about the green tea and where it came from and instead of an answer, I was given a very attractive container decorated with women wearing kimonos at their tea-picking occupation. This was filled with green tea. It is still quite full a decade later. I didn't enjoy it quite as much once it was placed on an Australian shelf but it sits there as a very special memento. Once in a while I partake of it in a little traditional blue and white cup and think of Japan, a roaring river and the Headmaster and his family that happy evening. They also gave us some rice biscuits called Osembe and some sweet red bean confectionery. They are a nation of "givers" not just of compliments and showed overwhelming hospitality.

After dinner we were taken out to the garden and presented with hanabi (fireworks) to set off as part of the "Welcome to summer" celebrations.

We had listened to the traditional stringed instrument, the Koto, throughout dinner. The Headmaster was giving us the complete and elegant Japanese experience.

When we came inside again, after a lot of getting in and out of shoes, Rosy, who was getting tired and grouchy, whined and grizzled to our horror, saying that she wanted something to do that was *"fun"* and then burst into tears. The kids had been given lectures and the threat of death almost if they misbehaved at Kocho Sensai's house and up until then and for the rest of the visit Anthony had behaved. Rachel whispered threats through clenched teeth at Rosy. I laughed, trying to drown out her words, hoping no-one would interpret successfully what she was grizzling about and suggested it was probably time for her "futon."

"She is so tired." I said. Actually I think she was just fed up with the whole Japanese experience and that the evening of strained behaviour had pushed her over the edge. She was desperate for some easy going Aussie informality. Still, there was no room for this rudeness particularly from the Japanese point of view.

Kocho Sensai had many photo albums of his trip to Sydney, school photos with Anthony and Rosy and their letters of goodbye already placed in them. He said how Rachel was the "Number one AET, Assistant English Teacher. He said Rachel's children were clever and Rachel's mother was "very beautifor." He took photos of us all together and then it was agreed that it was indeed time to think about going home.

It was quite a journey home and he surprised us by turning off the main road towards some black trees that lined the river and in the total darkness, got out of the car with a torch, to search for rhinoceros beetles for Anthony. This was really too much. What else could he possibly do to try to please us? After much searching amongst the trees with all of us sitting watching him in the dark, he became very apologetic that there were "none of the right species" around. He got back into the car showing great disappointment at his unsuccessful quest and we set off again and arrived home towards midnight.

While Kocho Sensae was driving the one and a quarter hour's journey alone back to his home probably to "Let's Face the Music and Dance," Rosy was facing the music and a stinging lecture from Rachel on rudeness, selfishness and the virtues of Kocho Sensae that had been trampled.

We sat up talking for some time about Kocho Sensae's virtues after Rosy had been dropped into her bed and the importance to the Japanese of aesthetics rather than material values. They didn't boast about what they had. They seemed very humble people, but a very clever people who laughed a lot. It had always disturbed me that Rachel's Paul was so materialistic, something she had not been brought up with and I wondered where this would lead them in the future.

2013 – Au revoir Porte de St Cloud.

After my farewell to the Luxembourg gardens, I continue down Boulevarde St Michel and discover the little boutique I'd been hunting for just where I thought it was. It is only tiny and a steel door is covering its entrance and it's closed. That's why I missed it earlier. I try and translate the sign on the window and look at some very smart scarves, with my nose pressed to the glass. Think it's only open two days a week. I continue on down to Metro Cluny Sorbonne, sauntering, wondering with mixed feelings, when I will pass this way again. I am about to turn my back on the Musee, my little park and my little sparrows.

I buy my usual banana, *poir* and grapes and go up to room and almost finish packing luggage.

Amazingly my poor old faithful high heels have lasted the distance today and I carried a second pair around all day just in case they collapsed. I think it wise to carry a second pair of shoes anyway if you're on your feet all day in Paris.

I have nothing against Porte de St Cloud. They have a wonderful restaurant where I've enjoyed several good cappuccinos and three superb *dejeuners* and their Sunday Market was a colourful experience. It's a great place to be away from tourists. I've just been very lonely and without purpose. Too long in one place and I do really need to be close to Cluny Sorbonne/Luxembourg when in Paris. Still, the train got me there in fifteen minutes. It's my state of mind. Really, I can't believe it. I'm in Paris and making sounds like a captive rhinoceros beetle in a tin can.

Claude had asked me if it was worthwhile going all the way to Australia as he gets really bored in a couple of minutes. I'm the same and why do I push myself beyond my limits of isolation. Everyone I know who is travelling overseas at present is with company. I know of four couples, either husbands and wives or friends. I'm the only one I know who is travelling alone. My first week was with the group and I had purpose. Last year, for the second half of the French painting experience, we were in the Chateau in the Loire Valley with another international group. It's not that they weren't an interesting group this time, but being only five of us meant that there was not the diverse interaction that there was with fifteen last year. Yet comparing my stories of travelling alone with the stories of others who have travelled in company, I seem to receive more assistance from total strangers and experience more interaction with people in general than they get the chance to.

But home beckons. It's the beginning of October and the plum trees would be in blossom, the wisterias budding and the lilac beside the verandah would be predicting a heavy scent which would have once reminded me of my Nan and Pop's garden. But now in future I would also see the cheeky, questioning face of the little gypsy boy in the Metro (whom I could not resist) selling bunches of lilacs in the crowded train. He'd picked them over a fence on the outskirts of Paris, and thrusting them towards my face, with his other little hand held out for money and one word – "Madame?"

And I have to get back and plan my trip to Perth where the very *"beautifor"* Rosy has the lead role in her school production of a Jane Austen classic which I wouldn't miss for quids. She will be sixteen then. Drama is her chosen career path. Anthony is a charming 6'5" tall young gentleman, a twenty-year-old with a beard (which is the thing at the moment) and at Uni doing journalism, (he's too nice a guy for that profession) creative writing and next year editing. I wonder what he'll think of this attempt of mine! He has also been pondering the future of studying for the Christian ministry. Who would have thought? And I want some time with Rachel. Love wins and life is just too short.

7.30 I begin breakfast. A Chinese man who checked in last night is bewildered at the food. He asks the African maid "Beef or ham?" pointing at the meat.

"*Jambon – jambon.*" she says impatiently.

"But beef or ham?" he insists.

"*Jambon!*"

I call across the room to him "*Jambon* is ham."

He turns and looks questioningly.

"Pig!" I yell, about to snort.

"Oh pig – thank you – thank you." He leaves the pig.

As I leave the table, I tell the receptionist that I need to get to the airport at 10.30, believing that St Cloud is not that far away from it.

"Charles de Gaulle? Oh Madame, one and three quarter hours!"

"What? I thought it was closer to St Cloud!"

"No Madame it is a *long* way. I will book the taxi for 9 am." She picks up the phone.

I imagine myself using the Metro at peak hour. Could I manage it? No!

Back in my room I run back and forth to the toilet. I hate getting to airports! I should try the Metro – but no – I can hardly manage my luggage as it is. Imagine trying to get down all those stairs, buy tickets and fit through gates, let alone get on and off to change trains.

I will have to bite the bullet and pay the horrendous cost for a taxi. I'm getting too old for this!

I get dressed in the outfit I'd planned to wear home all week. I look like mutton dressed up as lamb! I change the geometric design leggings for black ones. Still the black top is too short. I tear clothes out of my case and come up with the grey pinafore. Looks fine with grey scarf – quiet and nondescript.

I sit and wait for the taxi. Woody is re-loading the fruit and vegetable stall.

Nine o'clock has come and gone and still no taxi.

Madame at desk asks for 2 euros that I owe for phone call that I never successfully made to Caroline.

She agrees *"Non non Madame"* when I tell her I contemplated the Metro.

The Chinese taxi driver arrives.

"Traffic – sorry." He takes my heavy luggage and we head off down the street. "Traffic slow. Down here Madame, this way!"

I point to my luggage that he wheels along *"Il est tres grand pour le Metro."*

"Yes" he says smiling, "But not too heavy for me."

Your English is very good." I comment panting after him.

"Three years I live in America."

We walk on for 100 metres and finally his car is there. The meter has already rung up 30 euros by the time I settle myself inside. It's already cost me for the 100 metre hike. Now a one and three-quarter hour's journey!

Au revoir Eiffel Tower – its highest point hidden by smog or mist.

At last after crawling for half an hour in traffic that is heading for places of employment as well as international destinations, we're away on the freeway to Charles de Gaulle Airport.

He charges me 75 euros for the trip "…because I was late" he grins. I was expecting at least 150 euros. That rogue who picked me up at the start of my holiday!

"Keep the change" which is only a few euros, and he thanks me and smiles *"Bon voyage."* And off I go to join queue after queue, feeling like a potential terrorist.

2004 – Sayonara

Saturday, the date of my departure from Japan has come quickly and Rachel and I rise at 6 am and eat breakfast together. She looks so tired and drawn. She is still worried about Rosy.

We sat over breakfast talking about the prospects of where I might live. My hands and wrists were developing arthritis rapidly and I just felt so limited at times with what I could do around a property as big and steep as mine at Warrandyte. I felt I should make another move again. Rachel asked about the feasibility of going down to Sorrento on flat land. I said that her Aunty Liz was thinking of retiring to their beach house in that area one day and I may at least have her there. Rachel wondered.

This led to a discussion on my relationship with my only brother. I knew that my mother was much closer to him than she was to me as they'd shared the war years together with Dad away. They had that special bond that I could not compete with and anyway, sons and mothers have a special relationship I think. I wished I'd had a sister as well. That's why I'd had Caroline – as a sister for Rachel – and they had both seemed like sisters for me too.

I was still analyzing my family when my father had died. I had resented his control and decisions on my life's choices when I was growing up.

I had paid my father a visit at the nursing home the week after I had discovered Nick. Dad was ninety-two – and more on the ball than I had thought. I knew he worried about me being alone and I thought he would be pleased with the news that I had found again the man I had always wanted to be with "after all these years."

He had looked enquiringly at the white-haired stranger and hesitatingly shook Nick's offered hand.

"Dad – You remember Nick?" I was so excited. I wanted him to be happy for me. The prodigal son had returned after so many years. All was forgiven! Or was it? After all, hadn't I inherited Dad's rather reckless adventuring spirit? But he looked defeated and I felt suddenly deflated when he caught my hand as we left, pressed it and said in a grey voice that matched his stony face "Just you be very, very careful."

Dad died some months later, while I was at work.

Now I was ashamed and full of regret as it hadn't worked out with Nick and I had caused my father unnecessary worry and heartache.

So, as I told Rachel, we all cart around baggage from our parents' relationships and theirs with us as well as lots of regrets about our own past – everyone did. You might succeed in avoiding your parents' mistakes but you create your own set. Maybe seeing Rachel as my friend and being a half-open book from an early age had been a big mistake.

Natsumi who had helped organize the Nikko trip and had believed Paul was "medicine for her eyes" rang and said she was coming over to say goodbye and she arrived with a present for Rachel. She gave me a hair-pin that looked like a chopstick for wearing with kimonos. She cried when she left.

Miko came and said goodbye.

I was worried about my luggage being too heavy. I had dressed ready for the Melbourne winter in boots, slacks and tights with a black t-shirt and I carried my favourite jacket. I was stifling hot.

Megumi was in and out all morning checking on arrangements and she said we were to leave at 1.30 pm for Omnia where the bus depot was. Rachel and the kids were already outside chatting with Megumi while Yuuta brought the 'people mover' around.

I turned at the door, dropped my luggage for a moment and went back to the kitchen sink where I had tried to find some peace on occasion. I looked out at the little clothes line now empty. I went into the tiny dressing-room and thought of the confusion I'd felt there.

I thought of how we left our DNA and the echo of our emotions behind us everywhere we went. I had felt an attachment to every place I'd stayed in since I was a child, going back bare-footed at the guest house by the sea to glimpse once more the bed I'd slept in, the hint of salt and sand and summer in the air, before closing the door and ending the relationship I had formed with it; and the white-washed walls and shuttered windows that looked out over the bay at fishing boats and swooping gulls on the Cornish coast; the narrow winding staircase that creaked with every step and led to a tiny room that peered down on Paris rooftops; always going back to say goodbye with a tinge of sadness to those walls that had held me and protected me for a time, part of me always there and part of it always in my heart, feeling a severing of something when finally the door closed and I whispered goodbye to it, most probably forever.

In the mountains the roaring Yu-gawa River would continue to tumble and churn til the end of time whether or not I was there to witness it. That lion would continue to pace and the stag-beetles would continue their struggles with each other and with captivity at the hands of foolish boys all over Japan. Not to mention the poor little bunnies.

I went back to my luggage at the door and looked at the collection of children's shoes in the genkan for the last time, shoes that would shortly disappear, soon to re-emerge once more on Perth's sandy streets.

We arrived at the bus-station too early and Rachel suggested we look at the shops. I was boiling hot in my winter clothes but wandered along with her, struggling to carry my bag.

I was still worried about my luggage and wondered whether to take the large picture of Mt Fuji, out of my case and dump it – maybe hide it in the airport toilets. But I didn't want the story to get back somehow and hurt the feelings of the school nurse, so I left it in the lap of the gods amongst my tired and squashed clothing.

Megumi hugged me and showed a sad face as I was about to board the bus.

"Rachel miss Mummy."

"No, Rachel will say Mummy gone – hurray!"

"Oh Obachan – naughty girl."

Then there were photos taken by Megumi's husband and when I said "Arigato Yuuta" very earnestly to him, he said with Rachel's translation.

"We will come and stay with you when we come to Melbourne."

I said "Of course" and imagined that if this was the case I may have a lot of Japanese visitors arriving soon to my house. I'd met some wonderful people who seemed to care so much and were very generous and I would remember them all with respect, affection and humour. They would be welcome if they ever did decide to come.

Rachel and I hugged again in an apologetic sort of way.

I climbed aboard the bus feeling a lot of mixed feelings and knew that when I returned to Melbourne and Rachel to Perth, there may be more than the Nullabor Plain that separated us. There had been for some time and I had not been aware of it. On top of all the other resentments, in her eyes I had abandoned her years ago when I returned to Melbourne with Caroline. I had put Caroline's needs and my father's needs and come to think of it, mine before hers. One makes decisions in life with the best of intentions at the time, and yet in hindsight....

The world keeps on turning with or without us. The butterfly seizes the day, bravely flitting amongst the roses and the cabbages, delighting in the sunshine. Dodging predators and beaten by the rain, it lives its brief life, delighting small children and angering vegetable gardeners. You can't please everybody!

I looked back at my daughter. Her expression was suddenly that of my vulnerable fifteen year-old and I had to relinquish the impulse to jump out of the bus and hug her to me and tell her how much I loved her, because as I rose in my seat, the doors closed abruptly.

She gave me a parting smile, one that said a lot and I wondered if she had read my thoughts. Suddenly I saw her as a three year-old, sitting bolt upright in bed one night between Ed and me, pointing upwards at something we couldn't see, that had woken her from her dreams.

"Look, Mummy, Daddy, up in the sky. Look – a little girl riding on a birdie!"

Was Rachel *really* experiencing her long-desired dreams? Was she that little girl on the back of the bird, soaring to great heights?

As the bus pulled out I realized my warm jacket was in Yuuta's van. They all looked aghast at me, probably thinking "Mummy" was having a fit, as I gesticulated and did charades illustrating the fact that my favourite jacket was in the van. I eventually just shrugged and sat down again as the bus did a U-turn away from them and they waved tentatively, turning to talk amongst themselves, obviously unable to fathom Mummy's strange behaviour once again, and I disappeared from their sight and they from mine.

My luggage went through OK. No questions asked. Mt Fuji with the gleaming speeding train and all.

It was a bit of a puzzle to follow the directions I was given and get on the shuttle train and I felt very vulnerable and quite lost but I reached the right waiting area and the right loading gate despite the crowds.

"Thank you God. I've done it."

I sat down and began my wait. It was noisy. What a shame I would be leaving all those generous compliments behind me in Japan. I had got so used to them. No longer would I be "beautifor." Anyway it was just because I had "blue eyes that they'd kill for."

I sighed, my thoughts now turning to images of raucous crows, black-winged *tombo*, stag beetles, sumo wrestlers, mossy steps to shrines and all the smiling, laughing faces.

It would be cold when I arrived at Tullamarine. I would walk out into that frosty air and I would look like everyone else, no more the foreigner and disappearing once more into obscurity.

Wouldn't it be wonderful, I thought to myself – if *he* suddenly appeared, the face I had hurriedly sketched, grey hair in the lion style – *"medicine for my eyes."* I'd almost forgotten him.

"No. No more of your idle dreams – not today." I told myself. I was leaving Japan.

Had I lost my grandchildren because of this visit? That thought made me despair. Had I been too impatient with them? Would they remember me as the cranky old woman who came to stay? They were too young to understand family dynamics.

I wondered if it was too late to change my flight to Nepal instead of Melbourne where I should have gone years ago. Why didn't I? But I had two dogs and a cat depending on me and Caroline would be at the airport. Nepal or the Amazon would have to wait.

A woman's lilting voice finally announced:

"Qantas Flight Number 534 now boarding at Gate Number 5....."

I hoisted my heavy bag onto my shoulder, and walked alone to join the single file leaving Japan and the blue roaring Yu-Gawa river behind. Would I dispose of my diary in that bin I was approaching? I probably should, but it had kept me occupied and almost sane for six weeks. I reached for it. But someone might retrieve it and read it and it might somehow get back to Rachel …and she'd kill me! I gave it an affectionate pat. It wasn't going anywhere.

As I took out my boarding pass something fell to the ground from my bag. I stopped to pick it up.

I was holding up the queue of impatient passengers but I unfolded the creased rather grubby piece of lined paper that had been folded again and again in to a tiny squashed square.

I recognized Anthony's writing – with obviously the same words in Kana below them.

I LOVE YOU PUMPKIN XXX

2013 – Paris

At Charles de Gaulle airport I remove my boots and they go through the screen. The Americans behind me say there's no way they're removing their sneakers. I explain that it is just if there's metal in them (mine have zips) that will set off the alarm. I whisper to them "It's in case you've got a knife in your boots."

"Oh well, better safe than sorry I say" she drawls.

"HELLO WORLD" screams the big red mural of the world map. My gaze lands on Australia – sitting out there in its isolation. The emotion I feel is almost like seeing my Mum's familiar smiling face at the school gate – reassuring, welcoming, maybe a trifle embarrassing?

I'm now at Starbucks. I always say I don't drink Starbucks coffee but the latte is wonderful here at 11 am.

Middle Easterners with a hysterical toddler are at the next table. He does not stop shrieking. Their baby in a stroller happily ignores his older brother. The toddler coughs, nearly chokes, gags, and the father is about to really lose it.

Outside it is grey and pouring rain bounces on the tarmac. I find my way to Gate 39.

I ask the Asian woman with the broom *"Ou est la toilette?"* She looks irritated by my question and I pick up the word *"ascenser"* in her gabbled French. She continues sweeping. I walk in a small circle, again a pigeon ready for lift-off and after pressing the button on the elevator which refuses to obey, I spy a sign on an escalator *"Toilettes."*

A few minutes later I stand at the counter of a snack bar waving a five euro note in the air. The Chinese man takes so long taking the order being given by a big American, that I put my five euros back in my wallet and leave. That note converted to Australian dollars will buy me a coffee or two at home when I start on this new regimen I plan.

As I sip my red wine somewhere over Turkey I wonder. Maybe I should have gone on that hiking trip through the jungles of Borneo with Greenpeace after all. No plumbing to worry about on *that* holiday. I had seriously considered it. Maybe that's because I'm half way through a glass of *vin rouge*. I hold my glass up where the sunlight catches the ruby-red effect for a dazzling moment and I am reminded of stained glass windows.

Paint the inside of St Severin Church one colour?

But really, I think I allowed my tooth disaster and vanity to handicap me and ruin this trip. I've been hiding. Yet that young woman at the hotel said "Madam, I would not have noticed had you not told me." Maybe Caroline won't notice it when we meet either.

I just realize - wandering in my Spring garden gives me a buzz almost like when I wander around Paris, yet there are times when neither lives up to my expectations of perfection. But there *is* no such thing as perfection in life – in cities, friends, husbands, daughters, lovers, mothers – or cats. When my garden is covered in a swathe of onion-weed in winter I could turn my back on it and walk away, but spring returns eventually. In Paris, the mischievous plumbing, migrating wildebeest and clamouring beggars send me scurrying into the warm relief of a corner of my favourite cafe where *the sun is out and the sky is blue* and the café crème arrives with its little silver jug of hot creamy milk and Paris resides once again in my heart.

I take another sip – La verre de vin rouge is half full, and I'm a little tipsy – I think.

"And they all lived happily ever after," or "Be careful what you wish for." Too cynical? Too clichéd? OK.

Well, a stray vine with yellow flowers wanders through the garden, between the purple salvia and hard stony ground, suggesting pumpkin soup for the next six months. But "not *all* the flowers turn into pumpkins." That would be a better ending to fairy stories. And be really thankful for the odd pumpkin.

Many agonizingly uncomfortable hours later we touch down in Melbourne. Dawn is breaking and so is my left knee. With my fellow travellers who are obviously not morning people, we wander, irritated and complaining about the service, hoping the person we're following knows where he's going. Eventually we're standing waiting for our turn at the guillotine – Customs. I have nothing to declare – except that long haul travel, particularly the return journey, is a lot like childbirth. When it's all over you say "Well I won't be doing that again – but you do."

Thank God, there's Caroline.

"MUM - WHAT HAPPENED TO YOUR TOOTH?!"

ACKNOWLEDGEMENTS

Thanks go to my two wonderful daughters and my grandchildren who have allowed me to write about them and to the memory of those who are not here to give permission.

Thanks especially to my eldest daughter who provided me with a stage and a group of delightful players who inspired the beginnings of my book and for her great generosity in allowing me to share with others our awkward times together in the past.

Thanks to Kathleen Andrewartha for her editing advice and to Aunty Dot Peters for her encouragement.

To my cousin Graeme Mitchell for his ready help with my limited skills with technology, his endless supply of patience with me in my first and second editions and unintentionally giving my book it's title whilst walking with me through my garden.

Thanks to Kerry at Healesville Library's Writer's Group for her advice which led me to this revised edition.

Thanks to Tom Chapman for his support and the final help with this edition.

www.ingramcontent.com/pod-product-compliance
Lightning Source LLC
Chambersburg PA
CBHW020631230426
43665CB00008B/119